World Literature

Volume I: Greek, Roman, Oriental and Medieval Classics

COLLEGE OUTLINE SERIES

World

About the Author

An associate professor at the University of Alabama, Buckner B. Trawick was graduated from Emory University and received both his M.A. and Ph.D. from Harvard University, where he has undertaken additional study on a Ford Foundation Fellowship. Prior to his present position, Dr. Trawick held teaching positions at Clemson College, the University of Mississippi, and Temple University.

Literature

Volume 1: Greek, Roman, Oriental and Medieval Classics

BUCKNER B. TRAWICK

NEW YORK
BARNES & NOBLE, Inc.

Preface

For several years there have been available a number of admirable anthologies of world literature and continental European literature. There has been a need, however, for a convenient handbook to supplement these anthologies and to serve the student both as a guide through the great mass of writings and as a ready-reference work for factual information. It is the purpose of this outline to supply that need.

The objective of the author has been twofold: first, to provide enough biography, synopsis, and criticism to make the book useful to students who are employing the "great-works" approach, and, second, by means of copious introductions and cross-references, to render the outline serviceable to the students of comparative literature who are especially interested in trends and influences, including the interrelationships with English and American literature.

It has been difficult to decide which authors and works to exclude. In writing a short survey of nearly five thousand years of European and Oriental literature, there are only two alternatives: to give an extremely brief account of nearly all authors, or to omit many minor figures and thereby allow space for a more adequate coverage of the major writers. The latter alternative has been adopted in this outline. The selection of authors to be treated has been guided by two considerations: first, the contents of the five or six most popular anthologies now in use, and second, the influence that authors and their works have exerted on national and world literature. The great writings in the fields of history, philosophy, science, and literary criticism have been omitted except in a few cases where their intrinsic literary value has justified inclusion.

In a work of this sort, consistency in the use of foreign and English forms is virtually impossible. Both forms of the names of authors have been given in most cases. When an anglicized form (such as Virgil or Petrarch) has attained popular usage, that form has been employed in the discussions. The names of historical persons other than authors have usually been anglicized. As for titles of works, both original and translated versions have been given wherever they have seemed useful, especially in medieval Italian, French, Spanish, and German. Feeling that inclusion of foreign forms in such literatures as ancient Hebrew would be useless, pedantic, and precious, the author has given only the English titles.

The author has tried to give the most authentic dates available for authors' biographies and for their works. When a date has been found to be controversial, for sake of consistency _Webster's Biographical Dictionary_ has been used as the authority. The _c._ preceding two dates (for example, _c._ 429–378 B.C.) applies to both figures.

There has been no attempt to make the bibliographies exhaustive. At the end of each part is a list of the biographical, historical, and critical material in English which has appeared to be most useful for the average student of world literature.

Attention is called to the appendix, which is devoted to classical and Norse mythology; to the index, which lists authors, foreign and English titles, and some special genres; to the index to characters; and to the quiz and examination questions.

The author wishes to express his gratitude to Professor Werner P. Friederich (see _History of German Literature_) and Urban T. Holmes, both of the University of North Carolina, for their many suggestions and corrections.

—B.B.T.

Table of Contents

Part One
Ancient Oriental Literature

I

Egyptian, Assyro-Babylonian, and Persian Literature

It is believed that the world's earliest literature was written by the peoples who inhabited the fertile areas around the Nile, the Tigris, and the Euphrates rivers. The Egyptians, the Assyrians, the Babylonians, and the Persians all made valuable literary contributions in ancient times.

A. Egyptian Literature

Historical Background. The origin of Egyptian civilization is hidden in antiquity. That civilization, asserted by some to be the oldest in the world,* was already at an advanced stage as early as 5000 B.C. From archeological discoveries and from hundreds of existing inscriptions, it is clear that the ancient Egyptians brought architecture, sculpture, painting, mathematics, religion, government, and the art of writing to a high degree of development.

General View of the Literature. The discovery of the Rosetta Stone† in 1799 and its subsequent deciphering by Jean F. Champollion opened up four thousand years of Egyptian literature, of which the world had been ignorant before that time. Most of the literature of Egypt has been lost, but several pieces of great interest still survive. Tombs, pyramids, obelisks, stone tablets, and many papyrus manuscripts have preserved in literature three different forms of writing — the hieroglyphic, the hieratic, and the demotic. The earliest inscriptions were made about 6000 B.C., and the written record is almost continuous from 3700 to 200 B.C.

Most of the Egyptian writings that may be called literature fall into one of five groups: wisdom literature, religious literature, tales, love lyrics, and epic poetry.

---

* Some archeologists claim that Chinese civilization is older.   See p. 14.
† A stone bearing a trilingual inscription in hieroglyphic, demotic, and Greek.

Wisdom Literature.

THE PRECEPTS OF PTAHHOTEP,* preserved on papyrus roll of *c.* 2500 B.C.†   Called the "world's oldest book," *The Precepts* is a collection of shrewd and homely reflections on life, its conduct, and its meaning; it treats such current problems as divorce and labor relations.   Its style and tone are dignified and indicate a cultivated class of readers.

Religious Literature.

The ancient Egyptians, intensely religious and passionately eager for permanence (as evidenced by their pyramids, tombs, and embalming processes), were probably the first people to express belief in personal immortality.   Their principal deity was Osiris, the god of the Nile (sometimes identified with Ra, the sun-god).   Having been resurrected from the dead, Osiris was the symbol of immortality, the god of the afterlife, and the judge of the dead.

THE BOOK OF THE DEAD or Coming Forth by Day. Generally considered the most significant of ancient Egyptian writings.   It is preserved in about 2000 papyrus rolls.   There are 166 chapters of various dates, from *c.* 4266 to *c.* 2000 B.C.   This document is made up of prayers, charms, hymns, formulas, confessions, and the like.   Its purpose is to tell men how to obtain eternal life.   Its most famous chapters are the "Hymn to Ra" and the "Declaration of Innocence."

MISCELLANEOUS RELIGIOUS WORKS.   In addition to the poems found in The Book of the Dead, there have been preserved many hymns, dirges, and songs.   Among the best known are the following: "Antef's Festival Dirge" (written *c.* 2500 B.C.; on papyrus manuscript of *c.* 1500 B.C.), on the *carpe diem* theme; "Song for Neferhotep" (*c.* 1600 B.C.), a request for Ra's blessings; "Hymn to Usertesan III" (*c.* 3000 B.C.), a chant to one of the Pharaohs (representatives of the gods).

Tales.

The Egyptians gave us our first folk tales — ghost stories, stories of magic, romances, adventure stories, and fables.   The best and most famous tales are summarized below.   Other tales include *The Taking of Joppa*, *The Doomed Prince*, *Tales of the Magicians*, *The Peasant and the Workman*, and *The Exile of Sanehat*.

---

  * Only the English translation of a title has been given except where the foreign title is both current and well known.

  † Ptahhotep is said to have flourished *c.* 2650 B.C., but the *Precepts* are reputed to be of a far earlier date, perhaps as early as 3800 B.C.

THE TWO BROTHERS or *Anpu and Bata* (written *c.* 3200 B.C.; manuscript, *c.* 1300 B.C.). Perhaps the earliest extant story on the "Potiphar's-wife" theme. It involves magic, transformations, metempsychosis, and revenge. Two faithless women bring misfortune on their husbands, but the women are later repaid. The husbands prosper.

THE SHIPWRECKED SAILOR (manuscript *c.* 2500 B.C.). The lone survivor of a shipwreck reaches the Isle of Plenty, where a talking serpent prophesies his rescue. The prophecy comes true — the sailor returns to Pharaoh's court with wondrous gifts.

THE STORY OF SETNA (written *c.* 1300 B.C.; manuscript, *c.* 400 B.C.). This tale recounts a student's theft from a tomb of a book of magic, his repentance, the return of the book, and his expiation.

Love Lyrics. The people of ancient Egypt wrote a considerable number of love poems of varying dates. Many tell of the love between brother and sister (who frequently married each other). These poems are characterized by passion, tenderness, and subtlety. Some examples are "Beloved, It Is Only Thy Breath" and "I Lay Me Down upon My Bed."

Epic Poetry. There survives only a fragment of what may justifiably be called an epic. This is *The Epic of Panta-our* (*c.* 1324 B.C.), which tells about the victory of Ramses II over the Hittites.

B. Assyro-Babylonian Literature

Historical Background. It seems certain that the fertile area between the Tigris and the Euphrates rivers had reached a "high state of intellectual and manual activity"[1] by about 2000 B.C. Various tribes — Sumerians, Akkadians, Elamites, Chaldeans, and Cosseans — contributed their bits to the civilization. From about 1200 B.C. till about 608 B.C. the Assyrians were the ruling people; thereafter for about seventy years the Babylonians were the dominant power. The most famous leaders were the Assyrians Sennacherib (ruled 705–681 B.C.) and Ashurbanipal (ruled 669–626 B.C.) and the Babylonian Nebuchadnezzar (ruled 605–562 B.C.).

General View of the Literature. The Golden Age of Assyro-Babylonian literature was the middle of the seventh century B.C. Ashurbanipal was a great patron of learning and collected a vast library (in cuneiform characters on clay tablets), from which virtually all extant ancient literature of the region is now derived. In addition to official documents, the library contained myths, legends, hymns, chants, prayers, proverbs, folk tales, and accounts of battles. At least a specimen of each of these types survives. The poetry employs the devices of proportion, balance, and parallelism — devices which are characteristic of Hebrew poetry, too.

THE GILGAMESH EPIC (composed *c.* 2000 B.C.). Usually considered the greatest literary production of the ancient Assyro-Babylonians. In the middle of the seventh century B.C., the epic consisted of about 3450 lines; in the library of Ashurbanipal these filled twelve large tablets. Today only about 1500 lines survive wholly or in part; they are preserved on approximately 30,000 different tablets and fragments of tablets — some in Sumerian, others in Old Babylonian, and still others in Akkadian.

It is now generally recognized that the *Gilgamesh Epic* is a "compilation of material from various originally unrelated sources, put together to form one grand, more or less harmonious, whole."[2] It is believed that some of that material antedated by several hundred years the actual putting together of the poem. Although most of the sources are mythological, an attempt has been made to identify the hero with a ruler belonging to the First Dynasty of Uruk (eighteenth century B.C.),[3] to whose heroic figure dozens of myths and legends of various dates and origins (chiefly Sumerian and Semitic) attached themselves.

The epic recounts the exploits of the hero Gilgamesh, the son of the goddess Ninsun and a mortal, priest of the city of Uruk. The tyrannical deeds of the strong and arrogant young hero induce the people of Uruk to pray to the goddess Aruru for relief. Aruru answers their prayers by sending Eabani (Enkidu) as a rival and opponent to Gilgamesh; Eabani is a strong but bestial creature symbolizing primeval man. After a fierce encounter, in which Gilgamesh is victorious, the two become staunch friends (Tablets I and II). The following episode (Tablets III–V) is concerned with the friends' expedition against Khumbaba (Humbaba, Huwawa), guardian of a cedar forest wherein Irnina (an embodiment of the goddess Ishtar) lives; Khumbaba is defeated and killed. Tablet VI tells of Ishtar's wooing of Gilgamesh. When the hero rejects her, she becomes enraged and persuades her father Anu to send a bull to destroy him, but Gilgamesh and Eabani kill the bull. This episode has been interpreted as a nature myth — Gilgamesh representing the young solar god of the spring season, Ishtar being the goddess of love and fertility.   In Tablets VII and VIII Eabani is stricken with a disease and dies.   In order to avoid a similar fate, Gilgamesh sets out to find Utnapishtim, a human being who has learned how to escape death.   After many adventures Gilgamesh finds Utnapishtim (Tablets IX and X), who tells him the famous Babylonian tale of the Flood (Tablet XI), remarkably similar to the account of Noah's Flood found in Genesis 5–10.   Utnapishtim is eager to help Gilgamesh and informs him of the existence of a certain weed which will restore a person's youth.   Although Gilgamesh succeeds in obtaining the weed, a serpent almost immediately snatches it away and devours it.   In the last tablet Gilgamesh has an interview with the shade of Eabani, who tells him about the fate of the dead.

More than a merely entertaining story about a traditional hero, the *Gilgamesh Epic* has considerable allegorical significance.   It depicts man's quest for the meaning of life and his futile struggle to avoid death.   Its philosophical conclusion is that since death is inevitable and the afterlife usually gloomy, man should try to enjoy life and make the best of his earthly lot.

THE TIAMAT LEGEND (date uncertain; present form, *c.* 600 B.C.).   This is a series of cosmogonic poems concerning Tiamat, the female Principle of the Universe, and Apsu, the male Principle, who together form the first divine dynasty.   The series tells of wars between groups of deities.   Tiamat is overcome and mutilated by Marduk, wielder of the thunderbolt.   Accounts of the origins and wars of the gods are similar to those in Genesis, and in Greek and Norse mythology (see Appendix).

ADAPA AND THE SOUTH WIND (originated *c.* 1500 B.C.).   A folk tale of a fisherman who, in a rage, breaks the wings of the South Wind.   Summoned before Anu, the High God, the fisherman successfully defends himself.

BABYLONIAN CHANTS AND PRAYERS (various dates).   Many of these are similar in tone and subject matter to the Hebrew Psalms.   There are prayers for forgiveness of sin, poems of remorse, requests for mercy, and hymns of praise.   Especially noteworthy are "Look Down in Pity upon Me," "Besides Thee There Is No God Who Guideth Aright," and "A Light of Heaven."

C. Persian Literature

Historical Background. The language of the ancient Persians (Iranians) was of the Indo-European family, and the name *Iran* is etymologically related to the word *Aryan.* It has marked affinities with Sanskrit and with classical European languages.

Legends tell of an early Iranian dynasty of Bactria, but the earliest genuine historical reference to an Iranian state is dated about 850 B.C., when the Medes became prominent. The Median empire was overthrown about 558 B.C. by Cyrus the Great, founder of the Achaemenian dynasty, which, in turn, fell before Alexander the Great in 331 B.C. The successors of Alexander ruled till A.D. 226, when the native Iranian dynasty of the Sasanians was founded. The Arabian invasion of A.D. 642 brought this dynasty to an end.

General View of the Literature. Persian literature begins with the reign of Darius (521–486 B.C.). With the possible exception of parts of the Avesta, the earliest Persian writings now extant are inscriptions which record the ancestry and exploits of Darius and of his successors Xerxes (486–465 B.C.) and Artaxerxes (464–424 B.C.). These inscriptions, however, can hardly be called literature. It was not till early Sasanian days that real imaginative literature was written; by that time the language of Persia was Pahlawi (Parthawi, Parthian), a modification of the original Iranian.

The Avesta or Zend-Avesta — "Text and Commentaries" (first written down perhaps *c.* 625 B.C.; present form *c.* A.D. 375). The Avesta was formerly attributed to Zoroaster (Zarathustra), but now only a fragment of one section (the Gathas) is generally ascribed to him. Originally there were twenty-one books; now only one whole book and fragments of others survive. The Avesta is the Bible of Zoroastrianism.* It is made up of two parts: The Avesta and The Khurda Avesta.

The Avesta proper is, in turn, divided into five sections: (1) The Venidad, the only complete book, comprising Gathas (hymns), religious laws, and mythical tales; (2) The Vispered, made up of sacrificial litanies, prayers, and invocations; (3) The Yasna, litur-

---

* The religion of the ancient Persians before they were converted to Mohammedanism. It "teaches that Ormazd, lord of light and goodness, wars ceaselessly against Ahriman and the hosts of evil. Ormazd created man to aid him, and finally the good kingdom will be attained." (Webster's *New Collegiate Dictionary*, 1949.)

gical fragments and hymns; (4) The Yashts, twenty-one hymns, myths, and prayers; and (5) The Zend (probably later than the other four parts), commentaries and interpretations.

The Khurda Avesta, or Little Avesta, is a book of short prayers.

The present value of the Avesta is religious and philological rather than literary.

Pahlavi Literature. No Pahlavi poetry survives. There are, however, several important pieces of prose. In addition to a social code, forms for letter-writing, a history of chess, and a tale about King Khusrau and his page, there have been preserved two significant legends.

MEMORIES OF THE ZARIRS or *Yatkar i Zariran* (*c.* A.D. 600). An account of a war between two kings, Arjasp and Gushtasp; the armies of the latter defend the revival of Zoroastrianism and are victorious.

BOOK OF THE MIGHTY DEEDS OF ARDASHIR or *Karnamak i Artakhshir* (*c.* A.D. 600). A legend concerning the various adventures of Ardashir, reputedly a descendant of Darius.

2

Indian Literature

Historical Background. About 2000 B.C. a branch of the Aryan race — apparently fair-skinned — invaded India from the northwest. We know very little of their history until the conquest by Darius in 512 B.C. Their civilization, however, appears to be very ancient; religion, philosophy, ethics, and literature all seem to have reached a high level of development before authentic records were kept. Gautama Buddha (563–483 B.C.) made many changes in the old religious creeds and rituals; his teaching later became the basis for one of the five major religions of the world.

General View of the Literature. Most of the literature of ancient India was written in Sanskrit, the oldest extant Aryan language. A small portion of the literature was written in Prakrit, a vernacular form of Sanskrit. The history of Indian literature falls into two periods: (1) the Vedic period, which extends from about 1500 B.C. to about 200 B.C. and of which the writings are made up principally of religious and lyric poetry (although some fairly successful attempts to establish a prose style were made) and (2) the so-called Sanskrit period, which extends from about 200 B.C. well on into the Middle Ages and, in a sense, down to the present day. In the Sanskrit period many types of literature achieved distinction — epic, lyric, and didactic poetry; drama; fairy tales; fables; romances; and philosophy. Literary chronology prior to 500 B.C. is almost entirely conjectural.

RELIGIOUS WORKS

Poetry. The oldest sacred literature of India is found in the four Vedas ("Books of Knowledge").

THE RIG–VEDA (*c.* 1400 B.C.). An anthology of 1028 hymns to various gods — many of them impersonal nature deities. The prevailing religion of the Rig-veda is Hindu pantheism; its chief object of worship is Brahma, the eternal, self-existent god. The most notable single poem in this collection is the "Creation Hymn."

10

THE SAMA–VEDA or "Book of Chants" (date unknown). It consists principally of liturgies, of which most are repetitious of hymns in the Rig-veda.

THE YAJUR–VEDA or "Prayer Book" (date unknown). This is also liturgical and repetitious of the Rig-veda, but it contains, in addition, many original prose formulas.

THE ATHARVA–VEDA or "Book of Spells" (date unknown, but much later than that of the Rig-veda). Containing some hymns, it consists chiefly of spells, incantations, and notions about demonology and witchcraft.

Prose.

THE BRAHMANAS (date unknown, perhaps *c.* 1000 B.C.). Commentaries on the Vedic hymns and religious rites, these are possibly the earliest extant pieces of Indo-European prose.

THE UPANISHADS (*c.* 800–500 B.C.). A collection of 108 discourses on the Brahman religion. Though they fail to establish a coherent system of philosophical belief, they give a great deal of information concerning the conceptions of *maya* (the illusory world) and *nirvana* (absorption into the universal soul). The Upanishads were influential on Emerson and Schopenhauer.

THE SUTRAS (*c.* 500–200 B.C.). Extremely concise, often unintelligible treatises concerning ritual.

SECULAR WORKS

Epics. Though classified as secular works, the two epics contain a great deal of Indian mythological and religious matter.

THE MAHABHARATA (begun *c.* 500 B.C., added to during many later centuries). The longest poem in the world (about 200,000 lines, nearly eight times as long as the *Iliad* and the *Odyssey* combined), it is divided into eighteen books. The epic nucleus of the poem (about 80,000 lines) concerns the battle between the Kauravas (Kurus), representing the principle of evil, and the Pandavas (Pandus), representing the principle of good. The remainder of the *Mahabharata* contains glosses; descriptions; legends; and treatises on religion, law, philosophy, and military matters. Interpolations make the poem cumbersome and sometimes hard to follow. Two notable interpolations are (1) the *Bhagavad-Gita* ("divine song"), a long, didactic poem (eighteen cantos) in which Krishna (an incarnation of Vishnu, one of the great Indian gods) discusses philosophy and the good life with Arjuna, one of the Pandavas; and (2) *Nala and Damayanti*, a love story concerning conjugal patience and fidelity. The *Bhagavad-Gita* was influential on Emerson.

THE RAMAYANA (begun *c.* 500 B.C., finished *c.* A.D. 200). A poem of about 96,000 lines, in seven books. It concerns Rama (an incarnation of Vishnu) and his wife Sita; Rama's exile; Sita's faithfulness when tempted by Ravana, an evil spirit; and Rama's eventual destruction of Ravana. The poem is much more compact and readable than the *Mahabharata*.

Dramas. Very little is known about the origin of Indian drama; literary historians disagree as to the amount — and even the presence — of Greek influence. It seems likely, however, that the origin was indigenous and that the first real drama arose out of ceremonies connected with the worship of Vishnu-Krishna. There was no special theater; the dramas were presented in the banquet hall or ballroom of the rulers' palaces. The chronology, too, is uncertain, but the sixty-odd plays of which we know were probably written between 100 B.C. and A.D. 600; most of them came after A.D. 400. Indian drama shows a mixture of joy and sorrow, but the ending is always happy. Each drama has a prologue and is divided into scenes and acts (from one to ten). Most of the plays have intricate though not very original plots, realistic characterization, a court jester, and a mixture of prose dialogue and lyrical poetry. The custom of employing both Sanskrit (for the men of high rank) and Prakrit (for the lower classes) in the same play probably led to the death of the drama.

THE TOY CLAY CART (*c.* 100 B.C.; present form, *c.* A.D. 450). Attributed to King Sudraka. It has ten acts. A courtesan saves the life of a merchant because of his former kindness and generosity. There are many romantic elements and some good portrayal of real human emotions.

SAKUNTALA OR THE FATAL RING (attributed to Kalidasa, the "Hindu Shakespeare," *c.* A.D. 500). While King Dushyanta is absent, a Brahman sage hurls a curse at Queen Sakuntala. As a result, Dushyanta fails to recognize her when they are reunited, especially as she has lost the ring he gave her. In deep despair, she is whisked away to heaven. When a fisherman returns the lost ring to the king, the curse is broken, and Dushyanta's memory ot Sakuntala returns. After years of sadness and vain searching, Dushyanta finds his wife on a sacred mountain, and all ends happily.

The play has superior plot construction and excellent characterization, especially of Sakuntala.

Tales.   The ancient Indians had a great talent for telling stories. The several collections of Indian tales have often been considered the sources of many of the folk tales which have appeared in various forms all over the world.   A large percentage of the tales were written for didactic or religious purposes.   The most important collections were the following:

THE JATAKAS (*c.* 300 B.C.?).   Imaginative legends concerning the 550 births of Buddha and his early life, supposedly related by himself.   Many are animal fables, and most are didactic folklore.

THE PANCHATANTRA or "Five Books" (*c.* A.D. 300–500).   A series of tales (derived chiefly from the *Jatakas*) probably intended as a manual of instruction for kings' sons.   The tales are arranged in a framework: a Brahman attempts to instruct six young princes by relating "moral" tales to them.   The "five books" are (1) "Separation of Friends," (2) "Acquisition of Friends," (3) "War of the Crows and the Owls," (4) "Loss of What Has Been Acquired," and (5) "Inconsiderate Action."   The collection shows much humor. It contains many animal stories and has often been considered the source of a large number of medieval tales, especially those in the *Gesta Romanorum.*

THE HITOPADESA or "Book of Good Counsels" (date uncertain, but later than that of the *Panchatantra*).   A series of forty-three tales, of which twenty-five are from the *Panchatantra;* in four books.   The tales are more sententious than those in the earlier collection.

THE SUKASAPTATI or "Seventy Stories of a Parrot" (date unknown).   A framework series of fairy tales.

Lyrics.   In addition to sacred poetry, many secular lyrics were composed in ancient India, most of them after 100 B.C.   Many contain great passion and real beauty.   The leading lyricists were (1) KALIDASA (*c.* A.D. 350–500), famous for a large number of poems of sentiment; for example, the "Meghaduta" ("The Cloud Messenger"); and (2) JAYADEVA (fl. *c.* A.D. 1200), author of the "Gitagovinda" ("Cowherd in Song"), a semidramatic lyric concerning the love-making of Krishna.

3

Chinese Literature

Historical Background. The origins of both the race and the civilization of China are unknown. Recent discoveries indicate that a civilization may have existed in Mongolia as early as 20,000 B.C. Legends tell of a government, agriculture, and the use of wheeled vehicles about 2800 B.C.; certainly the Chinese had reached a high degree of culture while Europe was in a semisavage state. Reliable records, however, do not begin till about the eighth century B.C. From then till the beginning of the T'ang dynasty (*c.* A.D. 600) the history of China is principally a story of chaos, invasions, and petty wars. These centuries may be divided into three eras: the feudal period (700–200 B.C.), the period of the Han dynasty (200 B.C.–A.D. 200), and the period of minor dynasties (A.D. 200–600).

General View of the Literature. The literature of ancient China is extensive and includes almost every form known. There are histories, books of philosophy, lyrics, tales, dramas, and letters. Much of the earliest literature is concerned with three of the four main religions of China — Confucianism, Taoism, and Buddhism (Christianity, which came later, is the fourth). The names and works of scores of Chinese philosophers, commentators, poets, historians, lexicographers, and letter writers from the ancient periods have been preserved.

PHILOSOPHY

Lao-tse or **Lao-tzu** (b. 604 B.C.). To him is attributed (probably erroneously) the Tao-Te-Ching ("Way of Life"), which forms the basis of Taoism, the idealistic and pacifistic Chinese religion of inaction.

Confucius or **Kun'g Fu-tzu** (551–479 B.C.). Philosopher, statesman, teacher, "the founder of Chinese literature."[1] Although a religion was based on his teachings, he was far more interested in social, ethical, and political doctrines than in purely religious matters; he had virtually nothing to say about the nature of God or about life after death. His paramount interest was in how to act here and now. He was an intense student and had as his main object the preservation and dissemination of traditions.

THE FIVE CLASSICS. Collected and edited by Confucius *c.* 500 B.C.

Classic of Changes (*Yi King*). Ascribed to Wan Wang (*c.* 1140 B.C.), it is made up of geometrical combinations of six lines, plus sixty-four explanatory essays. This book was used by the Chinese for divination, and it was supposed by some to present a secret and profound philosophy, but no key has been found.

Classic of Ceremonies (*Li Ki*). A voluminous work on etiquette. It was re-edited about 100 B.C. by the two Tai cousins, and it was based on documents allegedly written by Confucius. A sixth Classic, *Rites of the Chou Dynasty* (*Chou Li*), was at one time coupled with the *Classic of Ceremonies.*

Classic of Historical Documents (*Shu King*). Dates of sources range from 2400 B.C. to 750 B.C. This is a formulation of the political ideals and the fundamentals of good government.

Classic of Poetry (*Shi King*). A selection of 305 best poems (reputedly from a collection of 3,000 poems written during several preceding centuries). The book stresses the cherishing of thoughts and sentiments of forebears. Some of the poems are odes written for various occasions; some are lyrics. The book is valuable for insight into the manners and customs of the ancient Chinese.

Classic of Spring and Autumn (*Ch'un Ch'iu*). So-called because, according to its admirers, "its praises were as stimulating as spring, while its censures were as withering as autumn."[2] It has little philosophical content, but it is noteworthy for a history of Confucius' native province of Lu from 722 to 484 B.C.

THE ANALECTS (*Lun Yü*). Compiled *c.* 450–375 B.C., *The Analects* make up a book of twenty-four chapters, composed of sayings of Confucius collected by his followers. This book gives us the best conception of Confucius that we have.

Mencius or **Meng-tzu** (372–288 B.C.). Statesman, philosopher, teacher. He wrote seven (unnamed) books of philosophy based on the teachings of Confucius. On a lower ethical plane than his master, Mencius was most interested in man's political economy.

Chuang-tzu (fl. *c.* 350 B.C.). He wrote a long, nameless work, of which parts are lost, attacking Confucianism and defending Taoism. He shows excellent wit and has a charming style. His work contains many fables and anecdotes.

POETRY

After the death of Confucius there flourished a school of poets noted for passionate expression, irregular meter, allusiveness, and allegory. There was some rhyme in early Chinese poetry (before A.D. 600). Lines varied in length, but were usually only four or five syllables long; after A.D. 600, the seven-syllable line was employed. (See also Confucius, *Classic of Poetry*, above.)

Chu Yuan (fl. *c.* 350 B.C.). Poet, statesman. Chu wrote *Falling into Trouble (Li Sao)*, a long poem recounting his own life and imaginary adventures. It contains many fanciful incidents, e.g., a ride in a dragon-drawn chariot and a visit to the Milky Way.

Mei Sheng (d. 140 B.C.). Poet. Mei was more classical in form than was Chu Yuan and reverted to Confucius' *Classic of Poetry* for models. He is famous for five-syllable verse, especially love lyrics.

Wang Ts'an (A.D. 177–217). Poet, scholar. Wang wrote a prose *ars poetica* and poetic laments concerning his own exile.

Liu Ling (fl. *c.* A.D. 250). Poet, one of the Seven Sages of the Bamboo Grove, a hard-drinking school of poets. Liu is famous for poems praising wine and Taoism.

T'ao Ch'ien or **Tao Yuan-ming** (A.D. 365–427). Poet. T'ao is memorable for resigning a magistracy because he could no longer "crook the hinges of his back for five pecks of rice a day."[3] He wrote allegorical, political, didactic, descriptive, and occasional poems. Many of his pieces show strong and genuine emotions and excellent workmanship.

Wang Chi (fl. *c.* A.D. 600). Known as the Five-Bottle Scholar. He wrote excellent poetry and prose; one noteworthy tale tells of a visit to Drunk-Land.

HISTORY

Ssu-ma Ch'ien (145–87 B.C.). China's "father of history." He wrote the *Historical Memoirs (Shih Chi)*, covering the history of China from 2697 to *c.* 100 B.C. There are 130 chapters under five headings: (1) annals of the emperors; (2) chronological tables; (3) rites, music, the calendar, astrology, sacrifices, watercourses, and political economy; (4) annals of the feudal nobles; and (5) biographies of eminent men.

Pan Piao, Pan Ku, and their sister **Pan Chao** (*c.* A.D. 50). They wrote a history of the Han dynasty, covering the years 100 B.C.–A.D. 1; it is a tremendous work in 120 volumes.

TRAVEL STORY

Fa Hsien or **Fa-Hien** (fl. *c.* A.D. 399–414). Explorer, narrator. In A.D. 414 he wrote *Travels in India*, an account of an overland journey from the heart of China to India, and of voyages thence to Ceylon, Java, and back to Shantung. His style is difficult and terse, but his information is invaluable for students of ancient China, India, and Buddhism.

4

Hebrew Literature

Historical Background. The people of ancient Palestine were of Semitic stock, rather closely related to the Arabs and the Assyrians. The Bible relates that Abraham (traditionally considered the progenitor of the Hebrew people) came from Chaldea. After several generations in Palestine, the Hebrews apparently were driven by drought and famine to Egypt, where they remained for a long time. They returned to Palestine and placed themselves under the rule of "judges," who were at once religious and military leaders. The Hebrews fought many petty wars against various enemy tribes. Eventually kings replaced the judges; the most famous Hebrew monarchs were David (*c.* 990 B.C.) and his son Solomon (*c.* 960 B.C.), under whom the Hebrews achieved their greatest political importance.

After the reign of Solomon the realm was divided into two kingdoms — Israel in the north and Judah in the south; Jerusalem was the capital of Judah. Wars with many neighbors continued. In 721 B.C. the people of Israel were carried into captivity by the Assyrians, and in 586 B.C. the inhabitants of the southern kingdom were led captive by the Babylonians. The Edict of Cyrus of Persia set them free in 538 B.C.; they returned to Palestine, rebuilt their cities, and achieved considerable prosperity.

As the Greeks and Romans in turn became the leading worldpowers, Palestine fell under their domination.* The Roman Emperor Titus put an end to all Hebrew hopes for political independence when he destroyed Jerusalem in A.D. 70.

General View of the Literature. Virtually all ancient Hebrew literature is concerned with religion. From the earliest days the Jews evinced a preoccupation with, and a genius for, religious matters. Their two most significant literary works — the Bible and the Talmud

---

* See also the account of the Maccabean rebellion against Antiochus Epiphanes (168–135 B.C.), p. 31.

— deal with the nature of God, with His laws, and with the ethical precepts of which He is claimed to be the source. At first crudely animistic and polytheistic, the Hebrews developed one of the highest concepts of the Deity that man has ever known. In the days of Abraham and Isaac, Yahveh (Jehovah) was believed to be a national god — stern, vengeful, capricious, and bloodthirsty. Over the centuries the concept was ennobled; the attributes of justice, mercy, holiness, morality, and universality were added.

The primitive Hebrew language was a mixture of Chaldaic and Phoenician; this language had few inflections, sparse syntax, and simple sentence structure; but it was forceful and capable of becoming eloquent. The numerous invasions, defeats, and periods of captivity suffered by the Jews effected the mingling of many foreign elements with the primitive speech. This debased language became known as Aramaic, and by 300 B.C. it had almost entirely supplanted Hebrew as the spoken language. Since Aramaic was a poor medium of literary expression, most Hebrew writers after A.D. 25 employed Greek instead.*

Though inevitably related to religion, ancient Hebrew literature contained many types of writing — histories, songs, folk tales, drama, biographies, epistles, short stories, and many other less distinct types.

THE BIBLE

The most widely read book in the world, the Bible has been translated into more languages and dialects than any other.† It is really a collection of sixty-six (or eighty‡) books, ranging in date (in their present form) from *c.* 750 B.C. to *c.* A.D. 100. It is divided into three parts: The Old Testament, The New Testament, and The Apocrypha.

THE OLD TESTAMENT. The Old Testament is made up of thirty-nine books, which may be classified conveniently in six

---

* There is some disagreement concerning the original language of the New Testament writers. See Ernest S. Bates, *The Bible Designed to Be Read as Living Literature* (New York: Simon and Schuster, 1943), p. 900.

† Despite some inaccuracies, the King James translation (1611) is generally recognized as the best literary version; John Livingston Lowes has called it "the noblest monument of English prose." This version will therefore be used as the basis for this outline.

‡ The books of the Apocrypha (see p. 30) were originally included in the King James translation.

groups:* History, Prophetic Books, Lyric Poetry, Drama, Wisdom Literature, and Tales.

History. These books trace the history of the Hebrews (with some gaps) from the creation of the world down through the rebuilding of Jerusalem after the return from the Babylonian exile.

Six of the history books (Genesis, Exodus, Leviticus, Numbers, Deuteronomy, and Joshua) form a group known as the Hexateuch. The first five of the six (called the Pentateuch) were for a long time erroneously attributed to Moses. In its present form the Hexateuch dates from *c*. 350 B.C.; parts of it were written perhaps as early as 950 B.C. It is based on four principal sources, the so-called J, E, P, and D Documents.

GENESIS. Chapters 1–11 contain accounts of the creation of the world and man (1–2), the fall of Adam and Eve (3), Cain's murder of Abel (4), Noah's flood (5–10), and the Tower of Babel (11). The remaining chapters deal with four cycles of legends, revolving, respectively, around the central figures of Abraham (12–23), Isaac (24–26), Jacob (26–36), and Joseph (37–50). Other famous passages relate these stories: how Lot's wife is turned into salt (19), Abraham's sacrifice of Isaac (22), Jacob's marriages to Leah and Rachel (29), Jacob's ladder (28), the sale of Joseph into Egypt (37), Joseph's temptation by Potiphar's wife (39), Pharaoh's dreams (41), and Jacob's moving to Egypt (45).

EXODUS. This book deals with the Hebrews' escape from Egypt and their journey back to Palestine under the able leadership of Moses. Some famous sections tell of the discovery of Moses in the bulrushes (2), the plagues of Egypt (7–11), the origin of the Passover (12), Moses' Song (15), the sending of manna (16), and the Ten Commandments (20). Most of the last half of the book is devoted to laws and their interpretations, rites, and ceremonies.

LEVITICUS. This document embodies a legal and religious system — laws, codes, rites, and sacrifices. One section ("Holiness Code," chapters 17—26) is of Exilic origin;† it emphasizes righteousness and goodness of motive as opposed to ritualistic details.

* The traditional division into Law, History, Poetry, Major Prophets, and Minor Prophets is neither logical nor chronological. Stith Thompson and John Gassner, *Our Heritage of World Literature* (New York: Dryden Press, 1942), pp. 411–415, suggest the following divisions: Historical Writings, Prophetic Writings, Dramatic Writings, Lyric Poetry, and Prose Fiction. Bates (pp. xv–xxiv) makes only three divisions: I, Historical Books; II, Prophetical Books; and III, Poetry, Drama, Fiction, and Philosophy.

† The Exile was the captivity (721–538 B.C.) referred to in *Historical Background* above.

NUMBERS. Numbers contains an unreliable census, more religious laws and customs, and some narratives concerning Moses. Its most famous episodes are Moses' smiting of the rock (20) and the speech by Balaam's ass (22).

DEUTERONOMY. Based on a "Book of Law" found in the Temple at Jerusalem in 621 B.C., it repeats much of Leviticus, but it contains some original narrative material concerning the wandering of the Hebrews in the wilderness, and it tells of the death of Moses (34).

JOSHUA. A historical book dealing with Joshua's assuming leadership of the Hebrews after the death of Moses. It tells of the entry into Canaan and of battles against hostile tribes; it is a deliberate attempt to create a national military hero. Its most famous passages describe the fall of the walls of Jericho (6) and the standing still of the sun and the moon (10).

JUDGES (earliest form, *c.* 850 B.C.; present form, *c.* 550 B.C.). This is a saga of the Hebrews soon after the death of Joshua. It recounts the life and the battles of the Jews under the judges. Its famous passages are: the exploits and song of Deborah (4–5), possibly written 1100 B.C.; Gideon's battles (6–8); the story of Abimelech (9); the story of Jephthah's daughter (11); and the story of Samson (13–16).

I SAMUEL (*c.* 550 B.C.). A continuation of Hebrew history under the judges and under Saul, the first king. Its famous passages include: the call of Samuel (3), the choosing and anointing of Saul (9–10), David's battle with Goliath (17), the friendship of David and Jonathan (18–19), and Saul's attempts on David's life (20–27).

II SAMUEL (*c.* 550 B.C.). This book is concerned principally with the reign of David. Its most famous episodes depict David's marriage to Bathsheba (11–12) and Absalom's rebellion (13–18).

I KINGS (*c.* 550 B.C.). A history written for the purpose of proving that God rewarded His worshipers and punished His enemies, it covers the period from the death of David to the accession of Ahaziah of Israel. Its most famous passages relate the building of Solomon's temple (6), the visit of the Queen of Sheba (10), the division of the kingdom (12), and the prophecies and miracles of Elijah (17–22).

II KINGS (*c.* 550 B.C.). Written for the same purpose as I Kings. It continues the history through the fall of the kingdoms of Israel (721 B.C.) and of Judah (586 B.C.). Its famous passages describe the miracles of Elisha (1–8), the fall of Israel (17), Sennacherib's raid (18–19), the reforms of Josiah (22–23), and the fall of Judah (25).*

NEHEMIAH (c. 300 B.C.). This is a personal memoir by the political leader of the Hebrews on their return from exile in Babylon. It tells of the rebuilding of the walls of Jerusalem, and of the religious reforms effected by Nehemiah.

Prophetic Books. The Old Testament prophet was not primarily a soothsayer; rather, he was a religious and social reformer. He was a spokesman for God — a spokesman who pointed out the people's evils to them and who often threatened the nation with disaster and destruction unless it repented. Elijah and Elisha (see I and II Kings, above) wrote nothing, but are considered the first two prophets. Their successors varied widely in approach and point of view — from Amos, who thundered out his threats, to Hosea, who gently persuaded; from the melancholy and pessimistic Jeremiah to the rhapsodic and confident Unknown Prophet (Second or Deutero-Isaiah). But all of them were inspired with a passion for righteousness, and many were endowed with a vision and eloquence which led to the production of superb poetry. The most important books of prophecy are summarized below. Others (omitted from this Outline) are Zephaniah, Nahum, Obadiah, Zechariah, Joel, and Malachi.

AMOS (c. 765–750 B.C., the oldest complete book in the Bible). Amos voices a stern and uncompromising warning to the Kingdom of Israel — a warning of utter annihilation unless social reforms are immediately effected. Amos is often considered the first to emphasize the justness of God.

HOSEA (c. 740 B.C.). This book of prophecy contains a far milder message than that of Amos. Hosea stresses God's mercy and forgiveness rather than His justice, and he entreats instead of denouncing. He emphasizes God's love and willingness to forgive.

MICAH (c. 720 B.C.). Here are combined the attitudes of Amos and Hosea: Micah foretells not only the punishment of the wicked but also an era of redemption and prosperity. He is probably the first author to express the hope for universal peace.

---

* I and II Chronicles (c. 350 B.C.) are feeble repetitions of I and II Kings and are omitted from this outline. The book of Ezra also is omitted.

ISAIAH (*c.* 740–701 B.C.), thirty-nine chapters.* Generally recognized as the greatest of the prophets, Isaiah was a statesman as well as a religious leader. He advocated collaboration with Assyria. Tradition holds that he was executed by being sawed in half during the reign of the wicked King Manasseh of Judah. Isaiah had no illusions about the complete moral regeneration of the people, but placed his hope in a "saving remnant," from whom eventually would spring a Messiah; this leader would be strong enough to establish righteousness in the land.

HABAKKUK (*c.* 600 B.C.). This book contains perhaps the earliest Hebrew discussion of the problem of evil.† Foreseeing that the tyranny of Babylon would succeed that of Assyria, Habakkuk wonders whether the wicked will really be punished and the righteous rewarded, but he soon answers confidently in the affirmative — though the course of justice may be long. Not vehement but sincere, he attacks social and religious evils.

JEREMIAH (*c.* 600–586 B.C.). A book of gloomy prophecy. Jeremiah opposed rebellion against Babylon and was later carried off as a prisoner by refugees who fled to Egypt when Jerusalem fell in 586 B.C. He held no hope for the survival of his nation, but placed his only reliance on personal righteousness.

LAMENTATIONS (*c.* 586 B.C.). Erroneously attributed to Jeremiah. Prophetic only in spirit, this poem bemoans the fall of Jerusalem. It is extremely artificial in form; in the original Hebrew it is "an acrostic, each line beginning with a different letter of the alphabet, and the lines are arranged in regular triplets or couplets, the whole carefully divided to form a series of dirges within a dirge."[1]

EZEKIEL (*c.* 585 B.C.). Written in Babylon by an exiled priest. This document helped maintain Hebrew morale by emphasizing the importance of ritualistic practices. Paradoxically, however, the author rejects the doctrines of vicarious righteousness and of the visitation upon the sons of the sins of the fathers; instead he stresses personal, individual responsibility. He is visionary and mystic. The book had great influence on Daniel, Dante, Milton, Blake, and others.

THE UNKNOWN PROPHET (Chapters 40–66 of the book of Isaiah as it appears in the King James translation; *c.* 540 B.C.). Of

---

* Chapters 40–66 in the King James version are obviously by a different and much later author. See The Unknown Prophet.

† See also Jeremiah and Job.

Exilic authorship, this book is exuberant and rapturous.   Its author suggests a new interpretation of Jewish history: the sufferings of the people are not divine punishment for sins, but vicarious suffering for the instruction and redemption of mankind. He suggests a Messiah of peace — the personification of the Hebrews — who will through his suffering atone for all human beings.   Bates calls the author "the first Christian, five centuries before Christ."[2]   He has the concept of a universal God and stresses God's holiness.   He also gives a picture of a new Golden Age.

Lyric Poetry.   Ancient Hebrew poetry employs some of the same poetic devices found in Germanic verse — parallelism of struc‧ture and idea, repetition, and balance.   There is no rhyme and no regular meter, but usually there is a distinct rhythm.

Bits of lyric poetry are, of course, to be found scattered through many of the prose books, e.g., the Song of Deborah, in Judges; and some of the prophetic books are almost entirely poetic.   The great collection of lyrics, however, is the book of Psalms.

THE PSALMS.   An anthology of 150 hymns, compiled *c.* 150 B.C.   A few of the hymns were probably written by David (*c.* 1000 B.C.); some were written during the periods of the Kingdom and of the Exile; most were post-Exilic.   These psalms vary widely in tone, content, and style.   Some are personal (e.g., 23, 121), others antiphonal and liturgical (e.g., 24); some are vindictive and violent (e.g., 137), others lofty and noble (e.g., 19, 42).   It is doubtful that any other comparable anthology has ever equalled the Psalms in sincerity, fervor, and passion.

Drama.   Although there was no theater in Palestine, there are two examples of dramatic writing.

JOB (*c.* 350 B.C.).   The book of Job is a philosophical drama, principally in poetic form; it was probably influenced by Greek tragedy — in content as well as in form.   It was not intended to be acted.   Its theme is the problem of evil.   Satan persuades God to let him try Job, a righteous and prosperous man, by afflicting him with boils, the death of his children, and the loss of his wealth. His three friends, Zophar, Eliphaz, and Bildad (ironically known as "Job's comforters"), suggest that the calamities are punishment for wickedness or that God is testing Job's love and loyalty.   Job pro‧tests that he is innocent; he is steadfast in his love for God; but he questions God's motives in making the innocent suffer.   The real philosophic conclusion of the book is presented by the Voice out of the Whirlwind (38–41): the question of why the innocent suffer is unanswerable by man, and man is presumptuous to question the motives of God. Job is humbled. Two passages have been interpolated into the original drama. The first (32–37) is made up of the speeches of Elihu, a fourth "comforter"; these tedious speeches add little to the philosophical discussion and break the dramatic action. The other interpolation (42) is contradictory to the conclusion found in Chapters 38–41: Job's health and possessions are restored.

THE SONG OF SONGS or Song of Solomon (*c.* 350 B.C.). A semidramatic poem intended to be presented with songs and dances as part of a wedding ceremony. Beautiful, sensuous, and sometimes highly erotic, the poems comprising this book are supposed to be spoken by the groom (in the role of King Solomon), the bride (the Shulamite), and choruses. Few scholars today accept the old beliefs that the book is an allegory of Christ's love for the Church, that Solomon was its author, and that the love described is spiritual.[3]

Wisdom Literature.*

PROVERBS (compiled *c.* 300 B.C.). A book of prudential sayings, chiefly poetic; erroneously ascribed to Solomon, probably of popular origin. Some of them are on a morally high plane, but many others are selfishly practical. Perhaps the whole book "smacks too much of the Ben Franklin ethics — it pays to be honest."[4]

ECCLESIASTES (*c.* 150 B.C.). Wrongly ascribed to Solomon. This is a series of heretical essays of profound pessimism, fatalism, and skepticism (except for many proverbs and pious passages interpolated by later editors[5]). The tone is that of a disillusioned old man who has found existence to be futile and meaningless. "All is vanity."

Tales. Several stories (once considered true, now generally recognized as fictional) are included in the Old Testament. Each one has a special purpose or message.

RUTH (*c.* 350 B.C.). A short story containing a tactful protest against the forbidding of racial intermarriage. Ruth, a Moabitess, is revealed as the ancestor of David, the greatest king of the Hebrews. It is famous for Ruth's declaration of love for her mother-in-law: "Intreat me not to leave thee" (1).

---

* "Wisdom literature" is literature which aims primarily at teaching some practical or ethical lesson. It is generally in the form of proverbs, precepts, or essays.

JONAH (*c.* 275 B.C.).   A widely misunderstood tale about an early Jewish missionary who rebels when sent to Nineveh, who repents and carries out his mission, but who rebels a second time when God forgives Nineveh.   Often the religious and ethical lessons — the wickedness of the rebelliousness and selfishness of Jonah, the universality and mercifulness of God, the virtue of repentance, and the need for religious and racial tolerance — are disregarded in favor of an inconsequential argument over whether a man could exist for three days in a whale's belly.

DANIEL (*c.* 150 B.C.).   An allegorical tale written for the purpose of encouraging the Jews during the Maccabean struggle.*   The story is based partially on old legends about an Exilic prophet.   It has an apocalyptic† ending.   Its most famous passages depict Shadrach, Meshach, and Abednego in the fiery furnace (3); Belshazzar's feast (5); and Daniel in the lion's den (6).

ESTHER (*c.* 150 B.C.).   Probably the latest of all the Old Testament books and also the least moral.   Its purpose was the supplying of a historical basis for the Jewish Feast of Purim.   The tale is bloodthirsty and revengeful, but artistic and effectively written.   Esther, queen of King Ahasuerus (Xerxes), saves her uncle, Mordecai, as well as the other Jewish people by exposing the plot of the wicked Haman, who has sought to destroy the Jews.

THE NEW TESTAMENT.   The New Testament is an account of the origin and early development of Christianity.   It is made up of four biographies of Jesus (the Gospels), a Church history, twenty-one epistles concerning religious matters, and an apocalypse — twenty-seven books in all.   Most (or perhaps all[6]) of these were written originally in Greek; perhaps the Gospels appeared first in Aramaic.   All the books were composed in the period A.D. 40–125.

The Gospels.   Four accounts of the life of Christ.   They agree in most essentials but differ in minor details.

MARK (Greek version, *c.* A.D. 70–100; perhaps in lost Aramaic version, *c.* A.D. 40–70).   The earliest, shortest, and perhaps most authentic of the Gospels.   Mark is a sourcebook for Matthew and Luke (see below); the three are called the Synoptic Gospels.   The book of Mark is attributed to John Mark, companion of the Apostle

---

* For the historical background, see the discussion of **I** and **II Maccabees** below.

† An apocalypse is a piece of writing which attempts to foretell or reveal the divine purpose.

Peter in Rome. It tells of only the last three years of the life of Christ — his ministry, death, and resurrection. The author of this fast-moving narrative delights in the story for its own sake and in the miracles. He is careless in workmanship and is guilty of confusing ellipses and repetitions. The last portion of the book (16:9–20) is generally considered an interpolation by a later editor.

MATTHEW (Greek version, *c.* A.D. 80; perhaps Aramaic version, *c.* A.D. 55). Attributed to the Apostle Matthew; based to a large extent on the Gospel according to Mark. Addressed to the Hebrews, the book has two main purposes: (1) to prove to the Jews that Christ was a fulfillment of the old prophecies — that He was the Messiah; and (2) to record the ethical teachings of Jesus. It begins with a genealogy of Joseph, husband of the mother of Jesus, and it gives the birth, life, crucifixion, resurrection, and ascension of Christ. It contains the only account of the Wise Men and of the flight of Joseph, Mary, and Jesus to Egypt. This Gospel is more carefully and purposefully written than that by Mark.

LUKE (Greek version, *c.* A.D. 90; perhaps Aramaic version, *c.* A.D. 65). Written by Luke, a physician and the companion of Paul on some missionary journeys. Luke uses Mark and Matthew as sources, but draws on other material as well. The book was written for the Greeks and Romans. Its author stresses the humanity of Jesus. Luke delights in poetry; he alone preserves the songs of Mary (the Magnificat, 1:46–55) and of Simeon (the Nunc Dimittis, 2:29–32). The tone of this Gospel is gentle, tolerant, and humanitarian. Luke gives the entire life of Jesus and the most famous account of His birth (2:1–20).

JOHN (*c.* A.D. 100–125 in its present form). Attributed, probably erroneously, to the Apostle John; the extant form of the book is much too late for such authorship. The book shows the influence of Greek and Alexandrian philosophy, especially the doctrine of the *Logos.** Its emphasis is on the divinity of Christ, His personification of *Logos*, faith (as opposed to works), the identification of the love for God with the love for man, and mystical union with the Deity. After a prologue, the book begins with John the Baptist's

* Greek for *word*. In Greek philosophy it meant "the rational principle in the universe." In theology it has come to mean "the actively expressed, creative, and revelatory thought and will . . . of God, at once distinguished from and identified with him." (Both meanings taken from Webster.)

baptizing of Jesus; then it tells of Jesus' ministry, death, and resurrection; it does not mention the ascension.

Church History.

THE ACTS OF THE APOSTLES (*c.* A.D. 60–90). By Luke, the author of the third Gospel. The Acts is a vivid and moving narrative of the spread of Christianity over Asia Minor, the islands of the Mediterranean, Greece, and Rome. It tells of the Pentecost; the stoning of Stephen, the first Christian martyr; many early miracles; the struggles of the young Church; and the conversion and missionary journeys of Paul.

Epistles.

By Paul (all written A.D. 50–65). Of the thirteen letters attributed to Paul, six are of major significance.* Although topical and addressed to specific congregations or specific individuals, these letters have proved to be the most universally influential letters ever written. Theologically profound, they became the basis for a vast amount of later Christian doctrine and practice. The tone and style of the epistles vary with the occasion and with the emotion of the moment. Some are cool, clear, and rational; others are eloquent, passionate, or even rhapsodic. Many parts are very closely reasoned and make difficult reading.

I AND II THESSALONIANS. Written at Athens to the young Church at Thessalonica. In these letters Paul expounds his beliefs that Christ's Second Coming is imminent and that therefore all men should make haste to be righteous and devout so that they may be enabled to rise with Christ and inherit eternal life.

GALATIANS. Written at Rome; called by Goodspeed "a charter of religious freedom."[7] Here Paul energetically denounces the tendency of the Church at Galatia to emphasize Mosaic law and ritualism. This epistle is expressive of Paul's liberalism and his concept of Christianity as a universal rather than a local religion.

I CORINTHIANS. Written at Philippi. Here Paul answers many questions which had been troubling the Church at Corinth. He inveighs against personal pride and ambition, and he proclaims (13 — the famous "Love" chapter) the vanity of all gifts and accom-

---

* Scholars now believe that the Epistle to the Hebrews was written by some other author and that it is a sermon rather than a letter. Besides those summarized in the text, the other genuine letters of Paul are: two to Timothy and one each to the Ephesians, to Titus, to the Philippians, to the Colossians, and to Philemon.

plishments not motivated by "charity."* He repeats his conviction that Christ's Second Coming will soon take place, and he advocates, therefore, that people remain unmarried so that they may devote more attention to religious endeavors. Again (15) he states his belief in Christ's resurrection and in personal immortality ("O death, where is thy sting? O grave, where is thy victory?").

II CORINTHIANS. Written at Philippi; probably a combination of two other letters, the earlier one constituting the last four chapters. This book is memorable for the author's rather bitter defense of himself (10–13) — a defense which seems to have been the result of the revolt of a faction of the Corinthian Church against Paul's leadership. The defense was successful, and the first nine chapters of the letter indicate that a reconciliation had been made.

ROMANS. Written at Corinth. This epistle is the most thorough expression of Paul's doctrine of salvation by faith — a supplement to his beliefs about sympathetic understanding found in I Corinthians. The Epistle to the Romans is the most profound and most theoretical of Paul's writings; it represents the very center of his theology — "All roads lead to Romans."

By Other Writers. There are in the New Testament eight epistles besides those of Paul. Only three are of major importance. (The others are I and II Peter, II and III John, and Jude.)

HEBREWS (*c.* A.D. 70–80). An anonymous sermon (not really in epistolary form) once erroneously attributed to Paul. This document is in the Pauline tradition but is smoother, more flowing, and gentler than Paul's writings. Addressed to the Christian Jews, it emphasizes the superiority of Christianity over Judaism, and it lays a great deal of stress on Paul's doctrine of justification by faith.

JAMES (*c.* A.D. 40–90). Attributed (perhaps wrongly) to James, the brother of Jesus. This is an open letter or sermon addressed to the "twelve tribes which are scattered abroad." It seems to be the deliberate result of the author's reaction against Paul's theory of salvation by faith. James' emphasis is on salvation by works: "Be ye doers of the Word and not hearers only." James also makes an eloquent plea against social injustice.

I JOHN (*c.* A.D. 100–125). By the author of the Gospel according to John. Addressed to "a pious matron," this letter is an answer

* King James translation of the Latin *caritas*, which, according to Professor Kirsopp Lake, should here be translated "sympathetic understanding" (lecture at Harvard University).

to the Gnostic heresies concerning the nature of Christ.   John finds
no difficulty in recognizing in Christ the mystical unity of the human
and the divine.

An Apocalypse.

THE REVELATION OF ST. JOHN THE DIVINE (*c.* A.D.
90).   This book was almost certainly written by some unidentified
Ephesian mystic instead of by the Apostle John, to whom it has been
ascribed.   It is addressed, in epistolary form, to the seven Churches
in Asia.   Though nominally a revelation of Jesus Christ, the book
is more Hebraic than Christian in tone and represents a continuation of the Jewish longing for freedom from oppression — the same
longing found in many of the Old Testament prophets and in the
book of Daniel.   It was written soon after widespread persecution
of the Christians began under the Roman emperor Domitian.   This
apocalypse foretells the fall of Rome (the Whore of Babylon), the
Second Coming of Christ, the resurrection of the saints, the chaining
of Satan, the Millennium, the final battle (of Armageddon) between
the powers of Good and Evil — with the triumph of the former, the
Judgment Day, and the establishment of the New Jerusalem.*

Ethically inferior to the other books of the New Testament, the
Revelation is, nevertheless, a literary masterpiece.   Its mystical
symbolism (though often obscure), its graphic accounts of the battles
between Good and Evil, and its terrifying picture of the end of the
world place it high in the realm of descriptive writing.

THE APOCRYPHA.†   This is a collection of fourteen books
which were included in the Septuagint (Greek) or the Vulgate
(Latin) versions of the Old Testament, but which were not considered by the Palestinian Jews to have been genuinely inspired
and which were not in the original Hebrew.   During the Reforma-
tion these were excluded from the Sacred Canon by the Protestants,
but they were included in the King James version and placed
between the Old and the New Testaments.   The Church of Eng-

---

* The account of the war in heaven (12:7–10) is an important source of
Milton's *Paradise Lost*.

† This title is generally employed to designate the Old Testament books discussed here; there are, in addition, twelve apocryphal books which have at one
time or another attached themselves to the New Testament.   These are the
book of James, the Gospel of Nicodemus, the Ascents of James, the Acts of Paul
and Thecla, Letters of Abgarus to Christ, Epistles of Paul to the Laodiceans and
to the Alexandrians, third Epistle of Paul to the Corinthians, Teaching of the
Apostles, three books of the Shepherd of Hermas, and Logia of the Lord (Oxy-
rhynchus papyri).

land admitted them into the Canon for purposes of "edification" rather than for "the establishment of doctrine." From a literary point of view, it is regrettable that these books have been dropped from most Protestant Bibles since about 1890.

The Apocrypha consists of four books of history, five tales, two books of "wisdom," one epistle, one song, and one prayer. As literature, the books described below are the most noteworthy.*

History.

I ESDRAS (*c.* 390 B.C.). An account of the Jews' return after the Babylonian captivity. It is mainly a reworking of II Chronicles, Ezra, and Nehemiah and therefore has little original literary value. It does, however, contain the delightful story of Zorobabel, who wins from Darius aid in rebuilding Jerusalem and the Temple. The favor is granted when Zorobabel competes in a contest to name the strongest force in the world. His opponents nominate, respectively, wine and the king; Zorobabel says that woman is stronger than either wine or king, but that truth is the strongest of all.

II ESDRAS (*c.* 380 B.C.). This sequel is less historical than I Esdras, but more interesting as a piece of literature. It consists chiefly of visions, angelic revelations, and prophecies of the downfall of the wicked and of the salvation of the righteous.

I AND II MACCABEES (*c.* 130 B.C.). These books give a history of the Jews in Palestine during the middle of the second century B.C. Book II covers approximately the period 185–168 B.C. — the years preceding the rebellion of the Jews against the Syrian king Antiochus Epiphanes, who attempted to suppress the Jewish religion. Book I recounts the rebellion itself (168–135 B.C.), which ended in victory for the Jewish leader, Judas Maccabaeus, and in the establishment of a dynasty of Hebrew priest-kings, who ruled till 40 B.C. The history is highly colored by the author's imagination and religious bent; but it abounds in exciting events and startling pictures. Judas is held up as a hero who wins not only — or even primarily — because he is brave and strong, but because he is a devout worshiper of Jehovah.

Tales.

JUDITH (*c.* 150 B.C.). A fictitious story of a God-fearing Jewess who, when her native Bethulia is besieged by Nebuchadnezzar's men, makes her way (by means of her beauty and her wisdom) into

---

* The others are The Rest of Esther, Baruch (with the Epistle of Jeremiah), Song of the Three Children, Bel and the Dragon, and the Prayer of Manasses.

the tent of Holofernes, the leader of the Assyrian expeditionary force. She pretends willingness to submit to his desires, lulls him into a feeling of security, and succeeds in beheading him in his drunken slumber. Judith is a favorite heroine of the Hebrews and has been the subject of many poems and paintings.

SUSANNA AND THE ELDERS (*c.* 130 B.C.). An excellent little story about a beautiful and righteous matron whom two wicked elders attempt to seduce. Her obstinacy leads the elders to accuse her of infidelity. She is condemned to death at first, but is later exonerated when Daniel proves by cross-examination that the elders are perjuring themselves. The elders are put to death. The story is told with admirable economy of words and with suspense.

TOBIT (date uncertain, 350 B.C.–A.D. 75). A wildly romantic tale which shows both Egyptian and Persian influences. Tobit, who has lost both his property and his eyesight, sends his son Tobias to Media to recover some silver which he (Tobit) has formerly left there. The angel Raphael, disguised as a fellow countryman, accompanies Tobias. By burning various parts of a fish, they succeed in driving away Asmodeus, a devil who has killed seven successive bridegrooms of Sara, a cousin of Tobias. Tobias and Sara marry, receive half the property of Sara's father, and return to Tobit, whose blindness they cure with the gall of the fish. Raphael fetches the silver from Media, reveals his identity, and exhorts the other principals of the story to worship God for his goodness to them.

Wisdom Literature.

ECCLESIASTICUS OR THE WISDOM OF JESUS, SON OF SIRACH (*c.* 150 B.C.). This is a group of poetic, pithy proverbs. Like that of the book of Proverbs in the Sacred Canon, its wisdom is shrewd rather than deep or noble; its burden is that obedience to God will bring prosperity and happiness — a favorite Old Testament sentiment. The book contains, however, some lofty and majestic passages.

THE WISDOM OF SOLOMON (*c.* 50 B.C., written in Alexandria). Another collection of maxims and wise sayings. Its moral tone, partially a result of Greek influence, is on a higher level than that of either Proverbs or Ecclesiasticus, and it actually approaches the nobility found in Christian ethics.

THE TALMUD

This term is broadly used to denote the body of Jewish civil and religious law; originally it was applied only to that part known as the Gemara (see below). It consists of four parts: (1) The Mishnah (codified *c.* A.D. 200), a collection of rabbinical rules and precepts derived chiefly from the Pentateuch; (2) The Gemara, commentaries on the Mishnah (there are two recensions* — the Palestinian Talmud [finished *c.* A.D. 408] and the Babylonian Talmud [finished *c.* A.D. 500]); (3) The Halakah, a collection of petty regulations and rites, full of minute details; and (4) The Haggadah, a collection of tales, parables, anecdotes, and legends employed for the purpose of illustrating a point of the law (it has been very influential on medieval and modern European fiction).

LITERARY INFLUENCE OF HEBREW LITERATURE

Any attempt to give in a few words even an intimation of the enormous literary influence of Hebrew literature — and especially of the Bible — is perforce pitiably inadequate. To list those writers who have been significantly affected would be to compile a roster of virtually all European authors since the days of St. Augustine. In all European literature the incalculable influence of the Bible may be seen in the fields of religious philosophy, style, subject matter, and diction. Taking English literary criticism as an example, one finds many volumes tracing Biblical influence. A few quotations will give an indication of the debt English literature owes to the Holy Scriptures: "The Bible has been a greater influence on English literature than all other forces put together."[8] "The Bible is a book-making book. It is literature which provokes literature."[9] "The English Bible is the chief bond which holds united, in a common loyalty and a common endeavor, the various branches of the English race. The influence of the Bible can be traced through the whole course of English literature and English civilization, and, more than anything else, it tends to give unity and perpetuity to both."[10] And finally, "An intimate acquaintance with the English Bible is the best possible preparation for a study of English literature."[11]

* A *recension* is a critical revision made in an attempt to establish a reliable text.

Bibliography for Ancient Oriental Literature

Egyptian

Budge, E. A. Wallis (trans.) *Book of the Dead*. 2nd ed. New York: Barnes & Noble, 1949.

Holliday, Carl. *The Dawn of Literature*. New York: T. Y. Crowell Co., 1931.

Wilson, Epiphanius (ed.). *Egyptian Literature*. ("World's Great Classics Series.") New York: Colonial Press, 1901.

Assyro-Babylonian

Holliday, Carl. *The Dawn of Literature*. New York: T. Y. Crowell Co., 1931.

Persian

Holliday, Carl. *The Dawn of Literature*. New York: T. Y. Crowell Co., 1931.

Jackson, Abraham V. W. *Early Persian Poetry*. New York: Macmillan Co., 1920.

Levy, Reuben. *Persian Literature*. London: Oxford University Press, 1923.

Indian

Farquhar, John N. *An Outline of the Religious Literature of India*. London: H. Milford, 1920.

Frazer, Robert W. *A Literary History of India*. New York: Charles Scribner's Sons, 1898.

Holliday, Carl. *The Dawn of Literature*. New York: T. Y. Crowell Co., 1931.

Keith, A. Berriedale. *The Sanskrit Drama*. Oxford: Clarendon Press, 1924.

MacDonell, Arthur A. *A History of Sanskrit Literature*. New York: D. Appleton and Co., 1901.

Oman, John C. *The Great Indian Epics*. London: G. Bell and Sons, 1899.

Chinese

Giles, Herbert A. *A History of Chinese Literature*. New York: D. Appleton and Co., 1928.

Holliday, Carl. *The Dawn of Literature.* New York: T. Y
Crowell Co., 1931.

Hebrew

Bates, Ernest S. (ed.). *The Bible Designed to Be Read as Living
Literature.* New York: Simon and Schuster, 1943.

Cook, Albert S. *The Authorized Version of the Bible and Its Influence.*
New York: G. P. Putnam Co., 1910.

Crook, Margaret B. *The Bible and Its Literary Associations.* New
York: Abingdon Press, 1937.

Dinsmore, Charles A. *The English Bible as Literature.* Boston:
Houghton Mifflin Co., 1931.

Gardiner, John H. *The Bible as English Literature.* New York:
Charles Scribner's Sons, 1906.

Holliday, Carl. *The Dawn of Literature.* New York: T. Y.
Crowell Co., 1931.

Jastrow, Morris. *A Gentle Cynic.* Philadelphia: J. B. Lippincott
Co., 1919.

McAfee, Cleland B. *The Greatest English Classic.* New York:
Harper Brothers, 1912.

Moulton, Richard G. *The Literary Study of the Bible.* Revised ed.
Boston: D. C. Heath Co., 1903.

Nelson, Lawrence E. *Our Roving Bible.* Nashville: Abingdon-
Cokesbury Press, 1945.

Part Two
Ancient Greek Literature

5

The Age of Epic Poetry

(c. 900–700 B.C.)*

Historical Background. Greek people inhabited not only the southern part of the Balkan Peninsula (Hellas), but also part of the coast of Asia Minor, part of Italy, and many islands in the Mediterranean and Aegean seas, including Crete and Sicily. On the Balkan mainland, mountains and the surrounding sea led to divisions into many petty local states, which carried on continual warfare with each other.

The primitive inhabitants were a mixture of three strains: (1) *Pelasgians or Helladics.* The earliest known inhabitants of the Greek mainland, they were perhaps related to the inhabitants of Asia Minor, and they probably were not Indo-Europeans. Little is known of them except what can be learned from legends and from the archeological discoveries of Schliemann and Evans. (2) *Aegeo-Cretans.* They were probably of Mediterranean origin and probably blended with the Pelasgians *c.* 1800–1400 B.C. (3) *Northern Indo-Europeans.* Variously called Achaeans, Danaäns, and Hellenes, these people probably migrated from the north of Greece *c.* 2000–1000 B.C.

After 1150 B.C.[1] there were three rather distinct racial groups: (1) *Dorians.* Their main settlements were the Peloponnesus, the Corinthian Isthmus, the southwest portion of Asia Minor, Crete, Sicily, and parts of Italy; their principal cities were Sparta, Corinth, and Syracuse. The Dorians were warlike, reserved, and devout. Their dialect was terse and rugged. They perfected the "stately choral ode." (2) *Aeolians.* The principal Aeolian settlements were Boeotia, Lesbos, and northwestern Asia Minor. The Aeolians were "impressionable, luxurious, and imaginative." Their dialect was soft and melodious. They contributed "poetry of passion and intense personal feeling." (3) *Ionians.* The principal Ionian settle-

---

* The "*c.*" before approximate or uncertain dates will henceforth be used to apply to the date after the hyphen as well as to the date following the "*c.*"

39

ments were Attica, Euboea, and west-central Asia Minor. Their cities were Athens and Chios. The Ionian nature was versatile, energetic, and imaginative. The dialect was flowing, graceful, soft, full of vowel sounds, yet energetic. Their contributions to literature were two — a dialect which became the universal language of the Greeks and most of the classical Greek literary forms — epic, drama, lyric, and prose genres.

The preliterary history of Greece falls into four periods: (1) *Pelasgian or Helladic Era* (*c.* 3000–1800 B.C.). Little is known of Greek history before 1800 B.C. The early period was probably one of Stone Age and Bronze Age cultures. The aboriginal inhabitants were perhaps overrun by Northern Indo-Europeans or perhaps conquered by an invasion from Crete. (2) *Cretan-Minoan Era* (*c.* 1800–1400 B.C.). Supremacy during this period was held by Crete, a great maritime power. Cretan culture (showing traces of Egyptian culture) was predominant. Perhaps the people of this era were overcome by the Northern Indo-Europeans *c.* 1400 B.C. (3) *Mycenaean Era* (*c.* 1400–1100 B.C.). Characterized by an Indo-European modification of Creto-Minoan culture, this was an era of many petty kingdoms, wars, and invasions from the north. (4) *Dorian Era* (*c.* 1100–900 B.C.). There were major wars and migrations in this period (the Iron Age). Indo-Europeans broke up into the previously mentioned groups: Dorians, Ionians, and Aeolians. During this era nearly all vestiges of Aegean culture were destroyed. The Phoenician alphabet superseded Aegean characters *c.* 1000–800 B.C.

In the ninth and eighth centuries B.C. Greece was in a highly unstable condition. There were invasions from the north and migrations from one part of Hellas to another. Although there was no such thing as national unity, the tribes were beginning to seek stability and to become aware of themselves as units. Semifeudalistic, they tried to develop traditions which would justify their tribal and family pride.

Over each tribal state there was a hereditary ruler, or *basileus*, who possessed almost absolute political power and who, in addition, served as military leader, judge, and priest. He was assisted by a council (*boule*) of nobles, who served in an advisory capacity. Then there was an assembly (*agora*) of freemen, who were without political significance but who could vote "yes" or "no" on certain issues presented to them. By the middle of the eighth century the power of the ruler had been reduced by the nobles, and the city-state — later to be of great importance — had been evolved.

There were three social classes: nobles, freemen, and slaves. The nobles controlled the bulk of the wealth and bore the brunt of most of the warfare. The freemen were engaged principally in agriculture and in the manufacture of simple, necessary articles. Slaves performed much the same functions as freemen and were usually treated very humanely; many were female war captives. Social organization was patriarchal, but the mother was held in high esteem and enjoyed a great degree of independence. Home life was sacred, and generous hospitality to strangers was an obligation.

The principal occupations were farming, stock raising, simple manufacture, and warfare. There seems to have been ample leisure for banquets, recitations by minstrels, games, contests, and festivals. Athletic training was an important part of Greek life; four famous series of national games were eventually established: the Olympian in Elis, the Pythian at Delphi, the Isthmian at Corinth, and the Nemean at Nemea. The first Olympiad was held in 776 B.C.

Religion permeated all Greek life. The Greek gods were anthropomorphic — little more than glorified human beings. They were capricious, amoral, and sometimes even immoral; they possessed many human emotions — jealousy, anger, desire for revenge, and sexual passion. They made their wills known through soothsayers, dreams, and oracles (of which the two most famous were that of Zeus at Dodona and that of Apollo at Delphi). The Greeks believed in an afterlife — a shadowy existence in Hades for the average man, punishment in Tartarus (a special section of Hades) for the wicked, and an unending bliss in Elysium for heroes.*

General View of the Literature. In an attempt to establish traditions, the tribal leaders of the ninth and eighth centuries B.C. turned to legends of the preceding centuries, which they glorified as the Heroic Age. These leaders patronized bards who could tell wondrous tales about the exploits of the great men of the past — men who derived their ancestry from the gods and who associated on almost even terms with the deities. The tales (or lays, as they were called) comprised a large body of "floating" or orally transmitted literature which ultimately became the basis for Homer's poems and for other heroic literature written during the Epic Era.

* For a summary of Greek mythology, see Appendix.

HOMER

Few, if any, *facts* about the life of the great epic poet (fl. *c.* 850 B.C.) have been established.   He composed in the Ionian dialect and therefore probably lived in an Ionian district.   Tradition holds that Homer was blind and that he was born either in Smyrna or in Chios (five other cities have also claimed him as a native: Colophon, Salamis, Rhodos, Argos, and Athenae); he was most likely born in an Ionian section of Asia Minor.

The "Homeric Question."   This is a twofold question: (1) Did Homer write both the *Iliad* and the *Odyssey?* and (2) Did Homer write the major part of either the *Iliad* or the *Odyssey?*   The first question was raised by the unknown Xenon and by Hellanicus and has been continued by others down to the present day; those answering the question in the negative are known as Chorizontes or Separatists.   The bases of the Separatist argument are the discrepancies in the diction, erudition, tone, religion, and artistry of the two poems.   Objectors to the Separatist theory (of whom the first was Aristarchus [*c.* 222–150 B.C.]) offer as explanation that the *Odyssey* was written somewhat later than the *Iliad*.   Similarities between the two poems, they say, are more striking than the differences.

Multiple authorship of both poems was suggested by Friedrich A. Wolf in 1795 in his *Prolegomena* to Homer.   He based his argument on the beliefs (1) that Greek was not *written* before 700 B.C.; (2) that Homer lived *c.* 850 B.C.; (3) that the poems were too long and complicated to be "natural" and early literature; (4) that the poems were too long to have been transmitted orally or to have "found an audience"; and (5) that the poems are full of inconsistencies and contradictions.   Wolf believed that Pisistratus (tyrant of Athens, d. 527 B.C.) caused bits to be gathered and then unified by a group of scholars.   Hermann believed a small, original core to be by Homer, the inconsistent parts by later interpolators.   Lachmann suggested breaking the *Iliad* into eighteen separate lays, each by a different author.

The most widely accepted current opinion is that Homer used many sources, consolidated them, and then reworked them into two poems.   It is likely that there were some later interpolations.   Discrepancies in tone, artistry, and erudition are explained by the belief that the *Odyssey* was written much later than the *Iliad*.   Oral transmission of very long poems is now believed possible and likely.

The *Iliad* and the *Odyssey* perhaps were not written down till the middle of the sixth century.

Homer's Poems.

THE ILIAD.

Historical Basis.   The existence of a historical Ilios (Troy) in Asia Minor, about three miles southeast of the Hellespont, was proved by the excavations of Heinrich Schliemann in 1870.   Tradition says that Troy fell to the Achaeans in 1184 B.C.

Mythological Background.   Peleus, king of Thessaly, and Thetis invite to their wedding feast all the gods and goddesses except Eris (Discord).   Eris, angry at the slight, attends anyway and rolls among the wedding guests a golden apple inscribed "To the fairest." Hera, Athene, and Aphrodite all claim the apple and ask Zeus to decide who should get it.   Wisely, Zeus refuses to serve as arbiter and relegates the decision to Paris, son of King Priam of Troy. Hera tries to bribe Paris with riches and political power; Athene offers glory in war; but Aphrodite promises him the most beautiful woman in the world.   Being young and human, Paris awards the apple to Aphrodite, who then helps him not only to win Helen, wife of Menelaus, King of Sparta, but also to carry her back to Troy.   In accordance with an old agreement, many chieftains of Greece gather to help Menelaus regain his wife.   Under command of Agamemnon, King of Mycenae and brother of Menelaus, the expedition embarks and, after several misadventures, lands at Troy and lays siege to the city and its environs.*   The siege has lasted a little more than nine years when the action of the *Iliad* begins.

The Story.   Agamemnon holds as his concubine a Trojan captive, Chryséis.   Although Chryses, father of Chryséis and priest of Apollo, offers ransom, Agamemnon refuses to release the girl.   At the request of Chryses, Apollo sends a plague on the Greeks as punishment.   Agamemnon finally relents and gives up Chryséis, but to replace her he takes Briséis, the concubine of Achilles, the son of Peleus and Thetis and leading Greek warrior.   Thereupon Achilles refuses to fight and sulks in his tent.   The battle rages intermittently till Patroclus, the close friend of Achilles, borrows Achilles' armor and is killed in battle by Hector, the chief Trojan warrior and son of Priam.   Infuriated, Achilles becomes reconciled to Agamemnon, re-enters the battle, and kills Hector in combat.   After much plead-

* According to Homer, Troia is the country of King Priam, and Ilios is the capital city.   Later usage has dropped the distinction.

ing by Priam, Achilles accepts a ransom for Hector's body. The poem ends with the funeral of Hector and the burial of his remains.

THE ODYSSEY.

Historical Basis. None.

Mythological Background. After the death of Hector, Achilles is killed by Paris. At the suggestion of Odysseus (Ulysses), the Greeks prepare a huge, hollow wooden horse, fill it with warriors, pretend to lift the siege, and sail away. The Trojans are persuaded by Sinon, a Greek who poses as a deserter, to take the horse into the city. That night Sinon releases the warriors from the horse. The warriors open the gates of the city to the returning main body of Greeks, who then destroy Troy and retake Helen. The Greeks set out for their homeland.

The Story. There are three main threads to the story of the *Odyssey:* (1) Telemachus' search for Odysseus, (2) the wanderings of Odysseus, and (3) Penelope's struggles with her suitors. These threads are artistically woven together at (4) the conclusion of the poem.

(1) Telemachus, the son of Odysseus, sets out from Ithaca to find his father. He seeks in vain at Pylos and Sparta.

(2) Odysseus with his subjects leaves Troy to return to Ithaca, his own kingdom. He meets with many adventures en route: a battle with the warlike Cicones; an encounter with the Lotus-Eaters (the lotus fruit induces loss of vigor, initiative, and ambition); a fight with Polyphemus, a Cyclops; a near-shipwreck caused by the release of winds from a bag; a visit with Circe, an enchantress who changes Odysseus' men into swine — they are restored by *moly,* an herb furnished by Hermes; an interview with spirits of the dead; an escape from sirens, beautiful maidens who lure sailors to destruction in shallows; an eluding of Scylla and Charybdis, sea-monsters lurking in the straits between Sicily and Italy; the killing of the sacred oxen of the Sun and a consequent shipwreck; a sojourn for seven years with Calypso on the island of Ogygia; a shipwreck at the hands of Poseidon at the prayer of Polyphemus; rescue by Alcinous, king of the Phaeacians; and departure again for Ithaca.

(3) Penelope, wife of Odysseus, holds many suitors at bay for several years. The suitors have wasted much of Odysseus' wealth and have even plotted to murder Telemachus.

(4) Odysseus and Telemachus return to Ithaca and plot against the suitors. Penelope, unaware of her husband's return, agrees to

marry whoever can bend the old bow of Odysseus. Disguised, Odysseus succeeds at bending the bow, kills the suitors, and then reveals his identity to Penelope. An uprising of the suitors' relatives is quelled by Athene and Zeus.*

Epic Conventions Established by the Homeric Poems. These are as follows:

(a) The adventures of a hero (usually a national hero) as the theme.

(b) Invocation to the Muse (Calliope).

(c) The beginning *in medias res* (the action of the *Iliad* begins in the tenth year of the war; the *Odyssey* begins with Odysseus' request to leave Calypso), plus recapitulation of earlier events.

(d) Stereotyped epithets, e.g., gray-eyed Athene, white-armed Nausicaa, fleet-footed Achilles.

(e) Epic similes — long comparisons, usually of actions or processes and usually derived from nature.

(f) Extensive use of monologues, e.g., Odysseus' speech at Alcinous' banquet.

(g) Gods' intervention in human affairs.

(h) Meter — classical (quantitative) dactylic hexameter, with the last foot in some lines a spondee.†

Summary of Criticism. For more than two thousand years Homer has been recognized as the first truly great Western literary figure, and his stature as a giant of literature has not been diminished by the passage of centuries.

It is true that there are many inconsistencies and incongruities in his poems: "Homer nods." Furthermore, there are numerous dull passages, such as the catalogue of ships in the *Iliad* and the description of Achilles' armor. Many repetitions mar the narrative. Finally there is an absence of elevated religious views; the gods themselves are amoral or immoral and are sometimes ridiculed.

* The three threads are not followed in the order given here. Books I and V–XIII tell the story of Odysseus' wanderings; Books II–IV deal with Telemachus' search; Books XIV–XXIV give the account of Penelope's struggle and the conclusion.

† In Greek and Latin a dactyl is a metrical foot composed of one "long" syllable (i.e., containing a long vowel) followed by two short ones; a spondee is made of two long syllables. In English prosody strong accent is substituted for length of syllable. Here is A. H. Clough's attempt to render the first line of the *Iliad* in hexameter verse:

"Goddess, the anger sing of the Pelean Achilles."

(*The Poems of Arthur Hugh Clough*, ed. H. F. Lowry, A. L. P. Norrington, and F. L. Mulhauser [Oxford: Clarendon Press, 1951], p. 451.) This attempt is somewhat awkward and irregular.

To offset these defects, however, we find superb "architectonics" — balance in plot and contrasts in characters; and the beginning *in medias res* adds suspense.   Moreover, the diction of the *Iliad* and the *Odyssey* is rich and fluent, and the poems abound in fresh and powerful figures of speech.   Although the religion depicted in the poems is of a low order, they do champion some of the major ethical virtues — courage, wisdom, marital fidelity, patience, and especially justice.   Finally, Homer has a broad and deep insight into human nature; many of his characters are universal and timeless.

HESIOD

Hesiod (fl. *c.* 800 B.C.), an epic poet, was born and spent all his life in Ascra, a village of Boeotia, near Mount Helicon.   He tells us that at his father's death his brother Perses defrauded him of his inheritance.   Little else is known of his life.

Literary Works.

WORKS AND DAYS (ERGA).   A long poem in four parts, in dactylic hexameter.   Part I (1–382) consists of moral advice addressed to Perses and the judges who helped to deprive Hesiod of his legacy.   The author warns Perses against shiftlessness and ignorance.   Part II (383–694) contains advice about the operations of a farm and about navigation.   Part III (695–764) consists of general precepts and proverbial philosophy, practical rather than ethical.   Part IV (765–828) is a collection of superstitions about lucky and unlucky days.

THE THEOGONY.   In dactylic hexameter, it is an attempt at a systematization of mythology.   It gives a pedigree of the gods, an account of the war between the Titans and the Olympic gods, the stories of Pandora and Prometheus, and an account of the four ages of man: Golden, Silver, Brazen (or Bronze), and Iron.

Significance of Hesiod.   "Homer was reading for kings, Hesiod for peasants."[2]   Although embittered, narrow, bigoted, superstitious, egotistic, and almost entirely lacking in imagination, Hesiod succeeded in what he attempted, which, he tells us, was the presentation of "truth, not invention."[3]   And occasionally he exhibited some "real flights of poetry."[4]   He has preserved for us the "true peasant note";[5] he was shrewd and practical; and he always "took the side of right against wrong."[6]   His *Works and Days* contains some meaty proverbs still current (for example, "The half is greater

than the whole" and "The immortal gods placed sweat before
virtue"[7]); and his *Theogony* is a valuable depository of mythology —
perhaps the earliest (besides Homer) in existence.*

THE CYCLICAL EPICS

(*c.* 800–550 B.C.)

Only fragments and titles of poems comprising the cyclical epics
are now extant. These poems were principally attempts to supplement Homer. Those on Trojan themes were summarized, altered,
and augmented by Proclus, whose identity and dates are unknown.†

Theban Cycle. The principal epics of the Theban Cycle were
Theogonia, which told the origins of heaven and earth; and *Thebais*,
Oedipodeia, and *Epigoni*, which told the Oedipus story.

Trojan Cycle. *Cypria*, *Aethiopis*, *The Little Iliad*, *The Sack of Troy*,
The Return of the Atridae, and *Telegonia*‡ were the main epics of this
cycle, which told the background to the story of the Trojan War,
from thirty years prior to the action of the *Iliad* through the death
of Odysseus.

INDEPENDENT EPICS

Fragments (in dactylic hexameter) or names of ten other epics
have been preserved, of which none seem to fit into cycles. Three
deal with the story of Heracles (Hercules), two with the Thebes
story.

MOCK EPIC

THE BATTLE OF THE FROGS AND THE MICE (*Batracho-
myomachia*) (perhaps *c.* 400 B.C.§). Anonymous. This short poem

* Some of the Cyclical Epics perhaps antedate Hesiod. Other works
ascribed (perhaps erroneously) to Hesiod are *The Catalogue of Women*, *The Eoiai*
(probably at one time part of *The Catalogue*), *The Shield of Hercules*, *Aegimios*,
The Teaching of Chiron, *The Wedding of Keyx*, and *The Melampodia*.

† Probably Eutychius Proclus of Sicca (fl. *c.* A.D. 170), but see Frank B.
Jevons, *A History of Greek Literature* (New York: Charles Scribner's Sons, 1894),
p. 54, for another candidate.

‡ Between *Cypria* and *Aethiopis* in Proclus' summary comes Homer's *Iliad*.
The action of *Cypria* covers the thirty-year background to the Trojan War down
to the action of the *Iliad*. *Aethiopis* resumes the story where the *Iliad* leaves off.
Material of the *Odyssey* is omitted, but would fall between *The Return of the
Atridae* and *Telegonia*.

§ Although *The Battle of the Frogs and the Mice* was probably not written till
four or five centuries after the serious epics, it has been included in the discussion of the Epic Age for three reasons: its date is uncertain, it was formerly
attributed to Homer, and — most important of all — it is a burlesque of the
serious epics discussed above.

is a parody of the epics of Homer and his imitators. Frogs and mice are made to act with the dignity and solemnity of Homeric heroes; combatants reappear on the scene after being seriously wounded or even killed; and the relationship between the animals and the gods is treated in mock-serious fashion. The plot itself is a burlesque of an epic battle. While fleeing from a cat, Crumb-snatcher, a mouse, meets Puff-jaw, king of the frogs. Puff-jaw courteously offers to ride the mouse across a pond on his back. In the midst of the journey a water-hydra threatens, the frog thought-lessly dives, and Crumb-snatcher is drowned. In indignation the mice declare war on the frogs. The mice use bean hulls for armor, nut shells for shields, and pine needles for lances, while the frogs equip themselves with marshmallows, colewort, beets, and sea reeds. Rousing speeches from the leaders incite the warriors to battle. The gods hold a council meeting to decide which side they will help. When Athene refuses aid to either, the mice eat holes in her clothes, and the frogs croak till she has a headache. A band of gnats sounds the attack, and the mighty battle is joined. Many heroes fall. At length a multitude of crabs and a thunderstorm sent by Zeus put an end to the war.

Although the poem has little intrinsic literary merit, it does have a few really humorous spots. Furthermore, it has been widely influential on later writers of mock-heroic pieces, especially on Rollenhagen, Parnell (who made a free translation of it directed against Theobald and Dennis), and Pope.

HOMERIC HYMNS

The term "Homeric Hymns"* has been applied to thirty-four anonymous songs, ranging in date from the seventh to the fourth century B.C. Written in hexameter verse, they vary in length from three lines to six hundred lines, but most are short. Their subject matter also is varied; most of them are prayers, invocations of deities, or preludes to recitations. The most famous are the "Hymn to Aphrodite" (3), the "Hymn to Hermes" (2), and the "Hymn to Demeter" (4).

---

* Both "Homeric" and "Hymn" are misnomers, for the poems were erro-neously ascribed to Homer, and the Greek *hymnos* meant merely "lay."

6

The Age of Lyric Poetry

(c. 700–450 B.C.)

Historical Background. During the era from 700 to 500 B.C. the pattern of Greek life was greatly altered. The power of the monarch decreased, and the power of the hereditary nobility became dominant. Villages consolidated themselves into autonomous political units, or city-states, in which citizenship was highly valued; the most famous city-states were Athens, Sparta, Corinth, Thebes, Argos, and Ephesus. In the sixth century the power of the nobles was overthrown by tyrants — unconstitutional rulers supported by coalitions of the nonaristocratic classes. Many of the tyrants were progressive though despotic, and many of them were patrons of art and literature. Toward the end of the sixth century most of the tyrants were overthrown, and the city-states adopted either oligarchic or purely democratic government.

During this era overpopulation and political disturbances caused widespread colonization. The Greeks established colonies over much of the Mediterranean area, especially in Sicily and southern Italy. Commerce and manufacturing increased tremendously.

The tendency of the time was away from centralization of power and toward personal liberty and individual self-realization.

General View of the Literature. In literature the Heroic Age was almost forgotten; emphasis was shifted from glorification of hero-kings to self-expression of the individual. The spotlight was turned away from the past and directed at the present. Since the literary form most suitable for giving vent to the author's personal feelings and opinions was the lyric, it was the only significant form employed during this era.

TYPES OF LYRIC POETRY*

Elegiac†

Although the first elegy was probably a lament, the term did not originally denote a poem commemorating the death of a friend.

---

* The term *lyric*, though originally used to designate a poem to be sung to the accompaniment of the lyre, is used broadly, in reference to Greek poetry, to signify any poem expressing the personal sentiments of the author.

† Possibly from Armenian *elegu*, meaning "flute," which instrument was used to accompany the recital (not singing) of the earliest elegies.

49

On the contrary, an elegy might be on any subject — hatred, vengeance, or even love. The word *elegy* was applied to any poem written in a special metrical form — dactylic hexameter alternating with syncopated dactylic pentameter.

Principal Characteristics. (*a*) It was expository or argumentative, not narrative; and it usually was an appeal to contemporaries. (*b*) It was especially fitted for expression of sententious, aphoristic remarks and was usually short and precise. (*c*) It was introspective — a transition from the objective epic to the subjective poem of personal feeling. (*d*) It was recited to the accompaniment of the flute.

Principal Elegists.

CALLINUS OF EPHESUS (fl. *c.* 680 B.C.). The earliest writer of the patriotic lyric. He exhorted the Ephesians to the courageous repulse of the invading Magnesians. Only twenty-one of his lines are extant.

MIMNERMUS OF COLOPHON (fl. *c.* 630 B.C.). "Founder of the erotic elegy."[1] He bewailed the sadness of life, the transiency of beauty, and the short duration of youth. He reflected the decadence and luxury of Ionia.

SOLON OF ATHENS (638–559 B.C.). Best known as a lawgiver. He used the elegy for political teaching and for expressing opinions about life in general. About 250 lines of his poetry are extant.

Iambic

Iambic lyrics were intended to be recited instead of sung. Their usual line length was trimeter, and they were used mainly for satire and invective. The most significant iambic poet was ARCHILOCHUS OF PAROS (fl. *c.* 650 B.C.). He is often credited with the invention of the iamb. He is vitriolic, violent, and passionate. Most of his poems are full of hatred or scorn; but they are brilliant, terse, and full of vitality. He also wrote elegiac poetry, especially laments.

Melic

Melic poetry was intended to be sung to the music of the harp, cithara, or lyre. It was written in many metrical forms and on numerous subjects. There are two principal types, monodies and choral lyrics.

Monodies. A monody was a personal poem intended to be sung by one person. The chief monodic lyricists were as follows:

ALCAEUS OF LESBOS (fl. *c.* 612 B.C.). Alcaeus was an aristocratic reactionary and an energetic foe to democracy. Exiled, he wrote lyrics (in the Aeolic dialect) lamenting his treatment. He produced ten books of lyrics about war, politics, personal sorrows, love, and wine.

SAPPHO OF LESBOS (fl. *c.* 600 B.C.). Despite clouds of legends concerning Sappho, few genuine facts about her life are known. She was born of a very aristocratic family at either Eresus or Mytilene (probably the latter) on the island of Lesbos, and she lived most of her life in Mytilene. There she gathered about her a group of girls to whom she taught music, singing, and etiquette; one of the principal purposes of the group seems to have been the preparation of each girl for marriage. Various legends and traditions have held that Sappho was married and had a daughter, that she spent some time in exile in Sicily, and that she committed suicide by leaping from a "Leucadian cliff" because her love for Phaon, a shepherd boy, was unrequited. None of these assertions has been established as fact.

Whereas there has been a great deal of disagreement concerning events in Sappho's life, few commentators have disagreed over her merits as a poet. Virtually all join in proclaiming her the greatest of all Greek monodic poets and perhaps the greatest woman poet of all time; Plato called her "the tenth Muse." Her skill in prosody is indicated by her use of fifteen different meters. As is usually the case in lyric poetry, the charm of her verse lies to a large extent in her exquisite choice of words — a charm often lost in translation. J. A. Symonds says: "Of all the poets of the world, of all the illustrious artists of all literature, Sappho is the one whose every word has a peculiar and unmistakable perfume, a seal of absolute perfection and inimitable grace."[2]

Into her poems Sappho poured her intense Aeolic passion. Most of her lyrics are personal, intimate, and self-revelatory. Nearly all of them are on the subject of love, and a majority are addressed to young girls. Unfortunately, most of her poetry has been lost or destroyed; only about one twentieth survives. There have been preserved one complete lyric and fragments of many others. All are in the Aeolic dialect. Appropriately, the only complete poem is an ode to Aphrodite, asking aid in winning a young girl's love. Others are epithalamia (wedding songs), farewells to comrades, praises of girls' beauty, and songs of melancholy and lovesickness.

Sappho has exerted a profound influence on many writers since her day. Among those most indebted to her are Theocritus, Callimachus, Catullus, Horace, Grillparzer, Luis de Léon, Ronsard, Malherbe, Boileau, Racine, de Staël, Chateaubriand, Lamartine, Baudelaire, Sidney, Lyly, Herrick, E. B. Browning, Tennyson, Swinburne, Freneau, Poe, Hovey, Teasdale, Millay, and W. A. Percy.

ANACREON OF TEOS (fl. *c.* 540 B.C.). Poet laureate of the court of Polycrates; later served Hipparchus in Athens. Anacreon was the originator of *vers de société.* His principal themes were wine, love, the transiency of life and of beauty, *carpe diem,* and hatred of war. His verse was light, sophisticated, graceful, and polished. Although he has been accused of lack of depth and tenderness, he is more widely regarded as one of the three most important early Greek lyricists (the other two being Sappho and Pindar).

Choral Lyrics. The choral lyric was probably introduced first at Sparta by Thaletas (fl. *c.* 675 B.C.), who composed songs (both words and music) to be sung by a chorus, with accompanying dances, at festivals. Choral lyrics were generally rather formal and stately. They were usually made up of a strophe (sung by half of the chorus), an antistrophe (sung by the other half of the chorus), and an epode (sung by the whole chorus). There were many types — marriage songs, songs of victory (epinicia), laments, and hymns to Dionysus (dithyrambs). The most important choral lyricists were ALCMAN OF SPARTA (fl. *c.* 650 B.C.), ARION OF CORINTH (fl. *c.* 600 B.C.), SIMONIDES OF CEOS (*c.* 556–467 B.C.), and PINDAR OF THEBES.

PINDAR OF THEBES (522–443 B.C.). Often considered the greatest Greek lyric poet. Pindar was born at Cynoscephalae near Thebes, of a very aristocratic family. Little is known of his life. It is likely that he was a priest of Apollo. Early in his life he devoted himself to lyric poetry, which he studied at Athens as well as at Thebes. In 502 B.C. an important family of Thessaly, the Aleuadae, employed him to compose an epinicion on a member of the family who had recently won a race in the Pythian games. Thenceforth Pindar was in great demand by victors in various athletic contests. It seems probable that he visited in the homes of the wealthy patrons whom he celebrated in verse.

Pindar was a prolific poet. Seventeen books of his poems were known to the ancients. These included hymns, dithyrambs, paeans, dirges, encomia (songs of praise), and scolia (impromptu banquet songs); only fragments of these types survive. But there are extant four books of epinicia (forty-four separate odes in a mixture of Aeolic and Dorian dialects), on which his fame now rests and on which it chiefly rested even when all seventeen books were known.

The Pindaric epinicia are extremely complex poems. Although they vary in structure, in metrical pattern, and in length, each one normally contains three elements: (1) celebration of a patron's victory in an athletic event, (2) a myth, related somehow to the celebrated event, and (3) moral or philosophical considerations. These three elements are generally woven into "a kind of pattern, and on the whole, so to speak, superimposed on a metrical and musical pattern consisting usually of triads, groups of three strophes. The one pattern does not seek to conform to the other, it rather avoids it; the metrical scheme marches steadily on and bears no relation to the arrangement of subject-matter."[3] An excellent example is the *Olympian Ode I*, to Hiero, tyrant of Syracuse; it opens with a brilliant proem; then the patron-hero is introduced and his victory related; after that comes the myth — concerning Pelops' chariot race against Œnomaus; next the poem returns to praises of Hiero; and finally the ode ends with reflections concerning poetry in general and Pindar's poetry in particular.

Pindar took his poetry seriously. The contests he described were parts of religious celebrations, so the poems had some religious significance; moreover, lyric poetry itself was sacred to Apollo and the Muses. Pindar felt that in writing an epinicion he was to some extent performing a holy rite. In religion he was a traditionalist and a conservative.

Some critics claim that Pindar's faults are banality and triviality; two of his epinicia, for example, celebrate mule races. He has been accused, too, of sycophancy; and whether he is actually guilty or not, it is certainly true that his odes inevitably glorify men of wealth and influence. But, then, he himself was an aristocrat, and it would be only natural for him to be interested chiefly in the achievements of the aristocracy.

At any rate, his faults are counterbalanced by many excellencies. His brilliant and powerful diction, the "organ effects" of his rhythm, and his pictorial imagination have led posterity to place him in the first rank of the world's lyric poets.

He has influenced a great number of other poets, among them Ronsard, Horace, Jonson, Gray, Wordsworth, Keats, and Goethe.

7

The Attic Age

(500–323 B.C.)

Historical Background. The fifth and fourth centuries B.C. were the glorious age of Greece — politically, culturally, and aesthetically. Athens was its center and leader till defeated by Sparta in 404 B.C. The reforms of Cleisthenes in 508 B.C. had given Athens the first truly democratic government in the history of the world. All citizens enjoyed complete political equality; only 20 per cent of the whole population, however, were citizens; slaves, foreigners, and women were excluded.

In 490 B.C. the Persians invaded Greece. They were defeated three times: in 490 at Marathon by a band of Athenians under Miltiades, in 480 at Salamis by the Athenian naval forces, and, finally, in 479 at Plataea by a coalition of Greek forces. In 477 some of the eastern city-states formed the Delian League, a confederacy for defense against Persia. Athens assumed leadership of the League and in 454 B.C. moved the treasury from the island of Delos to Athens; other members of the League lost their independence and were forced to pay tribute to Athens. This was the beginning of the Athenian Empire.

The period from 461 to 429 B.C. is known as the Age of Pericles. During these years Pericles was the chief general and leader of the Popular Assembly — the unofficial ruler of Athens. The era was one of unparalleled prosperity, influence, and cultural development. Primary education in reading, writing, arithmetic, literature, music, and athletics was given to virtually all citizens.

The imperialistic rivalry between Athens and Sparta led to the Peloponnesian War in 431 B.C. After ten years of inconclusive fighting, the combatants declared a truce (the Peace of Nicias) in 421 B.C., but the peace was short-lived. From 415–413 B.C. Athens laid siege to Syracuse in an attempt to conquer Sicily; the expedition was a failure and so depleted Athenian resources that Sparta was able to renew its quarrel with Athens and ultimately achieve victory. Athens surrendered in 404 B.C.

The period from 404 till 359 B.C. was marked by internal struggle, class strife, and disillusionment. Sparta remained the leading power till 371 B.C., when Thebes defeated her in the Battle of Leuctra. Thebes maintained leadership till 362, when Epaminondas, the Theban leader, fell in the Battle of Mantinea, fought against Athens and Sparta. Chaos followed. In 354 B.C. Philip of Macedon began his conquest of Greece, which he completed in 338 B.C. at the Battle of Chaeronea. He died two years later and was succeeded by his son, Alexander the Great, who by 331 had conquered all the known world — Greece, Egypt, all of Asia Minor, Persia, and south-central Asia as far east as the Indus River. Alexander died in 323 B.C., the end of the Attic Period.

General View of the Literature. The Attic Age was the era of most of the illustrious Greek authors: Herodotus, Thucydides, and Xenophon in history; Aeschylus, Sophocles, Euripides, Aristophanes, and Menander in drama; Demosthenes in oratory; and Plato and Aristotle in philosophy.

HISTORY

The Greeks of the fifth century B.C. looked upon history as a specialized branch of learning. Though guilty of many shortcomings, the ancient Greek historians were the first to attempt a systematic, authentic, chronological account of national and world events.

HERODOTUS OF HALICARNASSUS (*c.* 484–425 B.C.). The "father of history" was born in Halicarnassus, in the southern part of Asia Minor. About 455 Herodotus himself fought against the Persians and the tyrant Lygdamis and was subsequently exiled by Lygdamis. After wandering over most of the known world for ten years — as far north as Byzantium and the Black Sea, as far south and west as Egypt, and as far east as Babylon — he helped found the Athenian colony at Thurii in southern Italy, where he lived till his death about 428–425 B.C.

Work.

THE HISTORY. Herodotus' *History* was divided into nine books by Alexandrian scholars, who named them for the Muses. Though the subject matter is diverse, the narrative has some unity in that it purports to be an account of world events leading up to the defeat of the Persians by the Greeks. Book I deals with the mythical accounts of hostility between the Greeks and the barbarians, leading to the Trojan War; conquests by Croesus of Lydia; and the establishment of the Persian Empire, down to the conquest of Egypt by Cambyses. Book II is made up of *Logoi* ("things told") of Egypt. Book III tells of Cambyses' reign over Egypt and of the rise of Darius. Book IV is concerned with the beginning of Darius' campaign against Scythia and with his conquest of Libya. Book V covers the reduction of the Scythians in Thrace and the beginning of the Ionian revolt against Persia; Athens, but not Sparta, joins the conflict against Persia. Book VI tells of the progress of the war down to the victory of the Greeks at Marathon. Books VII–IX give an account of the death of Darius, the preparation of a mighty army by Xerxes, the march across the Hellespont, the battles of Thermopylae and Salamis, and the final defeat of the Persians simultaneously at Plataea in the west and at Mycale in the east.

Philosophy of History. Herodotus had no such clear-cut philosophy of history as Thucydides later was to have, but the earlier historian repeatedly attempted to show the presence of the gods' hands in the determining of world events. The gods disapprove the insolence, the pride, and the overweening of the mighty (such as Persia) and will bring them low (cf. the attitude of the tragedians, below).

Style and Technique. Herodotus wrote in a smoothly flowing, conversational style, marked by the use of antithesis and by careful attention to sound effects. His method is epic rather than dramatic; he is interested in broad, panoramic effects. But he is interested in details, too — details which give intimate pictures of people and their customs; consequently the *History* abounds in digressions from the main theme. Herodotus is romantic and imaginative, and he is more concerned with telling a story revelatory of people than he is with constructing a balanced, authenticated, cause-and-effect account of a series of wars.

Summary of Criticism. Although Herodotus is guilty of inaccuracies and discrepancies (especially in matters of dates), he never intentionally misleads us. Often he is naive and credulous, and he relies on untrustworthy sources; but he usually warns us when a piece of evidence is untrustworthy by labeling it hearsay, legend, prejudiced report, or the like. Concerning war, he knows little at first hand and is therefore a poor military analyst. He is to be commended, however, for his impartiality: he praises the Persians as well as the Greeks for courage and chivalry. Herodotus is perhaps too digressive and breaks his narrative too often. But his digressions are always informative and entertaining; they show him at his best — as a storyteller.

THUCYDIDES OF ATHENS (*c.* 470–398 B.C.). The "world's first critical historian."[1] Thucydides was born at Athens of a wealthy, influential family; he was related to Miltiades. In his youth he read and admired Herodotus. At the outbreak of the Peloponnesian War, Thucydides was one of the ten Athenian generals. In 424 B.C. the fleet under his command failed to prevent the Spartan capture of Amphipolis. He was punished by exile till the end of the war (404 B.C.), but was allowed great freedom by both Athenians and Spartans; thus he was enabled to make a close study of the war. He returned to Athens in 404 B.C.

Work.

HISTORY OF THE PELOPONNESIAN WAR. In eight books. Book I surveys about fifty years of Greek history, with special attention to the three years preceding the outbreak of the war; it reviews the underlying causes of the conflict. Books II–V cover the indecisive first ten years of the war, the Peace of Nicias, the renewal of hostilities, and the sack of Melos (416 B.C.). Books VI–VII tell of the disastrous Sicilian expedition. Book VIII (unfinished) relates the internal disorder and revolution in Athens (413–411 B.C.) following the Sicilian expedition.

Philosophy of History. Thucydides has been called the "first philosopher of history."[2] He discards the theistic theories of Herodotus and adopts a materialistic view of the universe. Events, he says, are determined not by the gods' intervention but by human nature — human selfishness, human frailty, human desire for advantage. Human nature never changes. Therefore history repeats itself, and hence Thucydides' history "is an everlasting possession"[3] — a useful guide for future emergencies.

Style and Technique. "All praise, but few enjoy, Thucydides."[4] He lacks the color and conversational tone of Herodotus; instead he is cold, rhetorical, austere, and obscure. He was influenced greatly by the rhetoricians and the Sophists (see p. 81). More annalistic than Herodotus, Thucydides has fewer digressions, and those are more relevant to his main theme. He carefully — rather contemptuously — rejects the myths, the legends, the traditions, and the hearsay evidence which make Herodotus entertaining but untrustworthy; Thucydides is severely critical of his sources.

Summary of Criticism. Thucydides is often guilty of dullness. He is too dry and annalistic to be entertaining. His theme is narrow: he shows no interest in aesthetic or social movements. But his works have many merits. Unlike Herodotus, he is very accurate; he is careful to criticize his sources and to follow them when they are trustworthy, and his chronology is especially accurate. As he was a soldier, he was able to give us an intimate, firsthand analysis of military happenings. In addition, he made the first critical and scientific attempt to interpret historical events. He had acute psychological penetration and was keen and impartial in the interpretation of human motives. Though Athens was the protagonist of his history, Thucydides shows no Athenian or Spartan bias.

XENOPHON OF ATHENS (*c.* 434–355 B.C.). Historian, soldier, associate of Socrates. Xenophon served under Prince Cyrus of Persia (not Cyrus the Great) against Artaxerxes (401–399 B.C.). Thereafter he settled at Sparta and fought with that city against Athens in the battle of Coronea (394 B.C.). As a result he was formally banished from Athens and lived at Olympia till 371 B.C., then at Corinth till his death.

Works.

DIALOGUES. Xenophon records his memories of Socrates in four dialogues: *The Apology of Socrates*, *The Symposium*, *The Memorabilia*, and *The Oeconomicus*. His estimate of Socrates is superficial. He admired the philosopher, but was unable to grasp his subtleties. Xenophon was interested not in theoretical speculation, but in practical philosophy.

HISTORICAL WORKS.

HELLENICA. An attempt to bring Thucydides' history from 411 to 362 B.C. It is valuable as a sourcebook, but hardly a worthy sequel to Thucydides, omitting important facts and being prejudiced in favor of Sparta.

THE ANABASIS. An account of "the most famous retreat in military history."[5] Here Xenophon tells of the ill-fated expedition of the ten thousand Greek mercenaries who, in 401 B.C., set out to help Prince Cyrus of Persia wrest the throne from his brother Artaxerxes. *The Anabasis* tells of the march from Sardis through Asia Minor and across the Arabian Desert to Cunaxa, where Cyrus was slain. The leaderless Greeks now faced surrender, joining the ranks of the enemy, or retreat.   Choosing the last course, they elected Xenophon general and retreated north through Carduchia and Armenia till they reached the shore of the Black Sea; from there they went to Chalcedon and Byzantium, where they served under the Thracian Seuthes.   Finally the remnant, about six thousand, returned to Asia in 399 B.C. in the service of Sparta.   Xenophon himself returned to Athens.

THE EDUCATION OF CYRUS (CYROPAEDIA).   In eight books.   Though long and tedious, this work is historically important for three reasons: (1) It is one of the earliest treatises concerning theories of education.   Xenophon here gives a synthesis of his ideas about the political and military instruction which should be given to a young prince.   He tells how Cyrus the Great of Persia (ruled 550–529 B.C.) was trained as a hunter, a soldier, an officer, a general, a victor, and a monarch; part of the account is historical, part fictional.   The important part of the treatise is Xenophon's own opinions; his "idea of the perfect ruler is a mixture of Spartan and Persian virtues and training."[6]   (2) The work is also one of the earliest Utopian documents.   Cyrus founds an ideal commonwealth, in which there is only one city.   Xenophon also suggests a public health service and a matrimonial agency.   (3) Parts of *The Education of Cyrus* are a sort of prototype of the historical novel.   The career of Cyrus is romanticized; and the story of Abradatas, Cyrus' follower, and his wife Panthea is almost a historical romance.

Philosophy of History.   Xenophon has no readily definable philosophy of history.   Although he is traditionally considered the successor of Thucydides, his purpose is very different from that of the earlier writer.   Xenophon is concerned chiefly with recounting adventures — partly to his own glory for participating in them. He makes no deliberate attempt at critical or psychological analysis of human events.

Style and Technique.   Xenophon's style is straightforward, simple, and graceful — the "words of a man of letters who was also a man of action."[7]   In his history his style is not so romantic or chatty as that of Herodotus, nor so sparse and rhetorical as that of Thucydides.

Summary of Criticism. . As a historian Xenophon is lesser in stature than either Herodotus or Thucydides.   He lacks both critical ability and intellectual and moral force: he has little grasp of spiritual subtleties; and he is guilty of prejudice (in favor of Sparta), personal vanity, and exaggeration. On the other hand, he is a careful observer of events, and he generally stands for what is noble, manly, and courageous. His writing is characterized by rapidity, directness, and practicality. He was the earliest Greek essayist. And, finally, "he awakened the Greeks to the essential weakness of the great Persian Empire."[8]

DRAMA

Tragedy

Origin and Development. Like the drama in England, Greek tragedy was the outgrowth of religious ceremonies. At festivals a chorus of men dressed up like goats (probably to represent satyrs) would sing dithyrambs and dance to honor Dionysus, god of wine and vegetation.*

About the middle of the sixth century B.C. Thespis of Athens, the "father of drama," introduced an "answerer" (*hypocrites*), or actor, who addressed spoken bits to the chorus during interludes in the lyrical parts of the performance. When these bits were expanded and when new mythological elements were added, drama was born.† Later, Aeschylus added a second actor, and still later Sophocles added a third. From the early days of the tragedy through the time of Euripides, the importance of the chorus decreased as the parts played by the actors increased; and the chorus was reduced in number from fifty in the days of Thespis to a total ranging from twelve to fifteen under Aeschylus; under Sophocles the number was fixed at fifteen.

Staging and Production. The cult of Dionysus, though widespread in Greece, was especially strong in Athens. In 635–4 B.C. a great new festival for the god was established — the City Dionysia

---

* William K. Prentice, *Those Ancient Dramas Called Tragedies* (Princeton: Princeton University Press, 1942), p. 3, believes that it is misleading to call Dionysus, as worshiped in the rites which led to Greek tragedy, the god of wine. Instead he should be considered "one of those supernatural powers, which, in some mysterious way, have to do with reproduction . . . and [therefore] all civilization, prosperity and happiness."

From these early performances we get the word *tragedy* (Greek *tragos*, goat, plus *aoide*, song). It is a mistake to think of Greek tragedies as necessarily sad dramas ending unhappily for the protagonist. Euripides' *Alcestis*, for example, not only ends happily but also contains some comic elements.

† Compare the *Quem quaeritis* trope in English church ceremonies about A.D. 900.

— to be held late in March.   The dithyrambic chorus, and later the full-fledged drama, became one of the regular features of the celebration.   Early in the fifth century B.C. it became the custom for the state to offer prizes for winning productions.   A choragus, or producer and director, was designated for each of three competing poets.   The choragus had to equip the chorus and actors at his own expense and then train them.   Each dramatist submitted four plays (a tetralogy), made up of a trilogy (three tragedies originally on one theme, e.g., Aeschylus' *Oresteia* trilogy) and a satyr-play — a shorter, less serious drama with many elements of comedy and satire (e.g., Euripides' *Cyclops*).

The actors were all men, chosen perhaps more for their strong voices than for their ability to act.   Properties, scenery, and costumes were elaborate.   Each actor wore a mask and a wig indicative of his nature and role, and he wore a high-soled shoe (cothurnus) to increase his height and impressiveness.   At the time of Aeschylus two actors (later three) were assigned to each choragus, so that each actor had to play several roles in *each* of the four dramas presented by his troupe.

The theater was an open-air structure.   The seats (at first of wood, later of stone) formed almost a complete circle around the orchestra, or stage.   Behind the orchestra was a skene, or dressing-place, of which the proscenium, or front wall, served as backdrop for the orchestra.   There was no curtain and usually no change of scenery.   An interior or specially propertied scene might be given on an eccyclema, a platform wagon rolled onto the stage.   A *mechane*, or cranelike machine, was sometimes used to raise a god above the stage (hence the deus ex machina; see page 62).

Structure.   The normal tragedy is made up of the following parts: (1) a *prologue* (omitted in early tragedies), an introduction and exposition spoken by one person; (2) a *parados*, the entrance song of the chorus; (3) *episodes* (either three or four), sections in which the main characters enact parts of the plot; (4) *stasima*, choral songs following each episode; (5) the *exodos*, action taking place after the last stasimon.

Subject Matter.   The subject matter of a Greek tragedy is either mythological or heroic or both.   The gods and the great men of the Heroic Age are ordinarily the dramatis personae.

Technique.

PLOT.   Greek tragedy has little plot in the modern sense of the term (i.e., a story built around an unstable situation which by its very nature must be resolved, and which, until the resolution, holds the audience or reader in suspense).   Some of the spectators already knew the general outline of each story and came not so much to see how it would end as to witness how the poet treated the subject matter.*

There was little or no action on the stage.   The limitations of the stage itself and the cumbersomeness of the costumes had a great deal to do with the absence of violent motions.   Such actions were generally performed off stage (as in the murder of Agamemnon) or were reported by a messenger (as in the suicides of Antigone and Haemon).

Sometimes (but not always) the unities of time and place were observed by the Greek tragedians; the unity of action was virtually always observed.†

Most of the plays of Aeschylus and Sophocles contain excellent dramatic motivation; Euripides often used the deus ex machina device — a god raised above the stage to resolve some impasse in the plot — instead of motivating his plots logically.   Foreshadowing,‡ which helped to achieve both suspense and dramatic irony, was often employed.   Oracles, divinities, and soothsayers as well as the chorus and main actors were frequently used in foreshadowing.

CHARACTERIZATION.   Though secondary to plot in importance (according to Aristotle), characterization in Greek tragedy was of great significance.   Some characters were little more than types, but many were both types and individuals; and a large number were so human as to be universally appreciated.

METER.   In Greek tragedies the spoken parts are chiefly in iambic trimeter or trochaic tetrameter.   The choral odes and lyric passages between an actor and the chorus, expressing grief or joy, are in numerous lyric meters.

---

* Philip W. Harsh, *A Handbook of Classical Drama* (Stanford, California: Stanford University Press, 1944), pp. 27–28, believes that only a few of the audience knew the stories.   It is to be noticed that in most of the dramas the chorus provides a fairly thorough exposition of the background of the story.

This discussion has drawn extensively on Harsh for historical, critical, and interpretive data too numerous to be recognized in every case by a footnote.

† A play observing the unity of time would have all its action taking place during a twenty-four-hour period.   One observing the unity of place would have no extensive shift in setting.   And one observing the unity of action would have only a single plot.

‡ Foreshadowing means giving intimations or hints of actions yet to come.

Leading Writers of Tragedy

AESCHYLUS OF ATHENS (*c*. 525–456 B.C.). The first great tragedian. His father, Euphorion, was a member of the Athenian nobility, of the deme (township) of Eleusis, where Aeschylus probably was deeply influenced by the mystical cults which flourished there. Aeschylus himself fought at the battle of Marathon and probably at Salamis and Plataea. He began competing in tragedy in 499 B.C. and won his first victory in 484. He continued to write for the Athenian stage till *c*. 459. Aeschylus made many visits in Syracuse, Sicily, to the court of the tyrant Hiero. Apparently he lived in Sicily after 468 B.C.

Innovations. Aeschylus contributed the following to the development of Greek tragedy: (*a*) addition of a second actor; (*b*) reduction of the number in the chorus to a total ranging from twelve to fifteen; (*c*) decrease in the importance of the chorus, with a corresponding increase in the importance of the actors' dialogue; and (*d*) origination of the trilogy on one theme. Less obvious changes effected by Aeschylus are mentioned in the paragraph "Summary of Criticism," page 65.

Works. Aeschylus wrote about ninety tragedies and satyr-plays, of which only seven tragedies are extant.

THE SUPPLIANTS (*c*. 490 B.C.). Probably the earliest surviving drama, and probably the first play of a tetralogy (the other three plays are lost). Its ethical message is uncertain; the play concerns the right and obligation of sanctuary even at the risk of war. Fifty daughters of Danaus flee from Egypt to Argos, whose king, Pelasgus, finally agrees to give them sanctuary — even though such an action may provoke Egypt to war. The play is thus little more than a prologue to the other two tragedies in the tetralogy. In matter of form, it is transitional between the dithyrambic lyric and real tragedy. Besides a herald, there are only two actors; the fifty suppliant maidens, who make up the chorus, are the protagonists. The drama contains little action or characterization, but it has some fine lyrics, grand language, and real dramatic conflict.

THE PERSIANS (472 B.C.). The only surviving play on a contemporary historical subject. Its theme is the humiliation of the Persians after their defeat at Salamis. The drama is the "least dramatic of all Greek tragedies. . . . The plot is one of tragic discovery by Atossa, mother of Xerxes, rather than tragic decision."[9]

There is fairly good dialogue, but the plot is poorly integrated. *The Persians* contains the first appearance of a ghost in extant drama.

THE SEVEN AGAINST THEBES (467 B.C.). The last play of a trilogy on the Theban cycle. (The other plays in the tetralogy were *Laius*, *Oedipus*, and *The Sphinx* [satyr-play].) The theme is the transmission of a curse to descendants (from Laius to Oedipus to Eteocles and Polynices). After the death of Oedipus, his sons (Eteocles and Polynices) quarrel over who is to rule the city of Thebes. Polynices brings in outside aid. He and Eteocles kill each other in battle.

PROMETHEUS BOUND (*c.* 466 B.C.). First of a trilogy on the Prometheus legend (the other two probably being *Prometheus Unbound* and *Prometheus the Fire-Bearer*). The theme has been variously interpreted; it concerns the conflict of injustice and brute force on one side against intelligence, justice, and altruism on the other. Because Prometheus has given fire to mankind, Zeus binds him to a rock on Mount Caucasus. Prometheus refuses to tell Zeus the secret to his (Zeus') downfall. Though almost entirely lacking in action, *Prometheus Bound* is perhaps the profoundest and most intellectually stimulating of the dramas of Aeschylus. Its influence has been enormous on ancient as well as modern authors. In addition to the plays by Shelley and Bridges on the theme, the works of Milton, Goethe, Byron, Browning, Swinburne, and Hardy were influenced.

✗ THE ORESTEIA (*AGAMEMNON*, THE CHOEPHOROI, THE EUMENIDES) (458 B.C.). The only complete extant trilogy,* it won first prize in the contest at Athens. Its theme is the inheritance, through generations, of a curse brought on by crime; crime breeds crime; retribution will follow; wisdom comes through suffering. The curse of Tantalus is handed down to Pelops, then to Atreus, then to Agamemnon, and finally to Orestes, who is pursued by the Furies (Eumenides), begs forgiveness (for killing his mother), and finally receives it. The trilogy had great influence on Sophocles, Euripides, Seneca, Voltaire, Alfieri, Wagner, O'Neill, and many others.

Agamemnon, the best play of the trilogy, has little plot. Clytemnestra, abetted by Aegisthus, her paramour and first cousin of Agamemnon, kills her husband, Agamemnon, who has been un-

* *Proteus*, a lost satyr-play, completed the tetralogy.

faithful as a husband and untrustworthy as the father of her children.* There is excellent characterization of Clytemnestra.

The Choephoroi (*Libation Bearers*) is the first play containing an intrigue as the main plot. Despite some unrealistic details, the play has good irony and suspense. The story is as follows: Orestes, son of Agamemnon, conspires with his friend Pylades to kill Clytemnestra and Aegisthus. He succeeds, but is pursued by the avenging Furies.

The Eumenides is the first play with a complete change of scene. The Furies pursue Orestes for having committed murder, but he is acquitted by Athene because he was avenging the murder of his father. The tragedy contains much effective pageantry.

The Thought of Aeschylus. Aeschylus deals with some of the profoundest of religious and ethical problems: the nature of the gods, the problem of evil, patriotism, and human responsibility. The following is a summary of his views: The gods are supreme and just. Man should submit to their decrees. Guilt is inheritable, but man has also personal and individual responsibility. Pride, murder, and other sins must be expiated by suffering, which brings wisdom to the sufferer. "Nemesis herself is not a personification of the jealousy of heaven, as in Herodotus, but a symbol of the victory of moral law over passion."[10]

Style and Technique. Aeschylus' plots are simple and loosely tied together; little happens. His characters are magnificent rather than human; they undergo little development. His diction is resounding, majestic, and exalted, perhaps bordering on bombast. Much is borrowed from Homer, Solon, Hesiod, the lyrical poets, Sophocles, the mystery cults, and colloquial sources. His method is objective, and he is aloof, detached, and remote.

Summary of Criticism. It is not for plot construction that Aeschylus is noted; his plots are not organically constructed, and his dramas have too little action. His characters, though graphically drawn, show little development; they are too often exaggerated — too extreme to be human. He is often guilty of bombast, wordiness, and obscurity. His merits, however, far outweigh his defects. In addition to the important innovations mentioned earlier, he

* The children are Orestes, Iphigenia, and Electra. Agamemnon had deceived Clytemnestra by sending for Iphigenia for the ostensible purpose of having her marry Achilles. His real purpose was to sacrifice his daughter to appease the wrath of Artemis.

gave "seriousness and dignity . . . to tragedy."[11]   Though sometimes diffuse and bombastic, his language is generally powerful and
dignified.   His grandeur and sublimity led Aristophanes (in *The
Frogs*) to rate him first among writers of tragedy.

SOPHOCLES OF ATHENS (*c.* 495–406 B.C.).   The second
great tragedian.   He was born at Colonus, a village about a mile
from Athens.   His father was a wealthy merchant.   Sophocles
received a good education as a boy.   He began writing early and
won the top prize in the Athenian contests for the first time in
468 B.C.   He wrote for sixty years thereafter.   He won twenty-four
victories in the contests and never placed lower than second.   He
was elected one of the ten Athenian generals.   Tradition reports
that he was embittered at the end of his life by a lawsuit brought
against him by his sons.   He died at Athens.

Innovations.   Sophocles made the following contributions to
the growth of Greek drama: (*a*) the use of painted scenery; (*b*) the
decrease in the importance of the chorus and the fixing of the number of the chorus at fifteen; (*c*) the addition of a third actor; and
(*d*) abandonment of the trilogy form — each play a separate unit.

Works.   Sophocles wrote about 123 plays, of which seven tragedies survive.

AJAX (*c.* 445 B.C.).   The theme of *Ajax* is the downfall of a man
as a result of insolence and pride (*hybris*).   Ajax has become enraged
because not he but Odysseus was awarded Achilles' armor.   Athene
has changed his anger to madness.   As the play opens, Athene
warns Odysseus that insolent conceit has caused Ajax' insanity.
Ajax regains his sanity, then falls on his sword.   Agamemnon and
Menelaus vengefully refuse him burial, but Odysseus finally changes
their haughty minds, and the body is interred.   The drama has
the following unusual features: an act of violence on the stage, the
exit of the chorus, and a change of scene.   The two crises of the
play are artistically bound together by the similarity of the insolence of Ajax and that of Agamemnon and Menelaus.   Ajax is a
real tragic hero — sinned against, but also possessing a tragic flaw
which effects his downfall.

ANTIGONE (*c.* 441 B.C.).   The theme of *Antigone* is the error
of stubborn pride (*cf. Ajax*) and the wickedness of allowing secular
law to conflict with divine law.   Creon obstinately refuses to allow
the equally stubborn Antigone to bury the body of her brother
Polynices.   She disobeys, and Creon orders her death, despite the

entreaties of his son Haemon, of the soothsayer Teiresias, and of the chorus. Antigone, Haemon, and Eurydice (Creon's wife) commit suicide, and Creon is humbled. The play has superb characterization; Antigone is very human. Ismene is depicted as a foil to her sister (Antigone) and Haemon as a foil to Creon. The tone of the play is unusually tragic. The suspense is exceptionally effective: will Creon relent before it is too late?

OEDIPUS THE KING (*Oedipus Tyrannus*) (*c.* 430 B.C.). The theme of this play is the "irony of fate. . . . No mortal man . . . can be pronounced happy until after he is dead."[12] In accordance with the prediction of the Delphic oracle, Oedipus kills his own father (without knowing that Laius is his father) and marries his own mother (whom he does not recognize).* The play is often considered the most powerful of all Greek tragedies. There is masterful revelation (Aristotle's "recognition") of the significance of Oedipus' deeds; and there is also an unsurpassed use of dramatic irony. The motivation is excellent, the action rapid. The inevitability of Oedipus' doom is possibly the best example in Greek tragedy of the inspiring of fear and pity in the audience. The influence of the play has been enormous; Seneca, Corneille, Dryden, Lee, and Voltaire all wrote adaptations.

MAIDENS OF TRACHIS (*The Trachiniae*) (*c.* 413 B.C.). A distinctly inferior play. Its theme is the death of Hercules as the result of the poisoned robe brought to him by his wife, Deianira. The interest is split between the deaths of Hercules and Deianira. The exposition is awkward and implausible, and the speeches are too long. The hero does not enter till the last quarter of the play. *The Trachiniae* influenced Seneca's *Hercules on Oeta*.

ELECTRA (*c.* 410 B.C.). Generally considered inferior to Aeschylus' *Choephoroi* and *Eumenides*, which are on the same theme. The main difference is that in Sophocles' play Electra instead of Orestes dominates the scenes. The speeches and characterization of Electra are the most notable features.

PHILOCTETES (409 B.C.). In a group which took first prize at Athens. This is a play of intrigue. Its theme is the conflict of justice and nobility on one side against base craftiness and worldly wisdom on the other. There is extraordinary characterization of

---

* Concerning Oedipus' guilt, Philip W. Harsh (pp. 119–120) points out that anger, insolence, and failure to reverence Apollo's oracle are real flaws and help bring on Oedipus' unhappy fate.

Neoptolemus (son of Achilles), Odysseus, and Philoctetes. The drama has a well-knit plot and steady movement, but the deus-ex-machina device is used at the end to effect the resolution of the plot.* En route to Troy, Philoctetes has been abandoned by the other Greeks; an incurable disease has caused them to leave him on the island of Lemnos. Ten years later, when the Greeks learn that they cannot take Troy without Philoctetes and the bow and arrows which he has inherited from Hercules, Odysseus and Neoptolemus return to Lemnos and try to enlist Philoctetes' help. He refuses to aid them till Hercules himself returns to earth and promises Philoctetes a cure for his disease.

OEDIPUS AT COLONUS (401 B.C.). Not presented till five years after the death of Sophocles. This along with other plays received first prize at Athens. Perhaps it is a reflection of the quarrel which may have taken place between Sophocles and his sons (especially Iophon) *c.* 408 B.C. The theme of the drama is the heroization of Oedipus. He curses his sons and prophesies their mutual slaying. He dies and is buried in a secret place. The plot is well constructed; the action is swift and dramatic. Characterizations of Oedipus — "the Lear of Greek tragedy"[13] — and of Antigone are outstanding. The play is probably indebted to both Aeschylus and Euripides.

The Thought of Sophocles. For Sophocles the gods are just, but not so prominent in human affairs as they are for Aeschylus. Guilt may be transmitted from father to son, but for Sophocles either pure fate or flaws of character (especially pride and arrogance) are more often the causes of man's ill. Sophocles evinces little belief in nemesis or retribution. Like Aeschylus, he believes that suffering teaches wisdom and strengthens character.

Style and Technique. Sophocles always builds his dramas around one "central issue, so contrived as to probe the depths of character in the principal agents."[14] This central issue so unifies his drama that every incident contributes directly to the climax. His plots, then, are very closely knit and generally rapid. The chorus is of minor importance. Sophocles is peerless in the use of dramatic irony, and his plots have excellent motivation. His

---

* According to Harsh (p. 152), the deus ex machina expedient is necessary to "perfect the characterization" of Neoptolemus and Philoctetes, i.e., to prevent Neoptolemus from stooping to base motives and Philoctetes from weakening — at the same time allowing the story to end according to the legend.

characterization is more normal, more human, and more realistic than that of Aeschylus, but still is often somewhat idealistic. Sophocles presents contrasts in characters to make characteristics more prominent. He is especially good at psychology, "sympathetic insight."[15] His characters sometimes change and develop during the course of a drama, e.g., Creon in *Antigone*. Few elements of humor appear in his dramas.

Summary of Criticism. About the only censure of Sophocles that can be justified is that occasionally his characters are too idealized. More often, however, his characterization is superb. His plots are unified and show excellent proportion and harmony; all events point toward one climax. As a technician he is superior to Aeschylus.

EURIPIDES OF ATHENS (*c.* 480–408 B.C.). Tragedian. Euripides was born on the island of Salamis, perhaps on the day of the great naval victory there. Tradition holds that he was a wrestler and boxer — probably because his father, Mnesarchides, insisted that he be an athlete. As a youth Euripides also made some attempts at painting. His first drama was written in 462 B.C., but none of his plays were produced till 455. He is reputed to have gone to Athens and become a student of Anaxagoras, Protagoras, and Socrates. He is traditionally believed to have had marital troubles and to have lived as a hermit in a cave on the shore of Salamis. About 409 B.C. he went to the court of Archelaus of Macedonia. About 408 he was killed, "perhaps by the hunting dogs of Archelaus."[16]

Innovations. Euripides is responsible for the following innovations in Greek drama: (*a*) further reduction of the importance of the chorus; (*b*) greater use of the prologue as an "introductory monologue addressed directly to the audience";[17] (*c*) use of romantic love as the principal motif of the drama; and (*d*) use of the monody and other musical novelties.

Works. Euripides wrote about ninety plays, of which eighteen are extant. Besides those discussed here Euripides wrote *The Children of Hercules, Andromache, Hecuba,* and *The Suppliants.*

ALCESTIS (438 B.C.). Fourth of a tetralogy — substituted for a satyr-drama. This is really a tragicomedy; it contains several humorous scenes (e.g., Hercules' drunken railings) and ends happily. Its theme is the rehabilitation of Admetus as the result of the death of his wife, Alcestis, who willingly sacrifices her life to save his.

There is touching characterization of Alcestis, who, at the end of the play, is brought back from Hades by Hercules.

MEDEA (431 B.C.). One of the most popular and influential of Greek dramas — Euripides' masterpiece. Its theme is that uncontrolled passions — especially anger and jealousy — may so overrule reason as to lead one into actions that are inhuman, disastrous, and self-destructive. Jilted by Jason, her husband, Medea avenges herself by poisoning Jason's new love, Glauce, and by killing her own children by Jason and then exhibiting their bodies to their father. There is powerful sketching of Medea as she is torn between love for her children and hatred for their father. Euripides creates a striking stage effect at the end of the play: Medea fleeing by means of a dragon-drawn chariot.

HIPPOLYTUS (428 B.C.). One of a prize-winning tetralogy (the other plays are lost). It has been influential on Ovid, Seneca, Racine, and d'Annunzio. Its theme is the necessity for moderation in love and for controlling one's passions. Theseus and Phaedra represent the extreme of excess of passion, and Hippolytus the extreme of Aristotle's "defect," or dearth. When Hippolytus, son of Theseus, refuses the love of Phaedra, his stepmother, she commits suicide but leaves a note to Theseus, accusing Hippolytus of having raped her. Hippolytus is killed by Poseidon at the request of Theseus, who discovers the truth too late.

MAD HERCULES (*c.* 422 B.C.). A political play glorifying Athens as a haven for the miserable and the exiled. Though somewhat inferior, the play attains some universal significance in its study of suffering and bravery. Hercules slays the usurper Lycus and then goes mad as a result, but Theseus takes him to Athens, where he is purified and comforted.

ION (*c.* 417 B.C.). A melodrama of intrigue and concealed identity. This play is an attempt to provide Ionians with divine ancestry and to show their kinship with Attic Greeks. It is "sensational rather than tragic,"[18] but it has good suspense. Ion, son of Creusa and Apollo, is about to be slain by his mother, who thinks he is the son of her husband by some other woman. Apollo reveals Ion's identity in time to save him.

THE TROJAN WOMEN (415 B.C.). A powerful play of "simple" plot — no complication, no intrigue, no "reversal of fortune" — a parade of Trojan calamities before Hecuba, who is about the only unifying element in the drama.

ELECTRA (*c.* 413 B.C.). An effective tragedy on the same topic as Aeschylus' *Choephoroi* and Sophocles' *Electra*. Euripides' treatment is more realistic and less heroic than the other two, but it is superior in plot construction. Euripides' unsatisfactory solution of the problem of guilt is that Clytemnestra deserved death but that Orestes should not have been her executioner. There are many differences in characterizations from those of the other two poets.

IPHIGENIA IN TAURIS (*c.* 414–412 B.C.). A romantic, sentimental, sensational drama bordering on melodrama. It was praised highly by Aristotle in his *Poetics*. Iphigenia, daughter of Agamemnon, recognizes a sacrificial victim as her brother Orestes. She saves him, and together they escape from Tauris and return to Argos. The play explains and celebrates cults of Artemis. It has excellent suspense and a happy ending. Naevius, Racine, Gluck, Goethe, Schlegel, and others have been influenced by it.

HELEN (412 B.C.). A melodrama of intrigue, based on a legend that Helen was carried not to Troy but to Egypt. The plot is almost identical with that of *Iphigenia in Tauris*. The drama is of mediocre merit. It inveighs against war, divination, and the belief in oracles. It contains many comic elements similar to those of New Comedy (p. 80).

THE PHOENICIAN WOMEN (*c.* 409 B.C.). A popular drama relating the entire story of the fall of the house of Oedipus. The minor plot concerns the quarrel of Polynices and Eteocles. The play has been influential on Accius, Seneca, Racine, Schiller, and others.

ORESTES (408 B.C.). A perennial favorite on the same subject as Aeschylus' *Eumenides*, but there are many changes in action and tone. The action of *Orestes* is poorly motivated; the deus ex machina ending is not plausible. The drama is imitative of earlier Euripidean plays, especially *Electra*, *Medea*, and *Iphigenia in Tauris*.

THE DEVOTEES OF DIONYSUS (*c.* 405 B.C.). Produced after Euripides' death. A "stark tragedy"[19] and, according to Goethe and Macaulay, one of Euripides' finest.[20] Its story is one of the oldest subjects of tragedy: Dionysus' punishment of Pentheus, a disbeliever, by having him torn to pieces by Maenads (female attendants or devotees of Dionysus) and Agave, mother of Pentheus. The interpretation is uncertain.* Its most memorable scenes are

---

* Wilmer C. Wright (*A Short History of Greek Literature* [New York: American Book Co., 1907], p. 263) thinks it Euripides' recantation of his earlier skepticism;

(1) insane Agave entering with her son's head on a wand and (2) her grief on regaining her sanity.

IPHIGENIA AT AULIS (*c.* 405 B.C.). Left unfinished by Euripides, produced posthumously along with *The Devotees of Dionysus.* This is a romantic and sentimental melodrama concerning the sacrifice of Iphigenia by Agamemnon to gain propitious winds at Aulis to blow the Greek fleet to Troy. The ending would probably have been the saving of Iphigenia by Artemis ex machina. Euripides gives a moving portrayal of the heroine. The drama has been used as a source by Racine, Gluck, and Schiller.

RHESUS. Its author and date are unknown; the play is attributed, probably erroneously, to Euripides. This is a dramatization of Book X of the *Iliad.* Aided by Athene, Odysseus and Diomedes sneak into the Trojan camp and kill Rhesus, the Thracian ally of the Trojans. The play is the poorest of all Greek tragedies; no character is tragic, and most of the technique is crude.

THE CYCLOPS (*c.* 423 B.C.). The only extant satyr-play.* The story of *The Cyclops* is a travesty (with many minor changes) of the Polyphemus episode from the *Odyssey* (IX, 105–566). The play is full of quiet as well as boisterous humor.

The Thought of Euripides. As a thinker, Euripides was far ahead of his day. In religion, although he was not an atheist, he criticized the orthodox views of the gods in "the light of morality and reason."[21] He changed at will the divine legends; he derided the traditional heroes; and he attacked the belief in oracles and divination. Though generally aloof from politics, he felt that the Athenian democracy of his time was debauched, that it was controlled by the rich and the aristocratic. He longed for a democracy based on reason, merit, and sincerity. His foreign policy was a championing of Athens against her enemies; but only rarely did he strike a martial note; far more often he attacked war as an unmitigated evil.

Gilbert Murray (*Euripides and His Age* [New York: H. Holt and Co., 1913], pp. 186–188) thinks it a glorification of Dionysus; Harsh (p. 239) interprets the drama as an exposition of the folly of transgressing the laws of human nature, personified by Dionysus. Still others have believed the play to be either an attack on popular religion or an argument for prohibition (quoted by Harsh, pp. 237, 469).

* A short dramatic piece presented as the fourth of the regular tetralogy and characterized by revelry, indecency, and satire; the chorus is always made up of satyrs and Silenus; the satyr-play is similar in matter and technique to Old Comedy (see p. 75).

"The principal point of his ethical doctrine is the importance of the individual's nature . . . his intellectual and moral endowment."[22] He sympathized with the man of humble birth, but he had little faith in *hoi polloi* as a group. His attitude toward women was doubtful, but tradition holds him to have been a misogynist. He was essentially pessimistic: nothing assures happiness — intellectual pursuits, love, children, or even lack of children. Aristotle (*Poetics.* XIII) calls him "the most tragic of poets."

Style and Technique. In matters of style and technique Euripides was a mixture of formalist and innovator, though his instances of disregard for traditional forms and methods far outnumbered his adherences to them. Formalism is noticeable in his treatment of prologues, his use of *stichomythy*,* his balance of speeches, and, occasionally, in his use of the deus ex machina.

In order to express his new theories, Euripides found it necessary to alter many of the old techniques. Perhaps his most significant change was in characterization. His men and women cease to be demigods or heroes of superhuman stature; instead they are more human, more commonplace. Many realistic details, sometimes bordering on naturalism, bring his characters down to the level of everyday life. Sophocles said that he himself portrayed men as they should be, but that Euripides portrayed them as they are.[23] Euripides was an excellent psychologist, especially in the portrayal of women — both noble and terrifying ones.

He made significant changes in the handling of plot, too. Sensationalism, melodrama, and startling effects often replaced the stark simplicity of Aeschylus. Euripides delighted in the depiction of madness and in the use of the deus ex machina perhaps for the purpose of shocking the audience. He used children for sentimental purposes. His plots were more complicated than those of his predecessors, a subplot occurring in one of Euripides' dramas. At best his plots were as good as the best of Sophocles', but sometimes they were lacking in motivation and continuity. He rarely based his plots on fate.

* *Stichomythy* or *stichomythia* is dialogue in which each speaker uses only one line for a speech. For example:

"Alcestis: Dark — dark — mine eyes are drooping, heavy-laden.
Admetus: Oh, I am lost if thou wilt leave me, wife."

(Quoted from Euripides' *Alcestis*, ll. 386–387; tr. A. S. Way, in Stith Thompson and John Gassner, eds., *Our Heritage of World Literature* [New York: Dryden Press, 1942].)

He reduced the importance of the chorus and virtually severed its organic relation to the action of the drama. His scenery, costuming, and stage effects were elaborate. He employed humor a great deal. And his language was simple, realistic, and sometimes rhetorically eloquent.

Summary of Criticism. Euripides is a far more controversial dramatist than either Aeschylus or Sophocles. Critics have found both much to blame and much to praise in his tragedies. His themes were sometimes ignoble and sometimes narrowly topical; but they usually dealt realistically with everyday matters and were often universal in application. Although some of his protagonists were unheroic, nearly all of them were human. His sensationalism, sentimentalism, and melodrama, though censured by some critics, have been defended by others as effective stage devices. Some of his plots were poorly motivated, especially in his use of the deus ex machina device; but some of the plots were well built and skillfully complicated, and sometimes the deus ex machina was used successfully for special effects. Finally, commentators have complained that Euripides' language was lacking in grandeur, but few can deny that that language was simple, direct, and often eloquent.

Comparison of Aeschylus, Sophocles, and Euripides

AESCHYLUS	SOPHOCLES	EURIPIDES
First great dramatist.	Second great dramatist.	Third and last great Greek tragedian.
Added second actor.	Added third actor.	———
Originated trilogy.	Abandoned unified trilogy.	———
Reduced number in and importance of chorus.	Set number of chorus at fifteen and further decreased its importance.	Still further reduced importance of chorus and virtually made it irrelevant to action of drama.
Used little scenery on stage.	Originated painted scenery.	Increased elaborateness of scenery, costumes, and stage effects.
Gods and fate supreme, not to be questioned. Man's suffering is the result of guilt, which is inheritable and which must be expiated. Suffering teaches wisdom.	Gods are just, but not so important. Fate still inexorable, yet man's suffering is sometimes (but not always) the result of guilt. Guilt is transmitted. Little insistence on retribution. Suffering teaches wisdom.	Orthodox gods often immoral and unreasonable. Life is tragic, but principally so as the result of conflicts in man's own nature.

AESCHYLUS	SOPHOCLES	EURIPIDES
Characters magnificent, superhuman. No development.	Characters somewhat more human, but still exalted personages. Excellent psychology. Character development. Characters used as foils.	Characters average human beings, treated sympathetically. More development than in Sophocles. Great emphasis on the individual. Excellent psychology, especially when depicting women.
Plots simple, little action; sometimes poor continuity. Little use of deus ex machina.	Plots more complicated; more action. Excellent motivation and continuity. Built around central issue, leading to powerful climax; closely knit plot. Little use of deus ex machina.	Plots most complicated. Action sometimes violent, sensational, melodramatic. Sometimes loose construction, poor motivation. Use of deus ex machina in twelve plays.
Diction dignified, magnificent, sometimes obscure.	Diction noble, serene, clear.	Diction simple, straightforward, rhetorically eloquent.
A little dramatic irony.	Great use of dramatic irony.	Some use of dramatic irony — sometimes comic.
Little topicality — one play (*Persians*) on a current event.	Little or no topicality.	Many plays dealing with current topics and current trends, though none with contemporary setting. Several comment on war and politics of the time.
No humor.	Brief touches of humor.	Many instances of humor — whole comic scenes.
Popular in own time. Won thirteen first prizes in contests.	Exceptionally popular in own time — won twenty-four first prizes.	Comparatively unpopular in own age — won only five first prizes, but he was the most influential of the three in later ages, especially on Latin drama and French classical drama.

Old Comedy*

Origin. The beginning and the development of Greek comedy are obscure. According to Aristotle, comedy originated late, and its first performers were volunteers. It is not known who introduced masks or prologues or who increased the number of actors.[24] Apparently, however, comedy derives from two sources. The first is the Athenian *comos* (hence our word *comedy*) or song of revelry in

* A term applied to Greek comedy written before *c.* 380 B.C. It is practically synonymous with Aristophanic comedy.

honor of Dionysus, sung on various occasions but especially at the two great annual festivals, the *Lenaea* in January and the *City Dionysia* in March. These songs were either incantations to avert evil or prayers for fertility. Revelers dressed in outlandish costumes paraded about, carrying phallic symbols, singing songs to Dionysus, and adding bits of ribaldry and personal jibes at bystanders. Later the revelers were divided into two parts, which sang antiphonally. The second source of comedy was a rude Sicilian mime or farce, made up principally of coarse, familiar allusions to persons in the audience — allusions perhaps ad libbed by the actors. Who brought the *comos* and the Sicilian mime together to produce the first comedy is unknown. The town of Megara claims the honor, but the claim is disputed by Athens. Magnes is credited with introducing choruses of birds, frogs, and the like.

Staging and Production. The staging and production of a Greek comedy were much the same as those of a tragedy. Five comedies, each by a different author, were usually presented at the festivals after the tragedies; a prize was offered for the best comedy. Masks and low-heeled shoes ("socks") were worn by the actors. The chorus was made up of twenty-four men, often in elaborate or grotesque costumes.

ARISTOPHANES OF ATHENS (*c.* 448–380 B.C.). The greatest writer of Greek comedy. Aristophanes was born of respectable and perhaps well-to-do parents, in the deme of Cydathene. He began writing comedy early; his first work was produced in 427 B.C. He probably acted in one or more of his own plays.

Structure of His Comedies. The structure of Aristophanes' comedies varies; no one pattern is followed consistently. Roughly speaking, one can say that each play falls into two parts (perhaps a hang-over of the two sources of comedy; see above): the first half, in which a "happy idea" is debated, and the last half, in which the idea is put into practice. The following parts are usually recognizable: (a) a *prologue*, which announces the "happy idea" or ingenious plan conceived by an actor; the plan is usually extravagant and impractical; (b) a *parados*, the entry of the chorus; (c) an *agon*, a debate between the proponent of the "happy idea" and its opponent; the proponent is always victorious; (d) a *parabasis*, a choral interlude spoken directly to the audience and giving the author's own opinions; the parabasis usually comes between the agon and the remainder of the comedy, but sometimes at the end of the play, and twice it is omitted altogether; two plays have two parabases each; (e) *episodes*, actions following the parabasis and illustrating the "happy idea"; sometimes the episodes are independent of each other; (f) *stasima*, choral lyrics between each two episodes; (g) the *exodus*, action after the last stasimon — usually a celebration or revel of some sort. Many lyrics, either serious or comic, are interspersed throughout the entire comedy.

Works. Aristophanes wrote about forty comedies, of which eleven are extant.

THE ACHARNIANS (425 B.C.). This comedy won first prize in the contest at Athens. Its theme is an appeal for peace with Sparta plus a parody of Euripides' support of war (in *The Children of Hercules* and *Andromache*). The leader of Athens decides to have the god Amphitheus negotiate a private peace with Sparta. *The Acharnians* is a superior play containing some effective scenes (e.g., the selling of the starving daughters of the Megarian and the Dionysiac revel at the end of the play). Its intellectual appeal is weak, but its emotional appeal is very strong.

THE KNIGHTS (424 B.C.). Winner of a first prize. Its theme is the satirization of the "tendency of democracy, once having begun a course of basic corruption, to fall victim to more and more depraved leaders."[25] The comedy also makes an appeal for peace between Athens and Sparta. "Happy idea": Nicias decides to supplant Cleon with a worse demagogue than Cleon himself. *The Knights* is a comparatively dull play, but it has some brilliant scenes, keen analysis of the political situation, and apt satire.

THE CLOUDS (423 B.C.). First form later revised. Its theme is the satirization of Socrates and the Sophists. "Happy idea": in order to be able to defeat his creditors in debate, Strepsiades decides to send his son to Socrates' university to learn how to argue. *The Clouds* is one of the most popular and influential of Aristophanes' plays. It tends toward higher comedy. The plot construction is loose; there are four main scenes and a verbal agon. The play probably contributed toward Athenian prejudice which led to Socrates' conviction.

THE WASPS (422 B.C.). The theme is an attack on the Athenian mania for jury duty — a mania induced by Cleon's increasing the pay of jurymen. "Happy idea": to have Philocleon (literally, "Cleon-lover"), who claims that he must serve on the jury or die of boredom, hold private court. This is an amusing play, but it is perhaps too topical to be of great interest today.

PEACE (421 B.C.). Another appeal for peace between Athens and Sparta. "Happy idea": Trygaeus decides to go directly to Zeus to ask him to impose peace and thereby save Greece. There is little dramatic conflict.

THE BIRDS (414 B.C.). The theme of *The Birds* is disputable. Some suggested interpretations are that it is a mere "fantasy of escape," a burlesque of the ambitious Sicilian expedition, or an advocation of either a real revolution or a change of government. "Happy idea": two men become disgusted with Athens and seek a Utopian existence in the land of the birds. The play has beautiful imagery, whimsical charm, excellent plot construction, and consistent characterization. There are no low-comedy elements. It is generally considered Aristophanes' masterpiece.

THE THESMOPHORIAZUSAE (411 B.C.). A parody of Euripides and a satirization of the women of Athens. "Happy idea": Euripides, upon learning that some women are about to debate the best method of revenge upon him for exposing the vices of their sex, persuades Agathon, another tragic poet, to masquerade as a woman and plead Euripides' cause. There is much parody of the style of Euripides. Most of the criticism is sound but somewhat exaggerated.

LYSISTRATA (411 B.C.). Aristophanes makes one more appeal for peace between Athens and Sparta. "Happy idea": Lysistrata suggests a sex strike against the men to force them to negotiate a peace. The result is uproarious low comedy, frankly obscene. The plot of intrigue is artistically constructed. The comedy is now considered one of Aristophanes' best plays.

THE FROGS (405 B.C.). Winner of first prize. Its theme is criticism of Aeschylus, Sophocles, and Euripides, with the last of the three receiving the worst censure. The drama is also an attack on Athenian political and literary decadence. "Happy idea": Dionysus decides to go to Hades to bring back a good tragedian, because the current writers of tragedy are very poor. Aristophanes gives a great deal of sound criticism of Aeschylus and Euripides, although he is prejudiced in favor of the former. The charge of Euripides' immorality in drama is false.

THE ASSEMBLY-WOMEN (*The Ecclesiazusae*) (*c.* 393 B.C.). A satirization of Athenian restlessness and debauched desire for novelty.* "Happy idea": Praxagora conceives the brilliant plan of disguising women as men, having them pre-empt the seats of the Assembly, and then letting them seize control of the state. The drama lacks the vigor, wit, and resourcefulness of Aristophanes' earlier plays. It contains elements tending toward Middle and New Comedy (see below).

PLUTUS (388 B.C.). An attack on mankind in general (and on Athenians in particular) for employing unjust or unworthy means to grow wealthy. "Happy idea": Chremylus has Asclepius restore the eyesight of Plutus so that he can redistribute wealth equably. The satire is universal and mild — almost benign, lacking Aristophanes' former biting wit and topicality. The play shows change in structure in the direction of New Comedy (e.g., a slave plays a leading role).

The Thought of Aristophanes. Aristophanes was a conservative and a believer in the sanctity of tradition. In his comedies there is usually discernible a longing for the "good old days," and there is nearly always a protest against the new — new manners, new religion, new philosophy, new rhetoric, and new literature. He felt that everything new was likely to be frivolous and degenerate. In a word, his dramas were a protest against the decadence of his age.

Characteristics of Aristophanic Comedy. The characteristics of the comedies of Aristophanes are as follows: topicality; satire; frankness, ribaldry, and abusiveness — sometimes personal; buffoonery; light, relatively unimportant plot; individual as well as type characters; use of two types of lyrics — light, clever *vers de société* (cf. Gilbert and Sullivan) and serious lyrics of great depth, feeling, and beauty; occasional and unexpected "gentleness and a quality akin to tears"; [26] sparkling wit and cleverness; unpredictability and inconsistency; appeal to the emotions rather than to the intellect; and, finally, disregard of the unities, of realism, and of verisimilitude.

Summary of Criticism. Although the humor in Aristophanes' comedies is often obscene and indecent, it is almost unfailingly hilarious; although he is prejudiced and unfair in his criticism, and although he exaggerates the faults of his objects of attack, he gen-

* Possibly a parody "in advance" of Plato's *Republic*, or perhaps a satire on women's rights. The *Republic* was not published till after 391 B.C., but some of Plato's ideas contained in it had probably been in circulation for many years.

erally puts his finger on real defects and shortcomings; although his plots are frequently flimsy and implausible, we accept those weak plots as mere frames on which to hang his satire; and although his characterization is poor (few of his characters are memorable, and many of them are mere caricatures or types), he has an exceptional gift of parody.

Middle Comedy

Middle Comedy was a transitional form between Old Comedy and New Comedy, presumably having some of the characteristics of each. It was more timid than Old Comedy, and it was concerned less with politics and living human beings. Instead, it travestied mythology and tragedy. Songs of the chorus became mere interludes. Unless Aristophanes' *Ecclesiazusae* and *Plutus* can be considered Middle Comedy, no examples of it are extant. It flourished *c.* 380–336 B.C.

New Comedy

New Comedy was essentially a comedy of manners, developing naturally from Middle Comedy. Gradually plots and characters from everyday life were substituted for those from mythology and Euripidean tragedy. Choral songs continued, as in Middle Comedy, to be nothing more than interludes; the number of these interludes was eventually fixed at four, thus dividing the play into the traditional five acts. New Comedy prevailed from 336 B.C. till *c.* 262 B.C.

Characteristics. The distinguishing features of New Comedy were three.

A CLOSELY–KNIT PLOT. It was usually based upon intrigue, concealed identities, discovery of long-lost friends or relatives, or a combination of any two or all three of these. The situation was usually farcical and improbable; there was often a subplot.

TYPE CHARACTERS. We find, for example, the duped husband, the miser-father, the mistreated but deserving son, the prostitute, the rascally slave, the parasite, the scheming valet, and the braggart soldier.

SUPERFICIALITY. New Comedy dealt with a narrow segment of society and was concerned more with manners and customs than with profound moral problems.

Playwrights.

DIPHILUS OF ATHENS (fl. *c.* 300 B.C.). Born at Sinope, he moved to Athens. He wrote about a hundred plays, of which one fragment of one play survives. He influenced Plautus.

MENANDER OF ATHENS (*c.* 343–291 B.C.). The best and most famous Greek writer of New Comedy. He was born of a rich family, in the village of Cephisia, near Athens. As a young man he was influenced by his uncle Alexis, an outstanding poet of Middle Comedy, by Theophrastus, by Epicurus, and especially by Euripides. His first play appeared in 321 B.C.; from then till his death he composed over a hundred dramas. Only moderately popular as a playwright during his life (he won only eight victories), he eventually became the favorite comic poet of the Greek and Roman world. It was Menander and not Aristophanes who set the style for Latin comedy and for the comedy of manners of northern Europe.

Of Menander's comedies only small bits of several and one considerable fragment of another survive. *Arbitration* (*c.* 300 B.C.) is a brilliant comedy, possibly indebted to Euripides' *Ion, Iphigenia at Aulis*, and (lost) *Alope*. The plot is characteristic: a man suspects his wife of infidelity, rages, later discovers her innocence, and is reconciled with her. An approach to seriousness is made in the discussion of the double standard of morality.

RHETORIC AND ORATORY

Early Rhetoricians. CORAX and his pupil TISIAS (fl. *c.* 430 B.C.), both Sicilians, were the inventors of the art of rhetoric. They were renowned for their subtlety, excellence at repartee, and use of the bon mot. They exercised great influence on later Athenian orators.

The Sophists. The Sophists were a group of professional teachers who flourished at Athens in the fifth and fourth centuries B.C. They gave instruction in all branches of learning necessary to fit a youth for a successful public life. They were famous (and infamous) for their cleverness, superficiality, showy dress and manners, subtlety, shallowness, and "disingenuous method of argumentation by which they professed to be able 'to make the worse argument appear the better.' "[27] The principal Sophists were (1) PROTAGORAS OF ABDERA (b. 480 B.C.), a great humanist, "founder of grammar";[28] (2) HIPPIAS OF ELIS (fl. *c.* 450 B.C.), a man of wide knowledge, teacher of astronomy and geography; and (3) GORGIAS OF SYRACUSE (fl. *c.* 425 B.C.), a great orator and rhetorician.

Orators. From earliest days eloquent and forceful speech had been considered rarer than courage and equally estimable. (Peleus enjoined Phoenix to teach Achilles to be "both a speaker of words and a doer of deeds."[29]) Early leaders were usually not only soldiers but also orators, e.g., Themistocles and Pericles. Oratory developed as an art under the early rhetoricians and Sophists. It became a branch of literature about 450 B.C.

DEMOSTHENES OF ATHENS (385–322 B.C.). Greatest of all ancient orators. Demosthenes decided early in life to train himself in speaking so that he could attempt to regain in the courts the inheritance of which he had been deprived by his guardians. Tradition says that he overcame a lisp by practicing speaking with pebbles in his mouth, and that he developed vocal strength by shouting against the noise of ocean breakers. He regained a remnant of his fortune after five orations. Thereafter he became a professional speech-writer. He also spoke before the courts and the Senate, and he participated in state affairs. Later he attacked the aims of Philip of Macedon and succeeded in persuading Thebes to join Athens. After Philip's victory at Chaeronea (338 B.C.), Demosthenes fled Athens and eventually took poison to escape the Macedonians. He died on the island of Calauria in 322 B.C.

Principal Orations. Demosthenes is remembered principally for these orations: *For the Rhodians* (353 B.C.), a defense of democracy; *Three Philippics* (351, 344, 341 B.C.), against Philip of Macedon; *Three Olynthiacs* (349–348 B.C.), also against Philip; and *On the Crown* (330 B.C.), his masterpiece, an apologia of his political conduct.

Style. Demosthenes was well trained in rhetoric. His orations were in the grand manner. His figures of speech were drawn from the mighty forces of nature — the ocean, thunder, lightning, the winds. Many of his speeches were carefully polished and revised. He used many proverbs, oaths, and ejaculations. He is famous for his periodic style and for his variety in the length of the sentence. He made much use of rhetorical amplification, antitheses, rhetorical questions, puns, variety of rhythm, and avoidance of hiatus.

PHILOSOPHY

The Greeks were the first people to attempt to set up a system of belief about the universe. Ridding themselves of superstition insofar as possible, they tried to solve, on the basis of observation and reflection, such problems as the origin and nature of matter, of mind, of the good, of the true, of the beautiful, and of the real.   The early materialists rejected the mythological explanation of the universe, relied on sense perception, and tried to explain the world in terms of material substance.   The idealists believed in the existence of mind or idea as an ultimate reality.

Principal Early Materialists.

THALES OF ATHENS (*c.* 640–546 B.C.).   The "father of philosophy," he believed water to be the ultimate material of the universe.

HERACLITUS OF EPHESUS (fl. *c.* 513 B.C.).   Heraclitus believed all things to be in a state of flux — that only change is real and that fire is the origin of all things.

ANAXIMENES OF MILETUS (fl. *c.* 500 B.C.).   According to Anaximenes, air is the first principle.

EMPEDOCLES OF AGRIGENTUM (fl. *c.* 444 B.C.).   He said that the universe is made of four elements: earth, air, fire, and water; that matter is indestructible; and that love is the unifying force of the universe, strife, the dividing.

Principal Early Idealists.

PYTHAGORAS OF SAMOS (*c.* 582–507 B.C.).   Pythagoras suggested the transmigration of souls; he was also interested in the relationship of numbers.

XENOPHANES OF ELEA (*c.* 576–480 B.C.).   Perhaps the first Greek monotheist.

ANAXAGORAS OF CLAZOMENAE (*c.* 500–428 B.C.).   Considered mind (*Nous*) the unifying principle of the universe.

SOCRATES OF ATHENS (470–399 B.C.).   The father of ethics, "the greatest figure in the history of Greek thought."[30] Although Socrates wrote nothing,* his influence upon the course of philosophy has been profound.   He spent some of his early life as a sculptor and soldier, but soon devoted all his time to philosophical speculation.   He mingled with people wherever he could find an audience, for he felt that he had a divine mission — to awaken men to their own ignorance and to inspire in them a desire for truth. There gathered about him a group of young men eager for knowledge (among whom were Xenophon and Plato); these he taught

---

* Our knowledge of him and his ideas is preserved by Xenophon and Plato. Which ideas are exclusively Socrates' it is impossible to say.

without pay. Most of his teaching was done by the question-and-answer (dialectic) method.

Socrates turned his back on science and materialism. He was interested principally in practical ethics. He rejected the empiricism of the materialists and attempted to establish absolute and universal standards of conduct. Although he did not expressly discard the old Greek polytheism, he believed in one supreme Deity who would guide men in matters of morality; and he believed in personal immortality.

His views were so radical and his methods of propagating them so likely to provoke hostility that he was soon attacked by many enemies. As early as 423 B.C. Aristophanes ridiculed him in *The Clouds*. Twenty-four years later he was charged with corrupting the youth of Athens and with attempting to undermine religion (see Plato's *Apology*, below). He was tried, condemned, and forced to commit suicide by drinking a cup of hemlock.

PLATO OF ATHENS (*c.* 427–347 B.C.). Philosopher, politician, teacher, essayist, poet. Born in Athens of an aristocratic family, Plato received an excellent education; he was a disciple of the Heraclitean philosopher Cratylus and later of Socrates. In his youth he wrote some poetry and essays. He also participated in politics, but gave it up about 399 B.C. Thereafter for about ten years he traveled — in Egypt, Italy, and Sicily. He returned to Athens about 389 B.C. and founded the Academy, the world's first university. Twice more he visited Sicily and attempted to put into practice there his political theories; in this he failed. He returned once more to Athens and taught and wrote till his death.

Works.

LETTERS. Thirteen extant letters are attributed to Plato. Probably only one is genuine.

THE APOLOGY. An account in monologue of the trial of Socrates, "Plato's idealization of his master's life and mission."[31]

DIALOGUES. Dramatized conversations in the form of questions and answers. The speakers are Socrates and his disciples. Forty-two dialogues are attributed to Plato; probably only twenty-six are genuine. The most important ones are as follows: (1) *Phaedo*, which tells of the death of Socrates and gives Plato's theories of immortality; (2) *Symposium*, Plato's theory of love; (3) *Crito*, a discussion of the respect due to laws; (4) *Republic*, perhaps the most important of all the dialogues; it portrays Plato's ideal state, founded on justice; (5) *Gorgias*, a claim that truth and righteousness will ultimately be victorious over falsehood and injustice, plus a statement of belief in rewards and punishments in the afterlife; (6) *Phaedrus*, a defense of true rhetoric versus false; it contains the famous simile of the charioteer (Man's soul or reason) driving two steeds (the spiritual and sensual elements in man). The other dialogues are *Euthyphro, Hippias Minor, Hippias Major, Ion, Charmides, Laches, Lysis, Protagoras, Meno, Euthydemus, Menexenus, Cratylus, Theaetetus, Parmenides, Sophist, Politicus, Philebus, Timaeus, Critias*, and *Laws*.

EPIGRAMS. Thirty-three are included in *The Greek Anthology* (see p. 90).

Plato's Thought.

THEORY OF IDEAS. Plato is opposed to materialism. True reality for Plato is made up of intellectual concepts or Ideas, which he considers eternal and unchanging. The material world is made up of "appearances," or phenomena, which are only shadows of reality; these phenomena may be perceived by the senses, but are unreliable as sources of truth, which may be attained only by reasoning and arguing about Ideas, and perhaps attained by the soul only after death. All Ideas are arranged into a hierarchy, with the Idea of the Good at the apex.

THEORY OF THE SOUL. This theory is related to the theory of Ideas. The soul is the divine and immortal part of a man, and it is closely akin to Idea, as the body is akin to matter or phenomena. The soul has existed before its sojourn in man's body, and it brings with it memories of its association with Idea (cf. Wordsworth's "Ode on Intimations of Immortality"). After the death of the body, the soul approaches again the realm of pure idea. Each man possesses a *daemon* or guardian spirit which acts as an intermediary between the gods and the man. The daemon is the higher part of the soul, kin to the divine.

ETHICS. Plato agrees with Socrates that virtue is knowledge and that wisdom alone will bring happiness, which is almost entirely intellectual; physical pleasures are to be avoided because they are hindrances to the pursuit of wisdom. Love is a yearning after perfect Beauty, Truth, and Goodness.

THEORIES OF GOVERNMENT AND SOCIETY. Plato condemns democracy, oligarchy, and despotism. His ideal commonwealth, based on justice, is a semicommunal state ruled by philosopher-kings, defended and maintained by soldiers, and supported by workers. He advocates equality of women, compulsory education, the universal brotherhood of man, and didacticism in art and literature.

Style. Plato's style varies. Sometimes it is simple, sometimes highly poetic. It "stands midway between poetry and prose, . . . and he becomes dithyrambic in moments of exaltation."[32] He often uses mythology to express symbolically or allegorically some abstract truth. Though not a Sophist, Plato shows the influence of the early rhetoricians and the Sophists. His writing is generally clear, calm, and eloquent.

ARISTOTLE OF STAGIRA (384–322 B.C.). Philosopher, teacher, essayist. Aristotle was born at Stagira in northern Greece. His father, Nicomachus, was the physician of Amyntas II of Macedon. Aristotle himself was a disciple of the orator Isocrates and later (for about twenty years) of Plato. On Plato's death he left Athens and stayed at Aterneus and Assos about three years. At the request of Philip of Macedon, he went to Macedonia as the tutor of Alexander, in which capacity he served *c.* 342–335 B.C. In 335 B.C. he established the Lyceum at Athens, the second university in the world. On the death of Alexander in 323 B.C. the Athenian reaction against Macedonia caused him to retire to Chalcis, where he died the following year.

Works. Many of Aristotle's writings are lost, but the remaining ones (about thirty-two of them) cover virtually all fields and attempt to systematize all knowledge. The most significant works are as ollows:

THE INSTRUMENT (*Organon*). Consists of the *Categories*, the *Topics*, the *Analytics*, and the *Sophistic Refutations*. These are treatises on deductive and inductive logic, with emphasis on the former. The syllogism originated in the *Analytics*.

THE POETICS. One of the earliest pieces of literary criticism (see also Aristophanes' *Frogs*). The *Poetics* defines tragedy and discusses its six component elements — plot, character, thought, diction, scenery, and song. It discusses motivation, the unities of time and action,* character flaw, probability, and catharsis. Aristotle praises Sophocles (especially *Oedipus the King*). The *Poetics* has been extremely influential on Italian, French, and English dramatic criticism and composition from the sixteenth century onward.

* But not of place; this remained for Lodovico Castelvetro (1505–1571) to add.

NICOMACHEAN ETHICS. (See *Thought, Ethics,* below.)

ON THE SOUL. (See *Thought, Psychology and Metaphysics,* below.)

POLITICS. (See *Thought, Political,* below.)

RHETORIC. Aristotle "created the art of rhetoric."[33] In this work he discusses kinds of proof, their origin and use, categories of rhetoric, audiences, application of psychology, style, and arrangement.

Thought.

PSYCHOLOGY AND METAPHYSICS. Aristotle rejects Plato's theory of Ideas; instead, he holds intellectual concepts real only as they exist in particular things. Form (Idea) cannot exist without matter, nor matter without form. Likewise, the soul cannot exist on earth apart from the body nor the body apart from the soul. God is the creator, the final Cause of the universe. The universe is teleological.

ETHICS. Aristotle believes that happiness is the highest good and that it is attained only through external (material) goods, wisdom, moral virtue, and moderation (the Golden Mean). Man has free will and should consciously seek virtue.

POLITICAL THOUGHT. Less communal-minded than Plato, Aristotle believes in a small, autonomous state, in which he would allow slavery. Education of citizens is of immense importance.

Style. Most of Aristotle's preserved works are sketchy, as if they are rough outlines to be used as class notes; they were probably not intended for publication. One work, the *Constitution of Athens,* is an exception; it appears to have been intended for the average reader. It is clear, austere, and plain. Aristotle has a penchant for categorizing and defining. He is less poetic, less emotional, and less fluent than Plato.

8

The Alexandrian and Roman Periods

A. The Alexandrian Period
(*323–146 B.C.*)

Historical Background. Alexander the Great died in 323 B.C., and his empire was divided among his generals. Ptolemy Soter, who became king of Egypt, soon made Alexandria, his capital, the greatest commercial city in the world. Furthermore, he invited to his court all the distinguished scholars, artists, and authors of the time. Finally, he began the great library of Alexandria, which grew speedily and eventually contained 700,000 volumes. The successors of Ptolemy Soter carried on his tradition.

General View of the Literature. With the death of Aristotle in 322 B.C., the great age of Greek literature came to a close. Some literary activity continued in Greece, but most of it was shifted to Alexandria. During the Alexandrian Period there was great learning and much technical facility, but little spontaneity or genius. Literature was produced for the sake of a small, sophisticated group and not for mankind in general. As Timon of Phlius says: "Many are fattened in crowded Egypt, scribblers on papyrus, endlessly squabbling in the bird coop of the Muses."[1]

CHARACTER SKETCH

Theophrastus of Lesbos (*c.* 372–287 B.C.). Pupil of Aristotle and successor to him in the Lyceum. Although Theophrastus wrote many works, only three survive in complete form. Two of them — *History of Plants* (nine books) and *Theoretical Botany* (six books) — are of little interest today; but the third work, entitled *Characters*, has been popular and influential for many centuries. *Characters* is a group of thirty short descriptions of character types which Theophrastus saw in Athenian society. These sketches may show the influence of Menander, who was the friend of Theophrastus; some of them resemble the portraits which Menander drew in his comedies of manners. They show a great deal of humor and psychological penetration. Each type of person described embodies some moral defect, and each is labeled by the name of his foible, e.g., Newsmaker, Flatterer, Skeptic, and Stupidity. Theophrastus' style is concise, simple, and direct. His descriptions have been copied and imitated many times. They have been influential on many, especially on Hall, Earle, Overbury, and La Bruyère.

POETRY

THEOCRITUS OF SYRACUSE (*c.* 315–264 B.C.). Lyric and semidramatic poet. Few facts of his life are known. He lived in Syracuse as a boy, visited Cos, and later moved to Alexandria, under the patronage of Ptolemy II (Philadelphus).

Works.

EPIGRAMS. Twenty to thirty epigrams are attributed to him; only nine are believed to be genuine.

IDYLS. Theocritus wrote thirty idyls in all, of four types:

Mimes, or semidramatic pieces. Probably intended to be read rather than acted. The most famous are "The Syracusan Women" (15) and "The Sorceress" (2).

Pastorals. Theocritus was the father of pastoral poetry and originated most of its conventions: (a) *themes:* singing contests, unrequited love, the death of a friend; (b) *setting:* lovely meadows beside a rippling stream, trees, sheep grazing; (c) *characters:* shepherds and shepherdesses; (d) *rewards or gifts:* ivory or wooden bowls, flowers, lambs, doves, fruit, milk, curds, wool, etc. His most famous pastorals are "The Death of Daphnis" (1), "Reluctant Polyphemus" (6), "The Harvest Feast of Demeter" (7), "the queen of eclogues,"[2] and "Polyphemus in Love" (11). Theocritus has been influential on Bion, Moschus, Virgil, Sannazaro, Spenser, Shelley, Arnold, and others.

Little Epics. Short narrative poems on heroic or mythological subjects. The most famous is "Hylas" (13), which tells of Hercules' grief for Hylas.

Encomia and Aeolic Songs. The best example is "The Distaff" (28).

Style. Theocritus' works are often sophisticated and artificial but sometimes spontaneous. They show a love of nature and some ability at drama, satire, and characterization.

Imitators of Theocritus.
BION OF SMYRNA (fl. *c.* 105 B.C.).   Bion wrote a "Lament for Adonis," reminiscent of Theocritus' pastorals.

MOSCHUS OF SYRACUSE (fl. *c.* 100 B.C.).   Author of a "Lament for Bion."   Both this poem and Bion's "Lament for Adonis" are pastoral elegies, and both were influential on Milton, Shelley, and Arnold.

The Greek Anthology.   In the sixth century A.D., Agathias of Aeolis began the collection of epigrams now known as *The Greek Anthology* or *The Palantine Anthology;* the final compilation was done by Cephalas of Byzantium in the tenth century.   The work contains about 4000 poems or epigrams by various Greek authors, ranging from the fifth century B.C. to the sixth century A.D.

PHILOSOPHY

Zeno of Citium (fl. *c.* 310 B.C.).   Founder of the Stoic school. Zeno believed happiness to be the result of freedom from physical appetites and of obedience to the gods' will.   Virtue is the highest good (*summum bonum*), and suffering should be ignored.   Zeno influenced Seneca, Epictetus, Marcus Aurelius, and many others.

Epicurus of Samos (*c.* 342–270 B.C.).   Founder of the hedonistic school bearing his name.   He taught that pleasure and the absence of pain were the principal aims of life.   Without precisely denying the existence of the gods, he believed that they troubled themselves very little about the world and human beings, that they were remote and almost amoral, and that therefore they should not be feared.   Epicurus advocated the life of a recluse, aloof from the affairs of the world.   His hedonism was not, however, the selfish pursuit of physical pleasures only, in which some of his later followers indulged.   Epicurus taught, instead, that virtue, reason, justice, and knowledge of nature led to pleasure.   He warned specifically that physical pleasures should be simple and indulged in with moderation.   Epicurus has had enormous influence on world philosophy, most particularly on Horace and Lucretius.

B. Roman Period

(*146 B.C.–A.D. 529*)

Historical Background.   Rome finished its conquest of Greece in 146 B.C., with the fall of Corinth.   History from that date onward is Roman rather than Greek. Justinian's suppression of the pagan schools of philosophy (A.D. 529) marks the end of ancient Greek literature.

General View of the Literature. Comparatively little of importance was written during the Roman Period. There was no significant poetry, and there were only a few prose writers of the first rank. The prose of the period was historical, biographical, philosophical, satirical, or critical.

HISTORY

Polybius of Megalopolis (*c.* 205–125 B.C.). Polybius was deported to Rome as a hostage in 167 B.C. There he became a friend of the Roman general and literary patron Scipio Africanus the Younger and (probably through Scipio's help) was allowed to return to Greece in 150 B.C. While at Rome he wrote most of his *Universal History*, in forty books, of which only five are extant in entirety. This work, which glorifies Rome, covers its history from 266 B.C. to 146 B.C. It is dull and lacking in artistry: it sticks too slavishly to facts alone. The sentences are long and awkward; the nouns, abstract and colorless. But it shows penetration, historical breadth, and a sense of justice.

Josephus of Jerusalem (A.D. 37–*c.* 100). Educated as a Jew, Josephus later went to Rome with the Emperor Titus. He learned Greek, in which language he wrote his *History of the Jewish War*, an interesting account of the revolt of the Jews and their suppression by Titus (A.D. 66–70). *The Early History of Judea* (*Jewish Antiquities*), his second work, treats the story of the Jewish people from the Creation to A.D. 66; this is less interesting and less vigorous than his other work.

BIOGRAPHY

Plutarch of Chaeronea (*c.* A.D. 46–120). Plutarch studied in Athens and later visited in Rome, where he lectured in Greek. He is remembered for his *Parallel Lives*, fifty biographies of great men in public life. All but four are paired off — one Greek with one Roman, e.g., Demosthenes and Cicero, Alexander and Julius Caesar. Men of letters are ignored. Each pair seeks to teach a moral lesson. The *Lives* are somewhat lacking in authenticity, but are noteworthy for dramatic and narrative skill, wealth of anecdotes, vitality, pathos, humanity, and wisdom. They were a sourcebook for Shakespeare (in North's translation).

PHILOSOPHY

Marcus Aurelius Antoninus (A.D. 121–180).   Roman Emperor (A.D. 161–181), the last great Stoic, opponent of Christianity and persecutor of the Christians.   He wrote *To Himself* (*Meditations*), in twelve books, a work of dignified self-admonition.   Aurelius holds that one's soul is the inner guide — all else is vanity; that one should forgive injuries, regard men as brothers, suffer and die with fortitude.   His style is "rugged and abrupt, crowded with Latinisms."[3] But the content is noble and human.

Plotinus of Lycopolis (A.D. 205–270).   This philosopher wrote the *Enneads* (*Nines*), fifty-four books of Neoplatonism.   He altered Plato's theory of Ideas by suggesting the *One*, or God, as separate from Ideas.   He accepted Plato's theory of daemons and believed that they accounted for the evil in the world.   His writings are poetic and mystical.   He exerted great influence on Henry More, Henry Vaughan, Spenser, Milton, and Wordsworth.

SATIRE

LUCIAN OF SAMOSATA (*c.* A.D. 125–200).   Born of a poor family, Lucian educated himself in travels.   He became thoroughly Hellenized and traveled in Greece, Italy, Gaul, and Egypt.

Principal Works.

DIALOGUES OF THE GODS.   Imaginary conversations ridiculing belief in the Greek gods.

DIALOGUES OF THE DEAD.   Imaginary conversations satirizing philosophers and contemporaries.   These dialogues point out the folly of living.   Sometimes they are cynical and melancholy.

HOW TO WRITE HISTORY.   An essay ridiculing the exaggeration, inaccuracy, and enthusiasm of historians.

THE TRUE STORY (*Veracious History*).   A narrative of imaginary travels, satirizing Greek mythology and history.   Lucian allows his characters to surpass all the marvelous feats formerly told about the Greek heroes; *his* heroes visit the sun, the moon, and the Elysian Isles.

Characteristics.   Lucian is critical of sham and hypocrisy in religion, literature, and society; but he is rarely bitter or savage. Instead, he is mild, good-natured, and gently cynical.   Sometimes he is melancholy, but never sentimental, and more often he is funny. As a craftsman, he has perfect assurance.   He is imitative of Homer, the Sophists, Plato, Greek comedy, and Xenophon; but much of his imitativeness is parody. He was influential on Apuleius, Erasmus, Wieland, Landor, and perhaps Swift.

LITERARY CRITICISM

Longinus or Dionysius (*c.* A.D. 80). Philosopher, critic, author of the critical essay *On the Sublime* (*On the Grand Style, On Excellence in Literature*). Nothing is known of his life. Modern scholars no longer identify the author of this essay with Dionysius Cassius Longinus (d. A.D. 273), secretary to Queen Zenobia of Palmyra.

The sublime in literature, Longinus maintains, must please always and everywhere, and it must of necessity be the product of a great soul. Excellent style consists in large part of distinctive and striking diction. Longinus urges imitation of the ancient Greek writers, especially Homer, Plato, Demosthenes, and the three great authors of tragedy.

Renaissance and neoclassical critics of Italy, France, and England considered *On the Sublime* a most valuable and authoritative guide. Among those most deeply influenced were Boileau, Dryden, and Pope.

Bibliography for Ancient Greek Literature

General

"Achians, The," *American Journal of Archeology*, XXXIII (1929), 206–218.

Capps, Edward. *From Homer to Theocritus*. New York: Chautauqua Press, 1901.

Hamilton, Edith. *The Great Age of Greek Literature*. New York: W. W. Norton and Co., 1942.

Jebb, Richard C. *Classical Greek Poetry*. Boston: Houghton Mifflin Co., 1897.

Jevons, Frank B. *A History of Greek Literature*. New York: Charles Scribner's Sons, 1894.

Murray, Gilbert. *A History of Ancient Greek Literature*. New York: D. Appleton and Co., 1897.

Myers, J. L. *Who Were the Greeks?* Berkeley, Calif.: University of California Press, 1930.

Prentice, William K. *The Ancient Greeks*. Princeton: Princeton University Press, 1940.

Robinson, Cyril E. *A History of Greece*. New York: T. Y. Crowell Co., 1929.

Sinclair, Thomas A. *A History of Classical Greek Literature*. New York: Macmillan Co., 1934.

Wright, Wilmer C. *A Short History of Greek Literature*. New York: American Book Co., 1907.

The Age of Epic Poetry

Bassett, Samuel E. *The Poetry of Homer*. Berkeley, Calif.: University of California Press, 1938.

Carpenter, Rhys. *Folk Tale, Fiction, and Saga in the Homeric Epics*. Berkeley, Calif.: University of California Press, 1946.

Clark, Frank L. *A Study of the Iliad in Translation*. Chicago: University of Chicago Press, 1927.

Clerke, Agnes M. *Familiar Studies in Homer*. London: Longmans, Green and Co., 1894.

Jebb, Richard C. *Homer*. 2nd ed. New York: Ginn and Co., 1887.

Scott, John A. *The Unity of Homer.* Berkeley, Calif.: University of California Press, 1921.

The Age of Lyric Poetry

Hudson-Williams, Thomas. *Early Greek Elegy.* Cardiff, Wales: University of Wales Press, 1926.

Norwood, Gilbert. *Pindar.* Berkeley, Calif.: University of California Press, 1945.

Pindar. *The Extant Odes of Pindar.* Translated and edited by Ernest Myers. London: Macmillan Co., 1904.

————. *The Odes of Pindar.* Translation and introduction by John Edwin Sandys. London: W. Heinemann Co., 1915.

Robinson, David M. *Sappho and Her Influence.* Boston: Marshall Jones Co., 1924.

Wharton, Henry T. *Sappho.* 4th ed. London: John Lane, 1898.

The Attic Age

Abbott, G. F. *Thucydides.* London: G. Routledge and Sons, 1925.

Adams, Charles Darwin. *Demosthenes and His Influence.* New York: Longmans, Green and Co., 1927.

Appleton, R. B. *Euripides the Idealist.* London: J. M. Dent and Sons, 1927.

Bates, William N. *Euripides, A Student of Human Nature.* Philadelphia: University of Pennsylvania Press, 1930.

————. *Sophocles, Poet and Dramatist.* Philadelphia: University of Pennsylvania Press, 1940.

Campbell, Lewis. *A Guide to Greek Tragedy.* London: Percival and Co., 1891.

Cheney, Sheldon. *The Theater: Three Thousand Years of Acting, Drama, and Stagecraft.* New York: Longmans, Green and Co., 1929.

Cornford, Francis M. *Before and After Socrates.* Cambridge, England: Cambridge University Press, 1932.

————. *The Origin of Attic Comedy.* Cambridge, England: Cambridge University Press, 1934.

Decharme, Paul. *Euripides and the Spirit of His Dramas.* Translated by James Loeb. New York: Macmillan Co., 1906.

Dobson, J. F. *The Greek Orators.* London: Methuen and Co., 1919.

Earp, F. R. *The Style of Sophocles.* Cambridge, England: Cambridge University Press, 1944.

Finley, John H. *Thucydides.* Cambridge, Mass.: Harvard University Press, 1942.

Flickinger, Roy C. *The Greek Theater and Its Dramas.* Chicago: University of Chicago Press, 1936.

Glover, T. R. *Studies in Herodotus.* Berkeley, Calif.: University of California Press, 1924.

Grube, G. M. A. *Plato's Thought.* London: Methuen and Co., 1935.

Harsh, Philip W. *A Handbook of Classical Drama.* Stanford, Calif.: Stanford University Press, 1944.

Jaeger, Werner. *Demosthenes: The Origin and Growth of His Policy.* Berkeley, Calif.: University of California Press, 1938.

Kitto, Humphrey D. F. *Greek Tragedy.* 2nd ed. rev. New York: Barnes & Noble, 1950.

Lamb, Walter R. M. *Clio Enthroned: A Study of Prose Form in Thucydides.* Cambridge, England: Cambridge University Press, 1914.

Lord, Louis E. *Aristophanes, His Plays and His Influence.* New York: Longmans, Green and Co., 1927.

Lucas, Frank L. *Euripides and His Influence.* New York: Longmans, Green and Co., 1928.

Murray, Gilbert. *Euripides and His Age.* New York: H. Holt and Co., 1913.

Norwood, Gilbert. *Greek Comedy.* London: Methuen and Co., 1931.

————. *Greek Tragedy.* London: Methuen and Co., 1920.

Pickard-Cambridge, A. W. *Dithyramb, Tragedy, and Comedy.* Oxford: Oxford University Press, 1927.

Post, Levi A. "Menander in Current Criticism," *Transactions and Proceedings of the American Philological Association,* 1934.

Prentice, William K. *Those Ancient Dramas Called Tragedies.* Princeton: Princeton University Press, 1942.

Ridgeway, William. *The Origin of Tragedy.* Cambridge, England: Cambridge University Press, 1910.

Ross, W. D. *Aristotle.* 5th ed. rev. New York: Barnes & Noble, 1955.

Sheppard, John T. *Aeschylus and Sophocles, Their Work and Influence.* New York: Longmans, Green and Co., 1927.

Shorey, Paul. *What Plato Said.* Chicago: University of Chicago Press, 1934.

Smyth, Herbert Weir. *Aeschylean Tragedy.* Berkeley, Calif.: University of California Press, 1924.

Snider, Denton J. *The Father of History.* St. Louis, Mo.: Sigma Publishing Co., 1907.

Stanford, William B. *Aeschylus in His Style.* Dublin: Dublin University Press, 1942.

Starkie, W. J. M. *The Clouds of Aristophanes.* New York: Macmillan Co., 1911.

Swayne, George C. *Herodotus.* Philadelphia: J. B. Lippincott Co., 1881.

Wallace, Edwin. *Outlines of the Philosophy of Aristotle.* 3rd ed. Cambridge, England: Cambridge University Press, 1883.

The Alexandrian Period

Lang, Andrew. *Theocritus, Bion, and Moschus.* London: Macmillan Co., 1906.

The Roman Period

Allinson, Francis G. *Lucian: Satirist and Artist.* New York: Longmans, Green and Co., 1927.

Collins, W. Lucas. *Lucian.* Philadelphia: J. B. Lippincott Co., 1875.

Part Three
Ancient Roman Literature

9
The Republic
(240–27 B.C.)

Historical Background. According to Horace,[1] Roman or Latin literature began with Livius Andronicus in 240 B.C., the year after the end of the First Punic War. For two centuries thereafter Rome was engaged in wars of conquest, with one after another of the Mediterranean powers — Macedonia, Syria, Greece, Carthage, Numidia, Spain, Gaul, and Egypt. Both Greece and Carthage ceased their resistance in 146 B.C. With the conquest of Gaul by Julius Caesar in 50 B.C., Rome became undisputed mistress of the Mediterranean world. Class struggles and civil wars added to the unrest of the period.

Although ostensibly a republic, Rome was actually governed by the aristocratic classes. Pompey, Julius Caesar, and others continually reduced the power of the Senate. The republic was virtually changed into an empire by Octavius Caesar in 27 B.C.

General View of the Literature. Prior to the time of Livius (below) there had been some indigenous *Italian* literature — litanies, songs for festive occasions (Fescennine verses), semidramatic verses (*saturae*), and primitive farces. Only fragments of these survive. The work produced by Livius and his successors were translations, adaptations, or imitations of Greek literature, and there was very little Latin prose or poetry before 27 B.C. which was not modeled on some Greek composition. Roman tragedy, comedy, epic, lyric, oratory, and history found their prototypes respectively in Euripides, Menander, Homer, Sappho, Demosthenes, and Thucydides. Satire as a separate genre was the only distinct literary type originated by the Romans during the period of the Republic.

DRAMA

Livius (Lucius Livius Andronicus) (fl. *c.* 272–207 B.C.). Teacher, actor, first Latin dramatist. He was a Greek, brought to Rome as a prisoner of war from Tarentum in 272 B.C. He became the slave of one Livius, whose name he took and to whose children he taught Greek and Latin. Later he was freed. In 240 B.C. he paraphrased the *Odyssey* into Latin, which is considered the first Latin literature. It is in crude Saturnian verse; fragments survive. Titles and fragments of nine tragedies and comedies are extant — all translations or paraphrases of Greek. The verse of the dramas is better than that of his *Odyssey*, but it is still stiff, wooden, and archaic.

Naevius (Gnaeus Naevius) (fl. *c.* 235–201 B.C.). Soldier, native Campanian, the second Latin dramatist. Naevius wrote thirty-four comedies and seven tragedies; only fragments are extant. His plays have freer movement and more lively language than the dramas of Livius. Naevius was the first native poet of consequence and the first to write on Roman topics.

Ennius (Quintus Ennius) (239–169 B.C.). Poet, the third Latin dramatist. The versatile Ennius wrote comedies, tragedies, history-dramas, epigrams, and an epic. Titles and fragments of twenty-two of his plays survive. He has been called the first "pure man of letters" in the Western world. He was a careful technician.

PLAUTUS (Titus Maccius [or Maccus] Plautus) (*c.* 254–184 B.C.). Playwright. Born at Sarsina of a poor family, Plautus came to Rome and worked in some capacity in a theater — probably as an actor or stage carpenter.* He made some money, but lost it in commerce; then he worked as a baker's assistant. Where he got his education is a mystery. He began writing plays and soon did well financially. He died at Rome.

Works. One hundred and thirty plays have been attributed to him; probably only forty or forty-five are his. Twenty are extant. All are New Comedy, modeled after works of Menander. These twenty plays fall into four classes:

PLAY OF MISTAKEN IDENTITY.

AMPHITRYON (*Amphitruo*). This drama is based on an old legend. Zeus has a love affair with Alcmena by means of disguising himself as her husband, Amphitryon; Mercury impersonates Sosia, a slave. This is a hilarious low comedy, full of spirit, verve, and bawdiness. There have been many later adaptations: Molière, Rotrou, Dryden, Kleist, and Giraudoux (*Amphitryon* 38).†

---

* "*In operis artificum scenicorum*," according to Varro, quoted by Gellius, III. iii. 14.

† *The Menaechmi*, *The Captives*, and *The Rope* are also concerned with mistaken identity, but all fall more exactly into other categories (see below).

PLAYS OF INTRIGUE.

THE CAPTIVES (*Captivi*). This has mistaken identity and recognition motifs along with intrigue. Two captives of war, a slave and his master, exchange clothes and identities in order to effect the escape of the master. The slave turns out to be the long-lost son of Hegio, who has bought him and his master. Humor is furnished by Ergasilus, a parasite. The play contains much comic dramatic irony. It is the most popular, least indecent, and least funny of the Plautine dramas. It influenced Ariosto, Jonson, and Rotrou.

THE MERCHANT (*Mercator*). In this excellent farce a father and son vie with each other for the love of a young girl. There are many funny scenes. The plot is fast moving, and the climax is especially effective.

THE HAUNTED HOUSE (*Mostellaria*). An amusing farce in which a young roisterer tries to hide his carousals from his father. The plot is very thin and degenerates into complete farce. The play was influential on Shakespeare (*Taming of the Shrew*), Heywood, Regnard, and Holberg.

PSEUDOLUS. An entertaining low comedy. It is concerned with the intrigue of a young lover who needs money to save his sweetheart from another. The drama has fast movement, but there are some minor inconsistencies of plot. The final scene of the drunken protagonist is delightful.

STICHUS. A formless but merry play showing the happy and untrammeled life of slaves. There is almost no plot, no suspense. A father tries to persuade his two daughters to desert their long-absent husbands, who, however, return wealthy and are welcomed back.

THREE–BOB DAY (*Trinummus*). The plot is barely one of intrigue; it is concerned with the inability of a young man to provide his sister with a dowry. The play begins as high comedy, but falls off into farce. An unusual feature is that there is no female role in the play.

THE TWO BACCHIDES (*Bacchides*). This begins as a "character" play, but soon becomes one of intrigue. It has a hackneyed plot based on a trick to get money. There is excellent character portrayal, but the drama is somewhat crude and indecent. It was influential on Molière.

CASINA. A highly indecent but very lyrical farce. It employs the motif of recognition in the denouement. The construction is skillful, the tone consistent.*

PLAYS OF "CHARACTER."

THE BRAGGART WARRIOR (*Miles Gloriosus*). A crude farce based on the character of a braggart soldier. The two parts of the double plot are poorly connected. The play has been extraordinarily influential on Terence, Udall, Dolce, Baïf, Mareschal, Gryphius, and Holberg.

THE POT OF GOLD (*Aulularia*). An excellent comedy based on the character of a miser. It was possibly copied from a lost play of Menander. Too great caution causes Euclio, the miser, to lose his treasure. The minor plot (violation of a daughter) is well connected to the main plot.†

PLAYS OF RECOGNITION.

THE CASKET (*Cistellaria*). This play has a stereotyped plot: by means of a little chest a slave girl is recognized as a person of high birth; a father then grants his son permission to marry her. The son is the "most violent lover of New Comedy."[2] There are some hilarious scenes. The text of the play is badly mutilated.‡

THE TWO MENAECHMI (*Menaechmi*). One of the most famous of Plautus' plays. The separation of twins leads to many amusing errors. Finally recognition of their kinship produces the denouement. The play is the source of Shakespeare's *Comedy of Errors;* Plautus' drama ends differently from Shakespeare's.

THE ROPE (*Rudens*). Similar to *The Casket*, but better. The heroine is recognized as a man's lost daughter by virtue of a rope tied around her box. The drama has a romantic atmosphere, important characterization, much dramatic action, dramatic irony, and vivacity. It was influential on Heywood.

Characteristics of Plautus' Plays. Plautus' plays are characterized by: (a) a mixture of Greek and Roman elements (scenes are usually laid in Greece, but references to places and customs are Roman, e.g., the Capitol); (b) closely knit plot (but not always); (c) stock characters; (d) free and varied meter — mostly trochaic

---

* Other Plautine plays of intrigue are *The Comedy of Asses* (*Asinaria*), *Epidicus*, *The Persian* (*Persa*), *The Carthaginian* (*Poenulus*), and *Curculio.*

† Another Plautine play of "character" is *The Boor* (*Truculentus*).

‡ Many critical, historical, and interpretive data for the discussion of Latin drama have been drawn from Philip W. Harsh, *A Handbook of Classical Drama* (Stanford, Calif.: Stanford University Press, 1944) and from Marcus S. Dimsdale, *A History of Latin Literature* (New York: D. Appleton and Co., 1915), pp. 37–70.

septameter or octameter, some iambic; (e) brisk dialogue; and (f) many songs.

Summary of Criticism. Perhaps Plautus' greatest fault was triteness and repetition; for example, four of his twenty plots are based on lovers' tricks to secure money. He is guilty, too, of repetition of character types, e.g., the indigent lover, the parasite, and the scheming slave. And some of his devices for gaining humor are trite, e.g., threatening of a slave. Yet he shows considerable variety of treatment within the narrow range of plot, characterization, and devices for humor. Contrast, for example, *The Captives* and *Amphitryon*.

Plautus deals with only a small segment of human life — generally a frivolous segment. But we must remember that he wrote primarily to amuse, not to instruct or even to hold the mirror up to nature; he succeeds in amusing.

His technique is slipshod. Hastiness in writing led to contradictions and redundancies. "He hurries across the stage in slippers down at the heel."[3] But he must be praised for his skill in meter, for his naturalness of dialogue, and for his racy language — popular, easy, and free of Grecisms.

Finally, Plautus has been censured for coarseness and obscenity. But he compensates by his unfailing good humor (except, perhaps, in *The Boor*), hilarity, and good spirits.

TERENCE (Publius Terentius Afer) (*c.* 185–159 B.C.). Writer of comedies. Born at Carthage, Terence was brought to Rome as a slave by Terentius Lucanus, who educated him and later freed him. Terence is reputed to have been intimate with Scipio Africanus the Younger. He produced six plays, of which five were well received. He left Rome for Greece, perhaps to collect some plays of Menander, but died either in Greece or at sea on his return trip.

Works. All of Terence's plays survive. Four are adaptations from Menander; the other two are adaptations from Apollodorus of Carystus, himself a follower of Menander.

THE WOMAN OF ANDROS (Andria). Primarily a translation from Menander. It has a single plot: a young man of Athens falls in love with a "foreign" girl, but is about to be forced to marry another. The "foreigner" is discovered to be an Athenian after all. The comedy influenced Steele, Bellamy, and Thornton Wilder.

THE SELF-TORMENTOR (Heautontimorusmenos). An adaptation from Menander. Its double plot of intrigue and recognition is essentially trite: Menedemus "torments" himself by distrusting his son and then repenting; the son woos and weds a girl acceptable to the father. Chremes brags about trusting his own son, but is "tormented" when the son is discovered to be in love with a courtesan. Menedemus' daughter-in-law is discovered to be the daughter of Chremes. The drama has a serious theme: one should mind his own business. Terence makes the traits of the various characters stand out in clear relief by contrasting father with father and son with son.

THE EUNUCH (Eunuchus). An adaptation of Menander's play of the same name. This is Terence's most successful play — gay, amusing, technically superior, though sometimes condemned as immoral. It has a complicated and skillfully unified double plot of love affairs, intrigue, disguised identity, and recognition. The characterization is good. The play has been influential on the works of Udall, on Shakespeare's *Taming of the Shrew*, and on modern comedy.

PHORMIO. An adaptation of a play by Apollodorus.* *Phormio* is a delightful farce with a double plot of recognition and intrigue for money. There is excellent characterization of Antipho and Demipho. The comedy influenced Molière's *The Rogueries of Scapin (Les Fourberies de Scapin).*

THE BROTHERS (Adelphoe). Based on Menander. This is the most intellectual of Terence's plays; it is a serious discussion of the education of children. There is a double plot, but neither intrigue nor recognition is involved: the drama is primarily a *débat* over discipline versus indulgence in education. A surprising twist comes at the end of the play. Characterization is elaborate. An unusual feature is the frequent use of the soliloquy. *The Brothers* influenced Molière's *School for Husbands* and Fielding's *The Fathers.*

Characteristics of Terence's Dramas. There is a limited range of subject matter; five of his six plots are based on uncertain betrothal or marriage, and in four of these, recognition of a girl as an Attic citizen resolves the plot. Five of his six plays have double plots, usually related to each other with great skill. The characterization is interesting. The absence of an omniscient prologue is noteworthy.

Summary of Criticism. Terence has little hilarity; his plays are too serious and are lacking in gaiety; there is an "absence of

* The other play by Apollodorus which Terence adapted is *The Mother-in-Law (Hecyra).*

comic force."[4]   Though his plots are well constructed, they are too stereotyped and repetitious.   His plays, nevertheless, have much merit.   They are noted for their refinement and a minimum of obscenity.   Real problems are discussed.   His character portrayal is consistent and detailed.   There is a homogeneity of scene — no mixture of Greek and Roman elements such as we find in Plautus. Finally, Terence's language is natural, simple, elevated, clear, and precise.

Comparison of Plautus and Terence.

Style.   Terence's style is more studied, more homogeneous, more artistic, more completely correct.

Tone.   Terence shows more refinement, less coarseness, less brutality.

Morality.   There is no improvement by Terence over Plautus in basic morality.

Humor.   Terence is less comic.   Humor is present in his plays, but it is quieter, less hilarious, and less farcical than in the dramas of Plautus.

Plot.   Terence is less varied, but more consistent, clearer, and better unified.   Terence has less action.

Characterization.   Terence's is less varied, has a narrower range, but is more distinct and more consistent.

Diction.   Terence's is simpler, more refined, less that of the man on the street.

SATIRE

Lucilius (Gaius Lucilius) (180–102 B.C.).   Originator of satire as a separate genre.   Lucilius was the mouthpiece of the circle of Scipio.   He produced thirty books of satires (from *saturae* = "mixtures"), which he called *sermones*, or readings.   Only about 1300 lines have been preserved, all in fragments, of which the longest is thirteen lines.   Lucilius addresses the average man.   He approaches the spirit of Old Comedy.   Some of his lines attack particular persons or public foibles.   But many others are not satirical in the modern sense; for example, there are accounts of travel, praises of Scipio, and descriptions of trials and prosecutions.   He is a great hater of shams.   His language is coarse, vehement, graphic, and unconventional.   His meter is trochaic septameter, iambic, dactylic hexameter, or elegiac.   He set the style and form for Latin satire — use of "anecdote, fable, scene, apostrophe, dialogue."[5]

PHILOSOPHY

LUCRETIUS (Titus Lucretius Carus) (99 or 95–55 or 51 B.C.).*
Poet, philosopher.   Little is known of his life; he was probably of a
patrician family and probably a friend of Cicero and Memmius
(proctor and patron of poets, including Catullus).   One (unreliable)
account† says that he wrote *On the Nature of Things* in lucid intervals
between spells of insanity brought on by a love philter, that Cicero
revised the poem, and that Lucretius committed suicide in his
forty-ninth year.

Work.

ON THE NATURE OF THINGS (*De Rerum Natura*).   An unfinished philosophic poem in six books (7415 lines), written in
dactylic hexameter.   The work shows the influence of Democritus,
Empedocles, Homer, Ennius, and especially Epicurus.   Its primary
purpose is didactic rather than scientific: it attempts to free man of
the fear of the gods and of death by giving a materialistic view of the
universe.   It contains some amazingly accurate guesses (according
to the scientific theories and discoveries of the last hundred years)
about the structure of the atom, evolution, anthropology, and
chance variations in biology.

Principal Ideas.

ATOMIC THEORY (Found mainly in Books I and II, derived
almost entirely from Democritus and Epicurus).   Nothing can be
created from nothing, and nothing can be dissolved into nothing;
matter is indestructible.   The universe is made up of matter and
space.   Matter is composed of atoms, indivisible and eternal par-
ticles, infinite in number and varying in size, weight, and shape.
They exist only in clusters, and they are always in motion.   Substances vary according to their atomic structure.

THEORY OF THE SOUL (Book III).   The soul is to be
explained entirely in terms of matter — very fine, smooth, and
swift atoms forming a unity made up of two parts, *anima* and *animus*.
"*Anima* was the center, the organ of life itself, *animus* the seat of
reason, feeling, and of will."[6]   At birth the soul atoms become part
of the body; at death they leave it, to become parts of the rest of

---

* St. Jerome in his translation of Eusebius' *Chronicle* gives the dates as 94–51
B.C. Donatus' *Life of Virgil* (6) gives 99–55 B.C. For a discussion of these dates,
see George D. Hadzsits, *Lucretius and His Influence* (New York: Longmans, Green
and Co., 1935), pp. 3 ff.

† St. Jerome, see note * above.

nature. Hence the soul is mortal (Lucretius adduces twenty-eight arguments for the mortality of the soul).

RELIGION. The orthodox belief in the Greek and Roman gods — creative deities of great power but of little ethics — is a false belief, growing out of fear and superstition. No such gods exist. (Lucretius' positive beliefs about a deity or deities are neither clear nor consistent. At one time he makes them aloof gods dwelling in the "lucid inter-spaces between worlds,"[7] completely serene and happy, oblivious of and unconcerned about the affairs of the world; at other times they are natural forces in the form of atoms, immanent everywhere in the universe.)

ETHICS. Lucretius is an Epicurean hedonist. True happiness, he says, is to be attained by the removal of the fear of the gods, the fear of death, and the fear of afterlife; by rather aloof individualism; and by the pursuit of wisdom and virtue (he never attempts to define virtue, but does *list* many virtues and vices).

Style. Lucretius' style is unusually straightforward and prosaic, but sometimes impassioned and eloquent. He uses many archaisms, strange linguistic forms, alliteration, assonance, and metaphor.

Influence. Lucretius exerted great influence on (perhaps) Catullus, Hobbes, Rousseau, and Voltaire.

LYRICS

CATULLUS (Gaius Valerius Catullus) (*c.* 84–54 B.C.). Poet. Catullus was born in Verona of a rich, aristocratic family. He probably met Clodia (the Lesbia of his lyrics) at his own home, *c.* 62 B.C.; he had a love affair with her for about five years; most of those years he spent in Rome. In 57 B.C. he made a trip to Bithynia as a member of the staff of Memmius. He returned to Italy, settled at Sirmio and Verona, and made occasional trips to Rome.

Works. Catullus was greatly influenced by the Greek lyricists, especially Sappho, Alcaeus, Callimachus, and the Alexandrian poets; he was also indebted to some young Roman poets who followed the Alexandrian school, especially Cinna and Calvus. One hundred and sixteen poems by Catullus are extant.

"LONG" POEMS. There are two wedding poems (61–62); one lyric (63); one short epic (64); and five elegies (65–68, 74). In general the "long" poems are more objective and less emotional than the "short" ones. Though listed separately from the lyrics, the wedding poems, epic, and elegies all contain many lyrical passages.

"SHORT" POEMS (107 of them).

Lyrics (about 65 of them). These may conveniently be classified in four groups: (1) *On Love* (chiefly to Lesbia), by far the most important group. These deal with his affair with Clodia, a brilliant, beautiful, unscrupulous, "emancipated" woman, wife of Metellus Celer, consul and governor of North Italy. The poems exhibit a wide range of emotions — violent passion (5, 51); praise of her beauty (86); doubt of her love (85, 92); jealousy (76, 77); indifference (11). (2) *Elegies.* Most famous: on his brother (101). (3) *Poems on Travel and Return Home* (31, 46). (4) *Miscellaneous.* This group includes anecdotes (10, 53); reproaches (30, 38, 40); invitations and greetings (9, 13, 28); a consolation (96); a hymn (34); a drinking song (27); and others.

Invectives and Satirical Poems (about 43 of them). Some are harsh, coarse, vituperous, violent (16, 22, 23, 41); others are mild, humorous, bantering (12, 25, 42, 84).

Style and Technique. The poems of Catullus are characterized by subjectivity, fervency, tenderness, pathos, passion, and sincerity. His diction is usually simple and colloquial — full of metaphors and diminutives. He uses about twelve different kinds of meter, especially elegiac, hexameter, iambic, hendecasyllabic, and choliambic.

Influence. Catullus has been extremely influential on later Roman literature (especially Virgil, Martial, and Ovid) and on Western literature after 1500 (especially Wyatt, Surrey, Sidney, Campion, Jonson, Waller, Herrick, Swift, Byron, Landor, Tennyson, and Swinburne).

Estimate. Although the volume of his poetry is very small (only about 2300 lines in all), Catullus is considered one of the three great Latin lyricists (the others are Horace and Virgil). The humanity, intensity, sincerity, and technical perfection of his poems have caused him to be ranked with Sappho and Shelley. Macaulay called him "an admirable poet,"[8] and Tennyson described him as "tenderest of Roman poets."[9]

ORATORY

CICERO (Marcus Tullius Cicero) (106–43 B.C.). Orator, statesman, essayist, philosopher, letter writer, poet. Cicero was born at Arpinum into a family of equestrian* rank. He was given

---

* The equestrian status was comparable to knighthood in England.

an unusually good education. He saw military service from 89
to 87 B.C.; then he went to Rome and studied law, rhetoric, and
philosophy. He became in theory an Academician (moderate
skeptic) but in practice a Stoic. His first public speech was made
in 81 B.C. He became quaestor of Sicily in 75, praetor in 66, and
consul in 63. He was banished in 58, but returned eighteen months
later and became proconsul of Cilicia in 51. He supported Pompey
against Julius Caesar, 49–48; he was pardoned by Caesar *c.* 47. He
opposed Mark Antony, 44–43; was proscribed by Octavian; and
was killed by Antony's soldiers.

Principal Works.

RHETORICAL TREATISES.

On Oratory (*De Oratore*) (55 B.C.). A dialogue in three books,
this treatise discusses choice of material, arrangement, expression,
memory, and delivery. It "never deals with the fundamental
problems either of style in general or of rhetoric in particular . . .
but is close in touch with practical realities."[10] The work gives a
good insight into Cicero's own methods.

Brutus (*c.* 46 B.C.). A dialogue giving a history of Roman oratory.

The Orator (46 B.C.). An important document in the form of an
open letter. It discusses ornamentation, pronunciation, diction,
arrangement of words, and rhythm.

ORATIONS ON PUBLIC MATTERS.

On the Agrarian Law (*De Lege Agraria*) (64–63 B.C.). Four speeches
(only three survive) attacking the democratic machinations against
the power of Pompey.

Against Catiline (*In Catilinam*) (63 B.C.). Four eloquent speeches
exposing the Catilinian conspiracy and suggesting penalties for the
conspirators.

The Philippics (*Philippicae*) (44–43 B.C.). The name is derived from
Demosthenes' orations. These fourteen orations were delivered in
the Senate against Mark Antony.

ORATIONS ON PRIVATE MATTERS.

For Archias the Poet (*Pro Archia Poeta*) (62 B.C.). A defense of citizenship, especially noteworthy as a eulogy on literature in general.

For Milo (*Pro Milone*) (52 B.C.). A defense of Annius Milo on a
charge of murder. This was one of Cicero's few failures in court.
The speech was reworked and improved before publication.

POLITICAL TREATISES.

On the Republic (*De Republica*) (54–51 B.C.). This treatise (in six books) on the constitution and government of a state pictures the perfect state as "an idealized Rome, guided by the wisdom and patriotism of her leading men."[11]   The work is famous for a vision of the other world ("Scipio's Dream," *Somnium Scipionis*).

On Laws (*De Legibus*) (*c.* 52 B.C.).   A treatise in five books (two now lost).   It is important for its information concerning actual law as well as legal theory of the time.

MORAL TREATISES.

On the Ends of Good and Evil (*De Finibus Bonorum et Malorum*) (45 B.C.).   An unoriginal but carefully written treatise (five books) in dialogue form.   It contains an exposition and criticism of Epicureanism, Stoicism, and Aristotelianism.   Cicero does not fully agree with any of the three, but leans more toward the last-named set of beliefs.

On Old Age (*De Senectute*) (44 B.C.).   A charming dialogue pointing out the comforts and advantages of old age.

On Friendship (*De Amicitia*, or *Laelius*) (44 B.C.).   A short, pleasant treatise on the nature of friendship in general.

On Duties (*De Officiis*) (44 B.C.). A treatise in three books, addressed to his son. It contains much Stoical doctrine, and it deals with the conflicts of duty and personal interest.

THEOLOGICAL TREATISE.

On the Nature of the Gods (*De Natura Deorum*) (*c.* 45 B.C.).   A refutation of atheism.   It discusses Epicureanism, Stoicism, and theism. Lacking in original and profound theology, the work is also inaccurate and inconsistent; apparently it was hurriedly written.

LETTERS.   Cicero's epistles are significant as works of art and also as sources of history and biography.

To Atticus. The largest and most important group (sixteen books).   These are intimate and informal.   They cover the period 67–44 B.C.

To Familiars (*Ad Familiares*) (published *c.* 41 B.C.).   Miscellaneous letters (in sixteen books) to many people on various subjects.   The collection contains also some replies by the addressees.

To Quintus (covering the years 60–54 B.C.).   Addressed to his brother; in three books.

To and from Brutus (44–43 B.C.).   In two books.   These letters deal with Cicero's last year of life.

Style.   Cicero attempted (successfully) to steer a middle course between the Asianic and the Attic styles.   The former was characterized by short, rhythmical clauses, short periods, rhyme, ornateness, cleverness in turning of phrases, and poetic diction. The Atticists tried to use everyday speech and to avoid extravagance and ornateness of all sorts. Cicero leaned toward the Attic side, insisting on purity of vocabulary, on accuracy of idiom, on avoidance of foreign or extraordinary words, and (usually) on straightforward speech and long rhetorical periods. He borrowed two Asianic elements, however: (1) ornateness and extravagance in moments of emotional elevation and (2) well-defined rhythm. Like Demosthenes, he often appealed to the emotions rather than the intellect. In the *Letters* and treatises he was, of course, less oratorical and more colloquial than in the orations; but at all times he maintained dignity, clarity, and eloquence. His language and his style are his chief claim to fame.

Summary of Criticism. Despite some long-windedness, Cicero achieved stylistic perfection. "He created a language which remained for sixteen centuries that of the civilized world, and used that language to create a style which nineteen centuries have not replaced, and in some respects have scarcely altered."[12] And Dimsdale adds that his style "is the basis of modern European prose."[13]

Cicero was egoistic, but his egoism was sometimes demanded by the nature of the argument, e.g., in the defense of Plancius.

He was sometimes irrelevant, but his irrelevancy was often effective in pleading — appeals to the imagination, emotion, and prejudices; for example, the defense of poetry in *For Archias the Poet*.

As a philosopher, he had no originality and no system of beliefs, but he was extremely influential as an exponent and preserver of philosophical ideas.

Finally, Cicero was supreme as a letter writer — "at the head of all epistolary artists."[14]

HISTORY

Caesar (Gaius Julius Caesar) (*c.* 100–44 B.C.). General, statesman, historian, dramatist, poet, letter-writer.

COMMENTARIES ON THE GALLIC WAR (*Commentarii Belli Gallici*), in seven books. *The Commentaries* cover the campaigns in Gaul and Britain, 58–52 B.C. They were written *c.* 52 B.C. as a defense of the author's military policy in Gaul and his constitutional position. They contain no self-praise, even by insinuation, but are a convincing justification of his conduct. They are famous for their simplicity, purity of diction, scrupulous accuracy, succinctness, and perspicuity — "the model and despair of later historians."[14]

COMMENTARIES ON THE CIVIL WAR (*Commentarii Belli Civilis*), in three books. These cover the conflict between Caesar and Pompey, 49–48 B.C. They were written probably in 44 B.C. They are less skillfully written than the *Commentaries on the Gallic War* — probably they were not revised by the author.

Sallust (Gaius Sallustius Crispus) (86–c. 34 B.C.). Statesman, historian, imitator of Thucydides. Sallust's style is characterized by austerity, antithesis, terseness, archaisms, and Grecisms. As a historian, he was usually extraordinarily honest and impartial, but sometimes careless about chronology. He was interested in motives.

ON THE JUGURTHINE WAR (*De Bello Jugurthino*). This history gives a lively account of the war between the North Africans under Jugurtha and the Romans under Metellus, Marius, and Sulla (111–106 B.C.). The work is memorable for good characterizations of the military leaders and good descriptions of Numidian customs and scenery.

ON THE CATILINIAN CONSPIRACY (*De Catilinae Coniuratione*). A political monograph written to disprove Caesar's complicity in the intrigues of Catiline. Cicero is cleverly and delicately condemned.

HISTORY (*Historium Libri Quinque*). An account of the ten years following the death of Sulla (d. 78 B.C.). The work is lost except for fragments.

Varro (Marcus Terentius Varro) (116–27 B.C.). Satirist, historian, author of six or seven hundred volumes, nearly all lost. Extant are six books on the Latin language (*De Lingua Latina*) and one treatise, *On Country Matters* (*De Re Rustica*). These works are tedious and lacking in descriptive and dramatic power, but valuable as source material. The lost *Portraits* (*Imagines*) (of famous Greeks and Romans) is said to be the world's first illustrated volume. About six hundred lines of *Menippean Satire* (*Saturae Menippeae*) survive.

IO

The Augustan Age

(27 B.C.–A.D. 14)

Historical Background. In 27 B.C. Octavian Caesar Augustus proclaimed the re-establishment of the Roman Republic, but from that date till his death in A.D. 14 he actually exercised the power of an emperor. For the most part, the era was one of enforced peace (*Pax Romana*) and of security. The relative serenity of the age provided leisure for national self-appraisal; there was an awakening of awareness of the past and present glories of Rome, and there was an enthusiastic hope for a still more glorious future.

General View of the Literature. Peace, security, leisure, antiquarianism, and nationalism all had tremendous effects on the literature of the Augustan Age. Writing as a full-time profession became respectable, and the rich and powerful — including Augustus himself — encouraged and patronized men of letters. Disappearance of political controversy led to the decline of oratory, and the sphere of history was restricted. The age was pre-eminently one of poetry. Greater leisure gave poets opportunity for more polishing, and much stress was laid on technical perfection.

THE EPIC

VIRGIL (Publius Vergilius Maro) (70–19 B.C.). Poet. Virgil was born at Andes, a village near Mantua, of a rather well-to-do peasant family. He was given a superior education at Verona, Milan, and Rome; he studied grammar, rhetoric, philosophy, and Greek. He was influenced by Epicureanism. His estate near Mantua was confiscated by Octavian in 41 B.C., but later possibly restored through the influence of the wealthy and influential statesman Maecenas, who became his patron. As he grew older, he became more conservative and abandoned some of his Epicureanism. He died while on a trip to Greece to authenticate some of the *Aeneid.*

Early Minor Poems. There are several poems of little significance which have been attributed, perhaps erroneously, to Virgil: *Catalepton*, *Priapea*, *Epigrams*, *Dirae*, *Ciris*, *Culex*, *Aetna*, *Copa*, and *Moretum*. Other early poems of more significance are as follows:

BUCOLICS or *ECLOGUES* (*Bucolica* or *Eclogae*). "Pastoral" or "Select" poems, written and published *c.* 42–39 B.C. These short poems made Virgil famous and were probably responsible for the patronage of Maecenas. The poems are indebted to Theocritus and other Greek pastoral poets. In turn, they have been influential on many later poets, especially Propertius, Spenser, Milton, Shelley, and Arnold. The most important single poems of the group are these:

Number 2. A lyric in dactylic hexameter — a love song by Corydon, a shepherd in love with Alexis; it is reminiscent of Theocritus' Idyll 11 ("Polyphemus in Love").

Number 4, "The Messiah." Most famous and most controversial of all Virgil's pastorals, it foretells the birth of a marvelous child who will bring peace and a new Golden Age to the world. Guesses as to the child's identity are as follows: (1) son to Octavian and Scribonia (best guess); (2) son to Antony and Octavia; (3) son to Octavia and Marcellus; (4) son to the consul Pollio; (5) Jesus Christ; (6) no one in particular.

Number 5. A pastoral elegy. Mopsus laments the death of Daphnis; Menalcas replies with a triumphant song that Daphnis is not dead but transformed into a benevolent, protective god. The poem is almost certainly a reference to the death and official deification of Julius Caesar. It is indebted to Theocritus, Bion, and Moschus.

Number 9, similar to Eclogue 1. Menalcas, a slave, fears the confiscation of his land.

Number 10. Gallus, a shepherd dying as a result of desertion by his mistress, resolves to sing "Sicilian strains," that is, write pastoral poems. At the end Virgil bids his own farewell to pastoral poetry, probably with plans for the *Georgics* (below) already begun.

GEORGICS. A propagandistic work in four books, written *c.* 36–30 B.C., at the request of Maecenas. It is indebted for some of its contents to Hesiod and Lucretius. Its purpose is to persuade free men to return to Italy's depopulated farms; the work was probably not successful as propaganda. It contains much praise of Octavian, but more of farming and the happy life of the rural man.

Book I concerns crops and meteorological prognostication; Book II, the orchard and the vineyard; Book III, stock and breeding; and Book IV, beekeeping (plus an account of the Aristaeus-Orpheus-Eurydice legend).

THE AENEID.

Environmental and Literary Influences. Virgil's quiet, rural life as a boy, his association with the circle of Maecenas, and the environment of the court of Octavian all had considerable influence on the *Aeneid*. The principal literary influences were Homer, Pisander, the Cyclic epics, the Greek dramatists (especially Euripides), Apollonius of Rhodes, the Alexandrians, Ennius, Catullus, and Lucretius. By far the most important single influence was Homer, from whose *Odyssey* Virgil borrowed many events and devices for the first six books of the *Aeneid*, and from whose *Iliad* he took many items of the last six books of the Latin epic. Virgil also used dactylic hexameter and all of the epic conventions established by Homer.

The Story. After the burning of Troy by the Greeks, Aeneas, the son-in-law of King Priam, escapes with his forces in twenty-one ships and is blown about the Mediterranean for seven years. He and his followers suffer many hardships, but at length land at Carthage. There they are befriended by Dido, the queen, who falls in love with Aeneas and tries to persuade him to remain in Carthage as coruler; but he knows that his destiny lies elsewhere and steals away to Sicily; Dido commits suicide. After a visit to the underworld (where the founding of Rome by Aeneas' descendants and the future greatness of the city are foretold), Aeneas proceeds to Latium in Italy, where he is hospitably welcomed by Latinus, the king. Latinus promises to give Lavinia, his daughter, to Aeneas in marriage; but she has already been betrothed by her mother to Turnus, prince of the Rutuli. Latinus decides that the two aspirants will have to fight for Lavinia's hand. After some indecisive battles Turnus suggests settling the matter by single combat, Aeneas accepts the challenge, and Turnus is killed. It is implied that Aeneas marries Lavinia and succeeds to the throne.

Purpose and Tone. One of Virgil's principal reasons for writing the *Aeneid* was to provide for Rome a glorious historical background, with a semidivine character as its national hero. This hero is both courageous and wise, but little emphasis is laid on such valor as Achilles and Hector displayed or on such shrewdness as made Odysseus famous. Instead, *pietas* is the attribute which is most characteristic of Aeneas, and *pius** is the epithet most often applied to him. Virgil was attempting to personify and glorify the traditional Roman virtues of bravery, fortitude, temperance, perseverance, sagacity, and devotion to duty.

These were serious purposes, and the *Aeneid* is a uniformly serious poem. It has virtually no humor. It is pervaded by an air of mild melancholy, of "brooding tenderness." It is lacking entirely in the spirit of daring and adventure, of yearning to "sail beyond the sunset, and the baths of all the western stars" which one finds in the *Iliad* and the *Odyssey*. These deficiencies are somewhat compensated, however, by a greater degree of moral earnestness than one finds in Homer. Homer's epics deal with a young, enthusiastic, vigorous world; "the Aeneid is the book of an old world."[1]

Style and Technique. As mentioned above, Virgil adopted all the epic conventions begun by Homer. The *Aeneid*, however, is a literary epic, intended for reading rather than recitation; consequently it is less repetitious, more subjective, more intimate, and more carefully written than Homer's poems. Virgil is supposed to have spent many years in its composition and revision (because his final revision was not complete, he wanted the entire poem destroyed at his death; only the order of Augustus himself saved it).

Influence of the Aeneid *on Later Literature.* "Virgil is that poet whose verse has had most power in the world."[2] In thought, style, and technique he has influenced European literature perhaps more than any other one poet. Almost all succeeding Latin literature, Dante, Petrarch, Boccaccio, Ariosto, Tasso, Leopardi, Carducci, Ercilla, Camoëns, Ronsard, Voltaire, Chaucer, Spenser, Milton, Dryden, Wordsworth, Shelley, Keats, Tennyson, and Arnold are deeply indebted.

Summary of Criticism. Ever since the *Aeneid* was written, it has been recognized as one of the world's greatest literary productions. Various critics have, however, both attacked and defended it. Some have suggested that Aeneas is a prig and sometimes immoral (e.g., when he deserts Dido), "devoid of spirituality, and . . . tinged with the so-called Babbittism of the self-made man."[3] But others have believed that he is the embodiment of Roman virtues as Virgil saw them; he is intent on achieving his manifest destiny, and he

---

* *Pius* is untranslatable, according to T. R. Glover, *Virgil* (2nd ed.; London: Macmillan and Co., 1912), p. 222; it is a combination of "pious," "conscientious," "dutiful," "compassionate," and "virtuous."

is always acting under guidance from the gods. Other characters, especially Dido, are also well drawn.

Most commentators agree that Virgil is tedious and lacking in humor; but he has high seriousness: the *Aeneid* is the "saddest book in the world."[4] Although it lacks the spirit of adventure and is stuffy, it is full of humanity: "The *Aeneid* is . . . the greatest single book written by man because of its inclusiveness of human life, of life long lived, in the things of life."[5]

Furthermore, the poem is marked by perfection of style and technique — diction, rhythm, meter, and balance. It has grandeur and majesty: "Stateliest measure ever molded by the lips of man."[6]

THE LYRIC

HORACE (Quintus Horatius Flaccus) (65–8 B.C.). Satirist, lyricist, moralist, literary critic. Horace was the son of a freedman. He was born at Venusia and was given excellent schooling at Rome and Athens. After joining the army of Brutus, he became a military tribune. When Brutus was defeated at Philippi (42 B.C.), Horace returned to Rome, "his wings clipped" — his father was dead, his property confiscated. He then became clerk in the Treasury and began to write verse to supplement his income. His poems soon attracted notice. Virgil introduced him to Maecenas (39 B.C.), of whose circle he became a leading member. In 33 B.C. Maecenas gave him a Sabine farm, which afforded him independence and leisure for writing. Horace had little enthusiasm for Octavian till about 25 B.C.; then he began to have faith in the emperor's plans for national regeneration. In 17 B.C. he was commissioned by Octavian to write an ode for the Secular Games. After this date his relation to the court was close, but he refused an invitation to become the emperor's private secretary; he preferred the independence and the seclusion of his Sabine farm.

Works.

SATIRES (*Sermones, Saturae*). "Conversation pieces,"[7] some serious, some gay, on a wide variety of subjects. They were influenced greatly by Lucilius. Book I (published *c.* 35 B.C.) is made up of ten monologues. The first three are concerned with moderation and tolerance; Numbers 4, 6, and 10 are defenses of himself and his poetry; Number 5 is an account of a trip to Brundisium with Maecenas; Numbers 7 and 8 are anecdotes; and Number 9 is an account of an encounter with a bore.   Book II (published *c.* 30 B.C.) consists of eight poems — some monologues, others dialogues. Again he defends himself as a satirist (11); he advocates the simple life (2 and 6); and he pokes fun at the bad taste of a rich man's dinner (8).

EPODES ("*Iambi*," implying invective).   Written *c.* 40–30 B.C., published 30 B.C.   Seventeen poems, varying, like the *Satires*, in tone and subject matter.   They were inspired principally by Archilochus.   Four are lampoons (4, 6, 10, and 12); two draw a horrible picture of a witch (5 and 17); one celebrates the victory of Actium (9); two point out the horrors of civil war (7 and 16); and one is a mock-serious description of the delights of the country (2).

ODES (*Carmina*).   One hundred and three poems, more often meditative than lyrical, in four books.   These are indebted to Sappho, Alcaeus, Simonides of Ceos, Callimachus, Pindar, Archilochus, and Anacreon.   The first three books were written between 30 and 23 B.C. and were published at the later date; the lyrics of Book IV were written during the following ten years and published in 13 B.C.   On numerous subjects, the *Odes* include dedications, invitations, farewells, nature poems, autobiographical sketches, poems on the pleasures of wine and love, poems on subjects of national importance, and hymns.   Book I consists chiefly of lyrics dealing with wine and love; Book II contains many "moral epistles"; Book III is made up to a large extent of ethical and patriotic pieces; and Book IV is devoted in large measure to eulogies of Augustus and members of his household.

EPISTLES (*Epistulae*).*   In two books (Book I, twenty letters; Book II, two letters), written 20–13 B.C., published 13 B.C.   All but four (3, 5, 8, and 9), which are genuinely personal, are addressed in some degree to the public at large.   Letters in Book I are concerned chiefly with manners, morals, and happiness.   The subject of Book II, Epistle 1, is a vindication of Augustan literature; the second epistle in the book is somewhat autobiographical — a series of excuses for not writing poetry any more.   Most of the letters abound in maxims, aphorisms, and flashes of wit.

JUBILEE HYMN (*Carmen Saeculare*).   Written and published in 17 B.C. for the celebration of the great national festival proclaimed

---

* "Of the literary epistle Horace may be regarded as the creator" (Marcus S. Dimsdale, *A History of Latin Literature* [New York: D. Appleton and Co., 1915], p. 298).

by Augustus. It was intended to be sung by a chorus of boys and girls. It contains high praise of Augustus and Rome.

THE ART OF POETRY or *EPISTLE TO THE PISOS* (*Ars Poetica* or *Epistula ad Pisones*). This work (written *c.* 10 B.C.) is ostensibly a letter to two young men named Piso (whose identity is uncertain), setting forth (at the request of the addressees) some rules for writing poetry (chiefly dramatic). It is a chatty discussion and rather formless. Part I (1–41) stresses the necessity for consistency. Part II (42–294) deals with form, diction, tone, and characterization, and it is concerned chiefly with dramatic poetry. Part III discusses the poet himself and holds that a poet must have both native ability and training; some rules for training are suggested.

The whole work stresses good sense as the foundation of good writing. It suggests a study of Greek models. It repeatedly attacks mere mediocrity, roughness, redundancy, inaccuracy of diction. Many of its vivid phrases have become bywords of literary criticism: "purple patch" (*purpureus pannus*), "labor of the file" (*limae labor*), "*in medias res.*"*

This work and Aristotle's *Poetics* are the two most significant pieces of ancient literary criticism. *The Art of Poetry* was especially influential on Boileau and the English literary figures of the late seventeenth and the eighteenth centuries.

Thought. As a philosopher, Horace has little new to offer, and he can hardly be said to have a system of belief. About religion he has little to say, but it is fairly obvious that he is not a devout believer in the Roman gods or in immortality. In ethics, his opinions are a mixture of Epicureanism and Stoicism, tempered by the application of Aristotle's Golden Mean. Although a hedonist and a believer in *carpe diem*, he is extremely conservative, and he always warns that excess — in wine, love, wealth, for example — leads to misery; he advocates the simple rural life, philosophic calm, and fortitude in the face of adversity. In politics, too, he is conservative and often admonishes the state when he foresees the approach of danger and civil war.

Style and Technique. Although he is remembered mainly for his lyrics and his literary criticism, Horace's most characteristic

---

* "Purple patch" means an especially noteworthy passage; "labor of the file" means careful revision and polishing; "*in medias res*" means in the chronological midst of the narrative.

attitude is the mildly satirical; not only the *Satires* but also most of the *Epodes*, many of the *Odes* and the *Epistles*, and even *The Art of Poetry* have satirical touches. A few of his earlier pieces show anger and lack of restraint, but his customary attitude in satire is one of good-natured amusement, and he rarely takes himself too seriously. Even in his love lyrics he adopts a bantering, detached tone, as of one who fears to be burned. Good humor, wit, friendliness, tolerance, and geniality are seldom absent from his poems.

Horace himself not only advocated but also engaged in "labor of the file." He composed extraordinarily slowly and carefully, and his technique was virtually flawless. He was a master of many genres and of many meters.

Influence on Others. Horace was not especially popular or influential during the Middle Ages, but after the Renaissance and through the eighteenth century he was very influential: in Italy, on Dante, Petrarch, Ariosto, Bembo, and Tasso; in France, on Ronsard, du Bellay, Montaigne, Malherbe, Boileau, La Fontaine, Corneille, Racine, Molière, Voltaire, Chénier, de Musset; in Germany, on Lessing, Herder, Goethe, Nietzsche; in England, on Spenser, Shakespeare, Jonson, Dryden, Addison, Steele, Prior, Pope, Richardson, Sterne, Smollett, Fielding, Gray, Johnson, Chesterfield, H. Walpole, Wordsworth, Coleridge, Byron, Shelley, and Browning.

Summary of Criticism. Horace has been censured for lacking deep emotion and spontaneity, for superficiality in social problems and in matters of love, and for aloofness. One critic thinks him only a "big little man" and that his self-possession was "incompatible with highest poetical achievement."[8] Some have accused him of complacency and egotism. His defenders, on the other hand, say that he writes understandingly and amusingly, even if from a distance. They say that he has excellent technique — in diction ("*curiosa felicitas*"[9]), in meter, and in restraint. Furthermore, he has great common sense and acumen as a literary critic, and his works are to be praised for their brevity and interest: "Horace is never tedious."[10] He is rarely offensive as a satirist, and he has excellent social tact; he "manages to probe his friend's every fault, while he makes him laugh."[11] In addition, he has a wide range of humor and the ability to laugh at himself. Finally, he has "intelligence, good sense, affection, kindness, loyalty . . ., *urbanitas* . . ., *humanitas*."[12]

THE ELEGY

For the Romans, an elegy meant a love poem in elegiac meter. The three principal elegists were Tibullus, Propertius, and Ovid.

Tibullus (Albius Tibullus) (*c.* 54–18 B.C.). Leading poet of the circle of Messala. Four books of amatory elegies are attributed to Tibullus, of which all of the third book and probably all but one poem of the fourth book are spurious. The first book is made up of ten lyrics; one is a birthday poem to Messala (7); five are devoted to the author's love for Delia (Plania) (1, 2, 3, 5, 6). The second book contains six elegies, three of them proclaiming Tibullus' love for "Nemesis, not the goddess, but a woman whose mythological name testifies to her low rank."[13] Six of the poems in Book III are probably by Sulpicia, niece of Messala. Tibullus is refined, "soft,"[14] gentle, considerate, direct, and clear; he is noted for smoothness and finish. But he is narrow in outlook and has a paucity of ideas. He is not a "supreme poet" but one possessing "a distinct, quiet charm."[15]

Propertius (Sextus Propertius) (*c.* 50–16 B.C.). Member of the circle of Maecenas. Propertius wrote four or five books of elegies. Nearly all of the first two books, half of the third, and three poems in the fourth (about sixty-seven poems in all) are concerned with his love for Cynthia (Hostia).[16] The others are on a wide range of subjects, e.g., religious rites, place names, the battle of Actium, sadness over the death of a noble Roman lady. Propertius is generally considered a poet superior to Tibullus — more versatile, more prolific. His faults are indirectness, vagueness, lack of unity, and monotony of meter. His merits are "richness of effect,"[17] dignity, freshness, real passion, grace, and tenderness.

OVID (Publius Ovidius Naso) (43 B.C.–A.D. 17). Epic poet, lyricist, dramatist. Ovid was born at Sulmo in central Italy, of a wealthy equestrian family. He was educated at Rome in rhetoric and law, but soon deserted an official career in the law and devoted himself to poetry. He married three times and divorced his first two wives. He was exiled by Octavian to Tomi (Tomis, Kustendje) on the shore of the Black Sea in A.D. 8.* He died at Tomi nine years later.

---

* Reasons for his banishment, he says (*Poems of Gloom.* II. 207), were "a poem and an error." The poem was *The Art of Love;* what the error was is a matter of guesswork, but probably it was implication in Princess Julia's adultery. It is believed that Ovid either abetted Julia in the scandalous affair or that he knew of it and failed to divulge the matter to Octavian, Julia's grandfather.

Works.*

LOVE POEMS.

LOVES (*Amores*).   A group of fifty poems in three (originally five) books, written in elegiac couplets, probably composed *c.* 23–15 B.C.   The *Loves* are principally erotic lyrics† attempting to picture not Ovid's own emotions but those of any lover.   Corinna, the subject of twelve of the poems, is probably a composite of several people.   The love depicted is frankly sensual and illicit, varying in tone from calm to stormy.   The poems are audacious, witty, and aphoristic, e.g., "Chastity is absence of opportunity."[18]   There is little continuity between the poems.

HEROINES (*Heroides*) (composed *c.* 22–15 B.C.).   These are fifteen imaginary letters from lonely heroines of mythology to the men who had been the cause of their distress.   Each letter is written at a moment of crisis.   The letters vary widely in emotional tone, from the "patient longings of Penelope . . . to the tumultuous passion of Sappho."[19]   Only two (Canace and Phyllis) are genuinely tragic, and some contain many humorous elements (e.g., Penelope, Briseïs, and Phaedra).   These letters are admirable studies of women's moods, but some are guilty of artificiality and poor taste.   They were influential on Chaucer's *Legend of Good Women* and perhaps on Landor's *Imaginary Conversations*.

DOUBLE EPISTLES.   Three pairs of letters attached to the *Heroines*.   Each pair consists of a love letter from a male and a reply by the female addressee (Paris and Helen, Leander and Hero, and Acontius and Cydippe).   The characters become real human beings.   Ovid uses much persuasive rhetoric.

WOMEN'S COSMETICS (*Medicamina Faciei Femineae*).   Fifty couplets suggesting some almost incredibly complicated formulas for cosmetics.   The work is too technical to be interesting.

THE ART OF LOVE (*Ars Amatoria* or *Ars Amandi*) (published *c.* A.D. 1).   A rather comprehensive textbook on love intrigue. Book I instructs men how to find and win a mistress; Book II, how to keep her.   Book III is addressed to women and tells them how to keep a lover.   The poem freely admits that it deals only with physical love.[20]   It is "a monument of art, of chiselled verses with

---

* Ovid's lost tragedy *Medea* was praised highly in antiquity.   Since none of it has been preserved, it is not considered in this outline.

† Exceptions are III. 9, a lament for the deceased Tibullus, and III. 13, a description of a procession honoring Juno.

the sparkle of diamonds. It is a monument of wit and delicate travesty, prompted by deviltry and restrained by no reluctance to shock."[21] Here Ovid "is no longer a servant of love [as in the *Loves* and the *Heroines*], but its master, and is proud of his dignity."[22] Despite the poet's protests to the contrary (I, 31), *The Art of Love* has often (especially during the Victorian era*) been considered distinctly immoral and was almost certainly the poem which, along with his "error," led to his exile.

THE REMEDIES OF LOVE (*Remedia Amoris*) (published *c*. A.D. 1). A sequel (in 814 elegiacs) to *The Art of Love*. It suggests antidotes (for men only) to love: work, travel, rehearse the beloved's imperfections, love somebody else. The work also suggests ways of *staying* out of love: avoid crowds where you might see her, wear slouchy clothes, eat properly, do not read poetry. It is less entertaining than *The Art of Love*, but is still enlivened by wit and cleverness.

NARRATIVE POETRY.

THE TRANSFORMATIONS (*Metamorphoses*) (composed *c*. A.D. 2–8). A long (12,000 lines, fifteen books) narrative poem in hexameter verse, considered an epic by some commentators. It attempts a chronological account of the transformations of men and inanimate objects from the beginning of creation through 43 B.C. It begins with the change of Chaos into Cosmos and ends with the deification of Julius Caesar. Actually the work is a series of 246 stories, each ending with a transformation of some sort; historical sequence is discernible only in Books I, II, and XI–XV. The poem is made up almost entirely of myths. Books I–XI consist chiefly of short, romantic fables, many of them sentimental; these are intense, graceful, and sometimes capricious. There is some humor and some burlesque of heroes and heroines. Books XII–XIV become somewhat heavier, more heroic, more ambitious; and Book XIV retells chiefly patriotic legends. Book XV tells of the Hellenization of Italy and exalts Rome as the center of the civilized world; it also includes an exposition of Pythagoras' philosophy and a defense of vegetarianism.

The Transformations is usually considered Ovid's masterpiece. In it he "gave ancient mythology its unexcelled, final, comprehen-

---

* Alfred Church, *Ovid* (Philadelphia: J. B. Lippincott Co., 1880), p. 37, says: "Of the 'Art of Love' the less, perhaps, that is said the better. The poet himself warns respectable persons to have nothing to do with his pages, and the warning is amply justified by the contents."

sive expression."[23] It is "second only to Virgil's epic . . . among the great monuments of Roman genius."[24]

POEMS WRITTEN IN EXILE.

THE ROMAN CALENDAR (*Fasti*). (Composed principally before exile, *c*. A.D. 8, revised while Ovid was at Tomi.) This is an unfinished poem in elegiac couplets. Six of its twelve books survive; the last six were intended but probably never written. The work is an almanac listing and discussing annual events of the first six months, with emphasis on Roman festivals and rituals. It gives a history of the calendar, some untrustworthy etymologies, and an account of zodiacal figures. Though not essentially a work of poetry, it has some brilliant passages. It was influential on Spenser's *Shepherd's Calendar*.

THE IBIS (*c*. A.D. 8). A harshly vituperative poem of 644 lines accusing "Ibis"* of many wrongs, including an attempt to appropriate Ovid's property while the poet is in exile.

POEMS OF GLOOM (*Tristia*) (composed *c*. A.D. 8–12). Five volumes of elegies devoted primarily to an apologia pro vita sua and to accounts of the miseries suffered at Tomi. It is an important autobiographical source, but somewhat inferior in inspiration.

LETTERS FROM THE BLACK SEA (*Epistulae ex Ponto*) (*c*. A.D. 12–14). A continuation of the subject of *Poems of Gloom*. There are four books, forty-four letters. These letters are addressed to specific people. The topics discussed are the poet's hardships; his wife and friends, whom he praises; and Tomi and its environs. The letters are important for the facts which they give about Ovid's life.

Evaluation of Ovid's Poetry.   Although often accused of immorality and of lacking high seriousness, Ovid is not completely devoid of ethical and religious content. To be sure, he protests against the injustice of the gods, and he adheres little to any belief in the orthodox Roman deities; but "a vague monotheism may underlie his story of creation . . . and he trusts in the gentleness of heaven."[25]

His faults are usually the faults of too great exuberance — "lack of restraint, discipline, and poise."[26] Macaulay says that Ovid "had two insupportable faults: the one is that he will always be clever; the other, that he never knows when to have done."[27] He

---

* Perhaps an imaginary figure, perhaps a real one. See A. E. Housman, *Journal of Philology*, XXXV (1920), p. 316. Dimsdale (p. 333) nominates the poet Labienus.

often "lacked severity of self-criticism and failed to eliminate the insignificant."[28]

There are, however, many compensations. His versatility, his unfailing gaiety, his creative imagination, his psychological penetration, his fluency, his facility, and his metrical skill have placed him in the front rank of narrative and erotic poets.

Popularity and Influence. "No other classical poet has been so widely and so continuously read."[29]   Though a standard author in Rome during the three hundred years after his death, he exerted a profound influence only on Martial.   He was submerged during the Middle Ages till the latter part of the eleventh century.   From then till 1800 only Virgil among the Latin poets exerted more influence on literature.   The authors most indebted to him are Dante, the Goliards, the troubadours, the Minnesingers, Chrétien de Troyes, Benoît de Sainte-Maure, de Lorris, de Meun, Petrarch, Boccaccio, Ariosto, Camoëns, Lope de Vega, Calderón, Erasmus, Goethe, du Bellay, Ronsard, Montaigne, La Fontaine, Molière, Chaucer, Spenser, Sidney, Drayton, Heywood, Lyly, Shakespeare,* Jonson, Milton, Herrick, Cowley, Dryden, Landor, Tennyson, and Swinburne.

HISTORY

LIVY (Titus Livius Patavinus) (59 B.C.–A.D. 17).   Historian. Livy was born at Padua, but came to Rome where he soon was on friendly terms with Octavian and perhaps Maecenas and his circle. He spent most of the last forty years of his life writing history.   He died at Padua.

Works.

THE ANNALS or *HISTORIES*.†   In 142 books, of which only 45 survive in two large fragments (Books I–X and XXI–XLV). These *Annals* cover the period from the founding of Rome down through the death of Drusus, the stepson of Augustus, in A.D. 9. The first fragment begins at 753 and ends at 293 B.C.; the second fragment begins with the opening of the Second Punic War (218 B.C.). The scale varies: the first ten books cover 460 years, but the last few books cover about one year each.   The *Annals* draws on several

---

* "Shakespeare is another of our poet's reincarnations.   There is hardly an aspect of Ovid's genius and art that one will not see reproduced somewhere in Shakespeare."   (Edward K. Rand, *Ovid and His Influence* [New York: Longmans, Green and Co., 1928], p. 164.)

† No official title, but Livy refers to them as *annales* and as *libri ab urbe condita*.

other written sources, especially Polybius, often without acknowl-
edgment. Livy's style was influenced by Virgil and Cicero.

Livy had two main purposes: to celebrate the growth and contemporary greatness of Rome and to "charm his readers by his
narrative and dramatic powers."[30] He was interested primarily in
the Roman people — their characters and their actions. He
leaned toward republicanism, and he believed that the era of the
Punic Wars was Rome's most noble. But he was proud of Augustan
Rome's power, wealth, and righteousness. He believed that history
should be edifying — he insisted on moral rather than material phenomena of society; this insistence made his record incomplete. Livy
was exceptionally popular in his own day; it is said that a citizen
of Cadiz journeyed to Rome solely to see him, saw him, and immediately returned to Spain. His history is a sourcebook for later
authors, notably Machiavelli, Shakespeare, and Macaulay.

Summary of Criticism. Livy was often inaccurate. He was
careless about his sources, and he was romantic rather than scientific;
he was not a researcher. But he had "poetic" if not historical
truth; the spirit of his history was true although the dates and
details were sometimes erroneous. Though nationally prejudiced,
he was politically fair. He lacked historical perspective; he colored
political development with ideas of his own time. He had little
knowledge of geography, politics, law, and military affairs; and he
did not digest his sources. And he had no consistent theory of
history; he gave only a series of annals. His works have survived
largely because of his mastery of style — "flowing and periodic . . .
milky richness."[31] They show much color, enthusiasm, vitality,
drama, and romance. Livy has been called the "most brilliant
stylist that the world has seen."[32]

II

The Empire

(*A.D. 14–476*)

Historical Background. The period from the death of Augustus in
A.D. 14 till the death of Emperor Marcus Aurelius in 180 was, on
the whole, one of increasing decadence. Most of the early emperors
(notably Caligula, who ruled 37–41, and Nero, who ruled 54–68)
were despotic and tended to suppress personal liberties. The
"good" emperors (Nerva, Trajan, Hadrian, Antoninus Pius, and
Marcus Aurelius), who ruled during the period 96–180, maintained
a rather high degree of prosperity and happiness; and Trajan
extended the boundaries of the Empire to their farthest extent.
After the death of Marcus Aurelius economic, social, and political
conditions grew continually worse, despite periods of comparative
stability, e.g., under Diocletian (285–305). Barbarian invasions
during the fourth and fifth centuries became more frequent and
more widespread. In 364 the Empire was divided; in 410 the
Goths under Alaric sacked Rome; and in 476 the Western Empire
fell to Odovácer. Significant dates during the period were as
follows: 30, the crucifixion of Christ; 64, the burning of Rome;
70, the destruction of Jerusalem; 79, the eruption of Vesuvius and
the burial of Pompeii and Herculaneum; 251, the first invasion by
the Goths; 330, Constantinople's becoming the capital of the
Empire; 364, the division of the Empire; 410, the sack of Rome by
the Goths; 455, the sack of Rome by the Vandals; 476, the fall of
the Western Empire.

General View of the Literature. As in Greece, so in Rome: the Golden
Age of literature was followed by the Silver Age. The social and
political decline was accompanied by a falling off in both volume
and excellence of Latin literature. Although most of the emperors
encouraged the production of literature, the first ten (after the death
of Augustus and prior to the accession of Nerva in A.D. 96) laid ever
greater restrictions on freedom of literary expression, and they dis-

couraged philosophy. Fearful of giving offense, the authors produced affected and artificial literature and tended toward dilettantism, a tendency fostered by an increased interest in rhetoric and by the new practice of authors' reading or reciting their own productions before an audience. Admiration for the great Augustan writers led their successors to attempt—unsuccessfully—to emulate or to surpass them.

This was an age of prose. Orations, letters, histories, biographies, tales, and (in the later days of the Empire) religious treatises were the principal forms. Poetry, though comparatively uninspired, was not entirely dead; Seneca wrote dramas in verse, Martial produced epigrams, and Statius composed an epic.

TRAGEDY

SENECA (Lucius Annaeus Seneca) (*c.* 3 B.C.–A.D. 65). Dramatist, philosopher, satirist. Seneca was born at Corduba (Cordova), Spain. He became tutor to Domitius (later Emperor) Nero; was subsequently exiled to Corsica (A.D. 41–49); but returned to Rome and became adviser to Nero (49–65), who gave him great wealth. As adviser, he did a great deal to restrain Nero in his vices. Seneca was accused of complicity in the conspiracy of Piso and was forced to commit suicide.

Tragedies. Nine of Seneca's tragedies have survived; these were composed at unknown dates, probably toward the end of his life. Most of them are rewritings of the works of the Greek tragedians.

MAD HERCULES (*Hercules Furens*). A free adaptation of Euripides' *Hercules.*

THE TROJAN WOMEN (*Troades*). A reworking of Euripides' *Trojan Women;* it contains some borrowings from Euripides' *Hecuba.* This is perhaps the best of Seneca's plays.

THE PHOENICIAN WOMEN (*Phoenissae*). Incomplete. Its few scenes follow Euripides' play of the same name.

MEDEA. The plot of this tragedy is essentially that of Euripides' *Medea.* This drama is one of revenge, and it emphasizes the "inhuman fury and weird sorcery of barbaric Medea."[1] It is important as a sourcebook of ancient magic. It probably influenced the witch scenes in Shakespeare's *Macbeth.*

PHAEDRA. Based on Euripides' *Hippolytus Veiled* (lost) and *Hippolytus* (*Crowned*), principally the former. *Phaedra* is one of

Seneca's best plays.   It was the source of Racine's *Phèdre* and of d'Annunzio's *Fedra*.

OEDIPUS.   On a plot borrowed from Sophocles' play of the same name, but Seneca lays more emphasis on Oedipus' tyranny and sense of guilt.

THYESTES.   A powerful but somewhat revolting tragedy of revenge.   It is the only Senecan play not based on an extant Greek drama.

AGAMEMNON.   A sequel to *Thyestes.*   It is modeled on Aeschylus' *Agamemnon,* and it deals principally with the return and murder of Agamemnon.

HERCULES ON OETA.   The main source of this play is Sophocles' *Trachiniae;* it was almost certainly influenced by Ovid's *Transformations* (IX. 134–272) and *Heroines* (IX).   It treats the death and rebirth of Hercules.   The spiritual tone is original.[2]

CHARACTERISTICS OF SENECAN TRAGEDY.   Extreme violence and minuteness of the description of the characters' actions on the stage make it seem unlikely that Seneca's dramas were ever acted or intended to be acted.[3]   They were probably intended to be recited publicly or read in private.   Declamation and rhetorical display are the most striking characteristics.   The dramas are marked, too, by vivid and detailed description of the sensational, by sophistry, and by epigrammatic dialogue.   There is frequent employment of the mystical and magical — ghosts, incantations, the underworld.   Horror is the predominant note.   The tragedies contain many theatrical and spectacular scenes.   There is little restraint or sense of proportion.   The characters are unreal and are lacking in subtlety.   The dramatic technique is poor: motivation is often lacking, the dialogue is unrealistic, the action is frequently handled awkwardly, and there is little preparation for entrances and exits.   Exposition is usually inadequate.   Other characteristics are the frequent usage of a messenger and of the long soliloquy.   "'Plot' . . . does not exist for Seneca at all. . . .   Suspense and surprise attached solely to verbal effects."[4]   The play usually begins with a prologue in dialogue or monologue form — a descendant of the Euripidean prologue; Seneca's prologue is used primarily for setting the tone of the play.

STRUCTURE.   Eight of the nine dramas are divided into five "acts" by the insertion of four choral songs; the chorus is not organic, but little more than an interlude.   Three speaking characters (four in *Agamemnon*) appear on the stage at once.   Seneca's tragedies do not regularly observe the unities.

METER.   The dialogue is principally iambic.   Seneca's prosody is monotonous.

SIGNIFICANCE AND INFLUENCE.   "No [other] classical writer is so important in the history of the modern drama."[5]   Alfieri in Italy, Corneille in France, and nearly all the English tragedians of the sixteenth and seventeenth centuries are deeply indebted to Seneca for certain features of form, style, and technique.   Especially Shakespeare and his contemporaries show Seneca's influence in the use of prologue, chorus, ghosts, messengers, long soliloquies, division into five acts, magic, horror, revenge, and philosophic fatalism (as opposed to the religious fatalism of Aeschylus and Sophocles).

Prose Works.   In addition to his tragedies, Seneca wrote a large amount of prose, chiefly philosophical.   His philosophy was a practical Stoicism.   It was not very original, but it exerted a great deal of influence on medieval thought and on that of Montaigne and Emerson.   Seneca's prose style is pointed and epigrammatic.   He uses short sentences, puns, and much antithesis.

DIALOGUES.   The title is a misnomer; the pieces are really moral essays.   There are ten treatises in twelve books: (a) *On Providence* (*De Providentia*), a discussion of the problem of evil; (b) *On the Constancy of the Wise* (*De Constantia Sapientis*): "The wise man can be neither harmed nor insulted"; (c) *On Anger* (*De Ira*), in three books, on the nature and restraining of anger; (d) *Consolation to Marcia* (*Ad Marciam de Consolatione*), comfort of his daughter after the loss of her son; (e) *On the Happy Life* (*De Vita Beata*), preserved only in part, a definition of Stoical happiness; (f) *On Repose* (*De Otio*), justification of his retirement from public life; (g) *On Tranquility of Mind* (*De Tranquillitate Animi*), more Stoicism; (h) *On the Brevity of Life* (*De Brevitate Vitae*): life is long enough if we do not waste it; (i) *Consolation to Polybius* (*Consolatio ad Polybium*), comfort to and flattery of the official in charge of petitions addressed to the Emperor Claudius;[6] (j) *Consolation to His Mother, Helvia* (*Ad Helviam Matrem de Consolatione*), consolation of his mother during his own exile.

MORAL EPISTLES (*Epistulae Morales*).   A hundred and twenty-four letters in twenty books, chiefly concerning manners and morals; addressed to Lucilius, procurator of Sicily.

ETHICAL TREATISES.   Seneca wrote two very long ethical works: (a) *On Clemency* (*De Clementia*), in two books (the second one is fragmentary), which probably influenced Shakespeare's "quality of mercy" speech in *The Merchant of Venice;* (b) *On Benefits* (*De Beneficiis*), in three books, a definition.

NATURAL QUESTIONS (*Naturales Questiones*).   A treatise in seven books, on natural sciences.   It treats the rainbow (I), thunder and lightning (II), water (III), rising of the Nile, hail, and snow (IV), wind (V), earthquakes (VI), and comets (VII).   It is worthless as science, but there is much ethical (Stoical) content.

PUMPKINIFICATION (*Apocolocyntosis*).   A scurrilous but witty Menippean satire on the Emperor Claudius.[7]

SATIRE

Petronius (Gaius Petronius Arbiter) (d. A.D. 65).   Satirist.   Little is known of the life of Petronius; according to Tacitus,[8] he was "master of revels" (*arbiter elegantiarum*) to Nero.   He was forced to commit suicide as the result of alleged complicity in the plot of Piso.

THE SATYRICON (*Saturae*).*   A prose tale or novel, interspersed with poetry.[9]   Only fragments (141 chapters) of the fifteenth and sixteenth books survive — probably about one eighth of the original.   The loose plot deals with the wanderings of three scapegraces.   The first section (Chapters 1–26) consists chiefly of a discussion of literature and oratory, with an implied condemnation of the Asianic (florid) style.   The second section (Chapters 27–78) is concerned with the "Dinner of Trimalchio," the most famous part of the novel; Trimalchio (considered by some commentators to be a satirical portrait of Nero) is a vulgar, vain, ostentatious, but not unkindly *nouveau riche*, at whom Petronius pokes much fun.   The last section (Chapters 79–141) contains a discussion of the decadence of art, a poetic account of the Greek capture of Troy, a poem on the Roman Civil War, the story of "The Matron of Ephesus,"† and an account of a voyage and shipwreck of the three rascals of the main plot of the book.

* "The Medley," the actual translation of the Latin title, is rarely used.

† A widow mourns her husband so inconsolably that she is about to starve herself to death.   She is eventually persuaded to eat — and love — by a sentry, who neglects to guard a crucified corpse.   When the corpse is stolen, the widow donates the body of her husband to keep the sentry from being punished for dereliction of duty.

The Satyricon has no real plot in the modern sense. Its construction is loose and episodic. There is not even a moral principle around which the author builds the story. The character portrayal is objective. The work contains little irony and no moral indignation; Petronius neither condones nor condemns vice; his attitude is amoral. The book has an utter lack of decorum; it is full of debauchery, sensualism, and depravity. There is some inane moralizing, but there are also some homely aphorisms and some humorous illustrations. *The Satyricon* shows an excellent vocabulary; it is especially noteworthy as a storehouse of the "vernacular of the half-educated Roman."[10]

Martial (Marcus Valerius Martialis) (*c.* A.D. 40–102). Satirist, epigrammatist. Born at Bilbilis, Spain, Martial went to Rome *c.* A.D. 64, where he had various patrons. In 80 he presented the Emperor Titus with a collection of epigrams on the inauguration of the Colosseum; as a result he was given special privileges, including an honorary military tribunate and equestrian status. Toward the end of his life he was given a small estate by a rich woman. He returned to Bilbilis in A.D. 101, where he died.

About A.D. 84–85 Martial published two books of mottoes or labels for presents; these were entitled *Xenia* and *Apophoreta.* They were written in elegiac couplets. Thirteen other books of epigrams appeared from 86 to 101; the fifteen books contain about 1200 epigrams in all. All are short. These epigrams are on a wide variety of subjects; some are funny, but usually there is more wit than humor. Many are sardonic and mordant. Some are neither satirical nor funny, but are, instead, complimentary, eulogistic, congratulatory, or supplicatory. Some are bold and full of effrontery. Martial himself says, "Some good pieces, some middling, some bad."[11] Actually the epigrams vary in merit. Some are extremely clever, pointed, and significant; some are trivial. Although he says that his page "smacks of humanity,"[12] the epigrams deal not so much with humanity in general as with the manners, foibles, hypocrisies, and scandals of contemporary Rome. Martial's writing shows formal perfection, cleverness, wit, metrical neatness, and brevity. He was influential in Spain, England, France, and Germany.

Juvenal (Decimus Junius Juvenalis) (*c.* A.D. 60–140). Satirist. Juvenal was born at Aquinum; practically nothing else is known of his life. He wrote sixteen satires in hexameter verse: I, the evils and principal offenders of the age; II, unnatural vice, especially among those who profess virtue; III, miseries of Roman life;* IV, a burlesque of Domitian's cabinet; V, wretchedness of clients and followers of the rich and stingy; VI, a tirade against women; VII, hardships of students and teachers; VIII, the "vanity of rank";[13] IX, debauchery; X, the vanity of human desires and the virtue of true prayer;† XI, gluttony and extravagant living; XII, rejoicing over a friend's escape from shipwreck, plus an "attack on will-hunters";[14] XIII, revenge and the conscience; XIV, the duty of parents in setting examples for their children; XV, cannibalism; XVI, soldiers' mistreatment of civilians.

Juvenal is full of righteous indignation at the evils of the time. His writings are realistic, vigorous, cynical, savage, sardonic, vitriolic, and resentful. He is a master of powerful invective. Occasionally he strikes a high moral tone. He has "unique pictorial power, a fine full-bodied rhetoric, and an unsurpassed faculty for coining phrases and aphorisms."[15] He influenced Boileau, Samuel Johnson, and the whole of Neo-classicism.

THE EPIC

Lucan (Marcus Annaeus Lucanus) (A.D. 39–65). Epic poet. Born at Corduba (Cordova), nephew to Seneca the Philosopher, he was brought to Rome in his infancy. He became quaestor under Nero, but was forced to commit suicide for an active part in the conspiracy of Piso.

PHARSALIA or *THE CIVIL WAR* (*Pharsalia* or *De Bello Civili*[16]). An unfinished historical epic, in nine and a half books, concerning the civil war of Julius Caesar's day. The work is historically inaccurate. It contains two innovations: (1) epic treatment of recent history and (2) the discarding of "divine machinery." The versification is smooth but monotonous. The style is highly artificial; the poem abounds in hyperboles, antitheses, and epigrams. There are too many dull and useless catalogues. The narrative structure is weakened by many digressions. The poem is noteworthy for characterizations of Caesar, Pompey, and Cato; some brilliant epigrams; some passages of powerful rhetoric and satire; and some weird accounts of witches and the supernatural.

* Model for Samuel Johnson's *London*.
† Model for Samuel Johnson's *Vanity of Human Wishes*.

Statius (Publius Papinius Statius) (*c.* A.D. 40–96).   Poet.   Born at Naples, he went early to Rome.   Almost nothing else is known of his life.

THE THEBAID.   An epic poem in twelve books, telling the story of the Seven against Thebes (p. 64).   Statius is deeply indebted to Virgil's *Aeneid;* the *Thebaid* echoes characters and episodes.   Its workmanship in general is superior.   Its meter (dactylic hexameter) is smooth, and its figures of speech are usually clever but somewhat too numerous and often exaggerated.   The poem is distinctly romantic, full of the strange, the unnatural, the pitiable, and the violent.   It has been censured for having "no national interest, no moral conception, no religious or philosophical doctrine."[17]   The influence of the *Thebaid* was enormous during the Middle Ages, especially on Dante and Chaucer; it was also great on English literature of the eighteenth century.

ACHILLEIS.   A fragmentary epic, intended to cover the career of Achilles.   Only one and a half books (1127 lines) were completed; these deal with the childhood of the hero.   The poem is sentimental and shows "Ovidian prettiness."[18]

MISCELLANIES (*Silvae*).   Thirty-two occasional poems, in five books, written in various meters.   These poems are on numerous topics, e.g., the virtues of Domitian and other, less exalted men, the death of a slave, the dedication of a statue, Lucan's birthday. They show some realism and are neat, ingenious, and erudite.

NATURAL HISTORY

Pliny the Elder (Gaius Plinius Secundus) (A.D. 23–79).   Historian, biographer, grammarian, rhetorician, soldier, natural historian.   Pliny the Elder was born at Comum.   He performed both military and naval service.   While directing the rescue of others, he was suffocated by ashes from Vesuvius.

Pliny was a voracious reader; he took 160 volumes of notes. His lost works include a treatise on the use of the javelin, a biography of Pomponius Secundus, a history of the German wars (in twenty books), a history of Rome (in thirty-one books), and a treatise on diction.   His most important work was the *Natural History* (*Historia Naturalis*), in thirty-seven volumes, compiled, he says, from 2000 sourcebooks.[19]   It is an "encyclopedia of nature and art."[20]   Its contents are as follows: I, introduction, preface, and index; II, an astronomical and meteorological account of the universe; III–VI, geography of the known world; VII, anthropology and physiology; VIII–XI, zoology; XII–XIX, botany; XX–XXVII, plants used in medicine; XXVIII–XXXII, animal substances used in medicine; XXXIII–XXXVII, minerals used in medicine and art.

His data are untrustworthy. The *Natural History* indicates little original observation or verification of his sources. He is hasty, credulous, and unreflective. His style is straightforward but formless, full of digressions and declamations. But the *Natural History* is invaluable as a sourcebook for ancient learning of many various sorts. It was especially influential during the Middle Ages, when it was accepted as authoritative.

LETTERS

Pliny the Younger (Gaius Plinius Caecilius Secundus) (A.D. 62–c. 113). Orator, statesman, poet, letter-writer, nephew to Pliny the Elder (above). Pliny the Younger was born at Comum; he studied under Quintilian (below) and later served as praetor under Domitian and as consul and governor of Bithynia under Trajan.

LETTERS (*Epistulae*). In nine books. These letters were carefully revised for publication. They are modeled on the letters of Cicero, but are less vivid, less spontaneous, and less significant. As a rule, each letter deals with a single topic. They are full of sententious remarks. Their style is graceful, light, and charming. They touch on a considerable number of topics — court activity, literature, matters of state, geography, current events; especially interesting is the account of the eruption of Vesuvius in A.D. 79. Pliny's *Letters* are important for the intimate picture they give of Roman life and manners between A.D. 75 and 112 — a picture in direct contrast to that found in Juvenal's satires.

THE PANEGYRIC ORATION (*Panegyricus*). Excessively eulogistic and overelaborate speech delivered on his acceptance of the consulship (A.D. 100). The speech is poor as oratory, but significant for historical information of the time.

LITERARY HISTORY AND CRITICISM

Quintilian (Marcus Fabius Quintilianus) (c. A.D. 30–96). Teacher, lawyer, critic, literary historian. Quintilian was born at Calagurris, Spain, but educated at Rome. He became a public teacher, a practicing lawyer, and a tutor to the sons of the Emperor

Domitian. He wrote *The Training of an Orator* (*Institutio Oratoria*), a treatise in twelve books, indebted to Cicero. Its contents are as follows: Book I, elementary education of the child; Book II, aims and methods of later education, and an outline of the principles and scope of oratory; Books III–XI, the manner and matter of oratory (*inventio, dispositio, elocutio, memoria, pronuntiatio;* cf. Cicero); Book XII, a portrait of the ideal orator. The treatise is significant as one of the earliest works dealing with theories of education (especially Books I and II). Furthermore, Books X and XI constitute a critical history of earlier Latin literature; noteworthy are comments on Virgil, Ovid, and Lucretius.

HISTORY AND BIOGRAPHY

TACITUS (Cornelius Tacitus[21]) (*c.* A.D. 55–117). Historian, biographer, statesman. Tacitus was born perhaps at Interamna. He was of the Senatorial and Republican faction opposed to the emperors (*c.* 80–90), but held office under three Flavian rulers. He married the daughter of C. Julius Agricola, governor of Britain under Domitian. He was the friend of Pliny the Younger, and he served as consul under Nerva and as governor of Asia under Trajan.

Works.

DIALOGUE ON ORATORY (*Dialogus de Oratoribus*) (written *c.* A.D. 80). This is a treatise in dialogue form deploring contemporary and praising ancient oratory. Its style is fuller and more Ciceronian than that of his later works.

AGRICOLA (*De Vita et Moribus Julii Agricolae*) (written *c.* 97). "The earliest artistic biography which we possess."[22] It tells briefly the life of his father-in-law. It is eulogistic, but exquisitely eloquent in places. The *Agricola* is exceptionally valuable as a record of part of the early history of Britain. It has been called "perhaps the most beautiful piece of biography in ancient literature."[23]

GERMANY (*De Germania*) (written *c.* 98). A sketch of the peoples of central Europe at the end of the first century A.D. There is some mixture of legend with fact. The crude but virile Germanic civilization is contrasted with the corrupt civilization of the Roman Empire — rather to the advantage of the former. The sketch is important as ethnology.

HISTORIES (*Historiae*) (written *c.* 104–109). An annalistic account of the Empire during the years 69–70. Four and a half books survive; perhaps many others have been lost.

ANNALS (*Annales*) (written *c.* 115–117). A history of the emperors from Tiberius through Nero (A.D. 14–69). Many portions are lost.

Thought.

POLITICAL VIEWS. Tacitus had a pronounced anti-Imperial prejudice. The injustices and atrocities of Domitian strengthened Tacitus' Republican bias. He distrusted absolutism.

RELIGION AND ETHICS. He had little interest either in monotheism of any sort or in the traditional worship of the Olympic gods. Most of his references to deities were for rhetorical purposes. He had no distinct ideas about immortality. He was a Stoic and especially admired the virtue of fortitude. His outlook was pessimistic.

PHILOSOPHY OF HISTORY. None is clearly defined, but he used history as a means to show the decadence of the Empire and the evils of despotism.

Style and Technique. Tacitus' works are generally concise, forceful, and epigrammatic. He employs short sentences and deliberately avoids balance, parallelism, rhyme, rhythm, and Ciceronian periods. Many of his apothegms have become proverbial expressions, e.g., "the sinews of war," "conspicuous by their absence." He is contemptuous of oratorical devices and mere prettiness. His works show Virgilian influence. His diction tends toward the colloquial. He depends greatly on the substantive and the adjective for color, and he neglects the verb. He lacks a knowledge of military affairs, but he gives a graphic description of battles — ignoring strategy and tactics. He is excellent at character study and psychological analysis. His works are characterized by authenticity, sincerity, veracity, and gravity. He at least attempts to find the facts and render them impartially, though his anti-Imperial bias often colors his facts.

SUETONIUS (Gaius Suetonius Tranquillus) (*c.* A.D. 75–140). Biographer, Imperial secretary, friend of Pliny the Younger.

Works.

LIVES OF THE CAESARS (*De Vita Caesarum*) (written *c.* 120 A.D.). His most important work. These are twelve biographies of the Roman rulers from Julius Caesar through Domitian.

LIVES OF EMINENT MEN (*De Viris Illustribus*) (written *c.*

140 A.D.). Biographies of famous men of letters; only fragments are extant. The important lives are those of Terence, Horace, and Lucan.

Characteristics, Merits, and Defects. Suetonius is lacking in psychological insight; he makes little attempt at characterization. Moreover, he has little historical perspective and is often apparently unconscious of the significance of the events he relates. But he has a wealth of factual details.* There is only halfhearted attempt at chronology within each biography; time order is often abandoned for divisions on other bases. His style is characterized by brevity, impartiality, directness, lucidity, and candor. He uses quotations a great deal, and he repeats many anecdotes and much gossip. He was influential on Racine's *Bérénice*.

THE TALE

APULEIUS (Lucius Apuleius) (b. *c.* A.D. 125).   Prose narrator. Apuleius was born in Madaura, Africa; he married a rich widow, Pudentilla, whose family accused him of practicing magic to win her and brought a lawsuit against Apuleius; he was acquitted.

Works.

APOLOGY (*Apologia*).   A defense of himself in the lawsuit against the family of his wife.   The defense is discursive and humorous.

TRANSFORMATIONS or *THE GOLDEN ASS*[24] (*Metamorphoses*). A picaresque romance, sometimes described as a novel; in eleven books.   The plot is taken from a shorter tale in Greek, wrongly attributed to Lucian.   *The Golden Ass* is the story of Lucius of Thessaly, who by misuse of magic turns himself into the form of an ass but retains his human mind.   After many adventures he is restored to human shape by eating roses provided by the Egyptian goddess Isis, whose devotee he becomes.[25]   The most famous episode is Lucius' listening to the folk tale of Cupid and Psyche, which is perhaps intended as an allegory on the salvation of the human soul (Psyche) by love (Cupid).

FLOWERS OF ELOQUENCE (*Florida*).   Twenty-four excerpts of purple patches from Apuleius' orations.

ON PLATO'S DOGMA (*De Platone et Eius Dogmate*).   A two-book outline of Plato's doctrines.

---

* As Hadrian's secretary he had access to many private Imperial documents, of which he made good use.

ON THE UNIVERSE (De Mundo). A free translation of a tract wrongly attributed to Aristotle.

The Style of Apuleius. It is flowery and diffuse, aimed at the senses rather than the intellect; and most of his works are full of alliteration, puns, parallelism, and even rhymes. His diction is "bizarre and lawless, a jumble of archaisms and neologisms, of the conversational and the poetic."[26]

Influence. Apuleius has exerted great influence on medieval and modern literature, especially on Boccaccio and Pater.

CHRISTIAN WRITERS

Since Christianity was at first a religion of the lower classes, of whom many could neither read nor write, it was not till the end of the second century A.D. that a real Christian literature began. The important early Church writers were Minucius Felix, Tertullian (Quintus Septimius Florens Tertullianus), St. Cyprian (Caecilius Cyprianus), and Lactantius (Lucius Caecilius Firmianus Lactantius).* Of greater significance were two later figures, St. Jerome and St. Augustine.

St. Jerome (Eusebius Hieronymus) (*c.* 340–420). Translator, scriptural commentator, biographer, historian. His most important work was the Vulgate, a Latin translation of the Bible (*c.* 383–405). He also wrote commentaries on all the major and minor prophets, numerous homilies, several biographies of saints, many "controversial" works, many letters, and a short history of Christian literature from the time of the Apostles down through his own day (*On Illustrious Men, De Viris Illustribus*).

ST. AUGUSTINE (Aurelius Augustinus) (354–430). Bishop of Hippo, theologian, philosopher. St. Augustine was born in Tagaste, Algeria, of a devout Christian mother and a pagan father. He was trained as a rhetorician, and he taught at Carthage, Rome, and Milan. As a young man he became a promiscuous pleasure-seeker. For a time he was a Manichaean, but was converted to Christianity by the sermons of St. Ambrose in Milan. Thereafter St. Augustine was a zealous theologian and writer. As Bishop of Hippo, he was engaged in continuous religious controversy, especially against

---

* Influential on Milton. See Kathleen E. Hartwell, *Lactantius and Milton* (Cambridge, Mass.: Harvard University Press, 1929).

Manichaeans, Donatists, and Pelagians.*   He died during the siege
of Hippo by the Vandals.

St. Augustine wrote an enormous amount of literature of five
principal sorts: (1) philosophy, somewhat Neoplatonic; (2) polem-
ics; (3) moral treatises; (4) sermons; and (5) dogmatic and
apologetic works.

As a theologian he has had a great influence; during the Middle
Ages his sermons were widely used.   Two of his most influential
doctrines were the immediate efficacy of God's grace and absolute
predestination — his interpretations of the Pauline doctrines found
chiefly in the Epistle to the Romans and the first Epistle to the
Corinthians.   St. Augustine's influence can be seen especially in
the theologies of Luther, Calvin, and Jansen.

Two of his works are widely read today.

THE CONFESSIONS (Confessiones) (finished *c.* 400).   A spiritual
autobiography.   Here he gives an account of his early life and of
his conversion.   The work reveals a great deal about his mind and
his personality; and it tells many interesting facts about the life,
religions, and philosophies of the Roman Empire of St. Augustine's
day.   W. R. Benét has called *The Confessions* "the first completely
honest self-analysis in the history of literature."[27]

THE CITY OF GOD (De Civitate Dei) (finished *c.* 420).   A
tremendous work defending Christianity against the charge that it
brought about the fall of Rome in 410.   St. Augustine holds that
all history is a conflict between the City of God (the principle of
good, personified by all devout Christians) and the Earthly City
(the principle of evil, personified by pagans and all other unbe-
lievers).   The conflict will lead to the Day of Judgment, when
those in the City of God will inherit immortality and those in the
Earthly City will be destroyed.

BOËTHIUS† (Ancius Manlius Severinus Boëthius) (*c.* 475–525).

* The Manichaeans were followers of the Persian Manichaeans or Mani
(third century) who founded a religion (Manichaeism) made up to a large extent
of Christian and Zoroastrian (see p. 8) elements.   The Donatists were a Christian sect who arose in North Africa in A.D. 311 as the result of a dispute over the
election of a bishop of Carthage; Donatus was either a supporter or a successor
of the bishop (Majorinus) concerning whose election the dispute began.   The
Pelagians were a heretical Christian sect of the fourth and fifth centuries A.D.
who denied the doctrine of original sin.

† As his dates show, Boëthius falls outside the chronological limits given for
this section.   Furthermore, it is perhaps misleading to place him among the
Christian writers; despite his canonization (as Saint Severinus) by the Roman

Boëthius was born in Rome. His father was a consul, and he himself was made a consul (510) under the Emperor Theodoric the Ostrogoth, whose favorite he became. In 525, however, he was accused of conspiracy against the emperor; he was condemned, imprisoned, and executed. It was in prison that he wrote his most famous work, the *Consolation of Philosophy*. In addition to composing this original piece, Boëthius translated Aristotle's *Categories* and *On Interpretation;* wrote commentaries on Aristotle, Porphyry, and Cicero and books on logic, astronomy, arithmetic, geometry, and music.

THE CONSOLATION OF PHILOSOPHY (*De Consolatione Philosophiae*). By far his most important literary endeavor, the *Consolation* is an allegory in five books; prose alternates with poetry. Here Boëthius attempts to reconcile many of the ethical tenets of Plato, Aristotle, Stoicism, and Christianity. In Book I, Philosophy in the form of a woman comes to the author as a comforter and guide; she warns him that man's misery is often a result of his ignorance of his own nature and destiny. Book II depicts Fortune as an untrustworthy donor of benefits (a conception adopted and elaborated by Chaucer). Books III and IV take up the perennial problem of evil that tormented Job — why the good suffer and the wicked flourish. Philosophy shows that evil is not real but only apparent and that the truly good people are also the happy ones. Book V attempts to solve another ever-recurrent ethical problem — the reconciliation of belief in the freedom of man's will and belief in God's omnipotence and omniscience. Philosophy argues that since God transcends time and is not bound by its limits, He may know of an event or a human act without being the cause of it. Hence man is responsible for his deeds and is exhorted to be good.

Boëthius is remembered today chiefly for the immense influence which he had on later writers and thinkers. His translations and commentaries were most important in the preservation and interpretation of classical philosophy; some of his minor works were widely used as textbooks in schools; and his *Consolation of Philosophy*, which was translated by King Alfred, Chaucer, Elizabeth I, and several others, was one of the most popular of all handbooks throughout Europe during the Middle Ages.

Catholic Church, there is no convincing evidence that he was a practicing Christian. Since the Middle Ages, however, regarded him as a Christian martyr (for opposing the Arian heresy endorsed by Theodoric), and since Boëthius came only a few decades after Saint Augustine, it has seemed permissible to include here a discussion of his works.

Bibliography for Ancient Roman Literature

General

Dimsdale, Marcus S. *A History of Latin Literature.* New York: D. Appleton and Co., 1915.

Mackail, John W. *Latin Literature.* New York: Charles Scribner's Sons, 1895.

————. *The Progress of Poesy.* Oxford: Clarendon Press, 1906.

Rose, Herbert J. *A Handbook of Latin Literature.* London: Methuen and Co., 1936.

The Republic

Collins, W. Lucas. *Plautus and Terence.* Philadelphia: J. B. Lippincott Co., 1880.

Duckett, Eleanor S. *Catullus in English Poetry.* Northampton, Mass.: Smith College Library, 1925.

Duff, J. Wight. *Roman Satire: Its Outlook on Social Life.* Berkeley, Calif.: University of California Press, 1936.

Ellis, Robinson. *A Commentary on Catullus.* 2nd ed. Oxford: Clarendon Press, 1889.

Frank, Tenney. *Catullus and Horace.* New York: H. Holt and Co., 1928.

Hadzsits, George D. *Lucretius and His Influence.* New York: Longmans, Green and Co., 1935.

Harrington, Karl P. *Catullus and His Influence.* New York: Longmans, Green and Co., 1927.

Harsh, Philip W. *A Handbook of Classical Drama.* Stanford, Calif.: Stanford University Press, 1944.

Havelock, Eric A. *The Lyric Genius of Catullus.* Oxford: B. Blackwell, 1939.

Norwood, Gilbert. *Plautus and Terence.* New York: Longmans, Green and Co., 1932.

Richards, George C. *Cicero: A Study.* London: Chatto and Windus, 1935.

Rolfe, John C. *Cicero and His Influence.* New York: Longmans, Green and Co., 1923.

Santayana, George. *Three Philosophical Poets.* Cambridge, Mass.: Harvard University Press, 1910.

Sinker, A. P. *Introduction to Lucretius.* Cambridge, England: Cambridge University Press, 1937.

Wheeler, Arthur L. *Catullus and the Traditions of Ancient Poetry.* Berkeley, Calif.: University of California Press, 1934.

Wright, Frederick A. *Three Roman Poets.* London: G. Routledge and Sons, 1938.

The Augustan Age

Church, Alfred. *Ovid.* Philadelphia: J. B. Lippincott Co., 1880.

Collins, W. Lucas. *Livy.* Philadelphia: J. B. Lippincott Co., 1876.

———. *Virgil.* Philadelphia: J. B. Lippincott Co., 1878.

Crump, M. Marjorie. *The Growth of the Aeneid.* Oxford: B. Blackwell, 1920.

Cruttwell, Robert W. *Virgil's Mind at Work.* Oxford: B. Blackwell, 1946.

D'Alton, John F. *Horace and His Age.* London: Longmans, Green and Co., 1917.

Davies, James. *Catullus, Tibullus, and Propertius.* Philadelphia: J. B. Lippincott Co., 1881.

Fiske, George C. *Lucilius and Horace.* Madison, Wis.: University of Wisconsin Press, 1920.

Frank, Tenney. *Vergil: A Biography.* New York: H. Holt and Co., 1922.

Frankel, Herman. *Ovid: A Poet between Two Worlds.* Berkeley, Calif.: University of California Press, 1945.

Glover, T. R. *Virgil.* 2nd ed. London: Macmillan and Co., 1912.

Goad, Caroline M. *Horace in the English Literature of the Eighteenth Century.* New Haven, Conn.: Yale University Press, 1918.

Horace. *The Complete Works of Horace.* Edited by Casper J. Kraemer. New York: Modern Library, 1936.

Hughes, Merritt Y. *Virgil and Spenser.* Berkeley, Calif.: University of California Press, 1929.

Jaffee, Harold B. *Horace: An Essay in Poetic Therapy.* Chicago: Harold B. Jaffee, 1944.

Mackail, John W. *Virgil and His Meaning to the World of Today.* New York: Longmans, Green and Co., 1922.

Martin, Theodore. *Horace.* Philadelphia: J. B. Lippincott Co., 1880.

Morgan, Junius S., Kenneth McKenzie, and Charles G. Osgood. *The Tradition of Virgil.* Princeton: Princeton University Press, 1930.

Myers, Frederic W. H. "Virgil," *Essays: Classical.* London: Macmillan and Co., 1904.

Nitchie, Elizabeth. *Vergil and the English Poets.* New York: Columbia University Press, 1919.

Noyes, Alfred. *Horace: A Portrait.* New York: Sheed and Ward, 1947.

Prescott, Henry W. *The Development of Virgil's Art.* Chicago: University of Chicago Press, 1929.

Rand, Edward K. *The Magical Art of Virgil.* Cambridge, Mass.: Harvard University Press, 1931.

————. *Ovid and His Influence.* New York: Longmans, Green and Co., 1928.

Saintonge, Paul F., Leslie G. Burgevin, and Helen Griffith. *Horace, Three Phases of His Influence.* Chicago: University of Chicago Press, 1936.

Sedgwick, Henry D. *Horace: A Biography.* Cambridge, Mass.: Harvard University Press, 1947.

Sellar, William Y. *The Roman Poets of the Augustan Age: Horace and the Elegiac Poets.* Oxford: Clarendon Press, 1892.

————. *The Roman Poets of the Augustan Age: Virgil.* Oxford: Clarendon Press, 1897.

Showerman, Grant. *Horace and His Influence.* New York: Longmans, Green and Co., 1931.

Smiley, Charles N. *Horace: His Poetry and Philosophy.* Chicago: Kings Crown Press, 1945.

Tibullus. *The Elegies of Albius Tibullus.* Edited by Kirby Smith. New York: American Book Co., 1913.

————. *Selections from Tibullus and Propertius.* Edited by George G. Ramsey. Oxford: Clarendon Press, 1900.

Wilkinson, L. P. *Horace and His Lyric Poetry.* Cambridge, England: Cambridge University Press, 1945.

Woodberry, George E. "Virgil," *Literary Essays.* New York: Harcourt, Brace, and Howe, 1920.

The Empire

Boissier, Gaston. *Tacitus and Other Roman Studies.* Translated by W. G. Hutchinson. New York: G. P. Putnam's Sons, 1906.

Cunliffe, John W.   *The Influence of Seneca on Elizabethan Tragedy.* New York: G. E. Stechert and Co., 1925.

Farrar, F. W.   "Seneca," *Seekers after God.*   London: Macmillan and Co., 1906.

Giulian, Anthony A.   *Martial and the Epigram in Spain in the Sixteenth and Seventeenth Centuries.*   Philadelphia: University of Pennsylvania Press, 1930.

Gummere, Richard M.   *Seneca the Philosopher and His Modern Message.*   Boston: Marshall Jones Co., 1922.

Haight, Elizabeth H.   *Apuleius and His Influence.*   New York: Longmans, Green and Co., 1927.

_____.   *More Essays on Greek Romance.*   New York: Longmans, Green and Co., 1945.

Holland, Francis.   *Seneca.*   London: Longmans, Green and Co., 1920.

Juvenal.   *Juvenal and Persius.*   Translated and edited by G. G. Ramsey.   New York: G. P. Putnam's Sons, 1918.

_____.   *The Satires of Juvenal, Persius, Sulpicia, and Lucilius.* Edited by Lewis Evans.   New York: Harper Brothers, 1860.

Lucas, Frank L.   *Seneca and Elizabethan Tragedy.*   Cambridge, England: Cambridge University Press, 1922.

Mendel, Clarence W.   *Our Seneca.*   New Haven, Conn.: Yale University Press, 1941.

Nixon, Paul.   *Martial and the Modern Epigram.*   New York: Longmans, Green and Co., 1927.

Petronius.   *The Satyricon.*   Edited by J. M. Mitchell.   London: G. Routledge and Sons, 1923.

Seneca.   *Seneca, His Tenne Tragedies.*   Introduction by T. S. Eliot.   London: Tudor Translations, 1927.

_____.   *The Tragedies of Seneca.*   Translated and edited by Frank J. Miller.   Chicago: T. Fisher Unwin Co., 1908.

Smith, Kirby F.   *Martial the Epigrammatist and Other Essays.* Baltimore: Johns Hopkins Press, 1920.

Suetonius.   *Lives of the Caesars.*   Edited by Joseph Gavorse. New York: Modern Library, 1931.

Todd, F. A.   *Some Ancient Novels.*   London: H. Milford and Oxford University Press, 1940.

Whipple, T. K.   *Martial and the English Epigram from Sir Thomas Wyatt to Ben Johnson.*   Berkeley, Calif.: University of California Press, 1925.

Part Four
Medieval Oriental Literature

Chinese Literature

Historical Background. The period of the T'ang dynasty in China (A.D. 600–907) was an era of great wealth, leisure, refinement, extravagance, dissipation, and romance. This era was succeeded by a short one of uncertainty and political turmoil; between 907 and 950 there were five dynastic changes. Thereafter till 1279 China was governed by the "fire-led" Sungs, a family of enlightened rulers, who encouraged the arts, the sciences, and literature. In 1279 the last of the Sungs fell before the Mongol Kublai Khan; the Mongolian dynasty was brought to an end in 1368 by the Mings.

General View of the Literature. The epoch of the T'angs was one of the most notable in Chinese literature. Besides being the most prolific and perhaps most brilliant era of poetry, the age produced many scholars, philosophers, essayists, and historians. As might be expected, in the interim between the T'angs and the Sungs there was little literary activity, but Feng Tao invented block printing about 945. The Sungs were enthusiastic patrons of literature; history, poetry, scholarship, and lexicography flourished under them. Their successors, the Mongols, continued to encourage literary production. Although a large quantity of poetry was written during the Mongol regime, the period is most memorable for its drama and novels.

POETRY

Chinese poetry "burst forth and reached perfection under the T'angs."[1] In 1707 a collection of T'ang poetry filled thirty volumes and contained 48,900 separate poems. After the advent of the Sungs, poetry suffered a decline in both quantity and excellence; and during the Mongolian dynasty, although a considerable amount of poetry was written (eight volumes have been collected), few poems of the highest merit were produced.

Medieval Chinese poetry is artificial and hard to understand. Each line is made up of five or seven monosyllables, arranged according to strict tonal patterns (or sharp and flat sounds) rather than to normal syntactical patterns. There is no inflection. Rhyme is regularly employed. Although some poems extend to several hundred lines, most of them are short — four, eight, or twelve lines.

Comparatively little medieval Chinese poetry deals with romantic love. Far more of it is concerned with friendship, wine, and the delights of solitude. Great emphasis is laid on brevity, suggestiveness, and originality.

Li Po or **Li T'ai-po** or **Li Tai-peh** (705–762). Probably the greatest of all Chinese poets. Very precocious, he wrote a commendable poem on a firefly when he was only ten years old. As a young man he led a dissipated life, but became, nevertheless, a court favorite. His tippling apparently had no ill effects on his poetic ability; legend tells, on the contrary, of instances when some of his best verses were written while he was drunk. Later he became the victim of an intrigue and was banished from court. It is traditionally believed that he was drowned when he leaned too far over the side of a boat in order to embrace the moon's reflection in the water.

Li Po is remembered especially for poems which suggest a great deal but which then leave much to the imagination. Some of his favorite topics are nature, court life, and the joys of wine. Some of his most well-known lyrics are "Drinking Wine," "In the Mountains on a Summer Day," "Self-Abandonment," "Waking from Drunkenness on a Spring Day," and "Clearing at Dawn."[2]

Han Yü or **Han Wen-kung** (768–824). Poet, statesman, philosopher. Although he held one of the highest positions in the court, Han was banished for criticizing the Emperor Hsien Tsung's enthusiasm over a bone of Buddha. He was, however, soon recalled and reinstated.

Han Yü wrote poetry on a tremendous number of different topics. Many of his poems are light, playful, and witty. Others show him to have been unusually humane toward animals. Some of his most famous poems are "To Stand upon the River Bank," "Oh, Spare the Busy Morning Fly," and "Alas, the Early Season Flies."[3]

Han's prose is superior to his poetry and on an equally great variety of topics. His most sensational piece of prose is his memorial to the Emperor concerning Buddha's bone; the piece is actually an attack on Buddhism and a defense of Confucianism. Other notable prose works are the farewell to his deceased friend Liu Tsung-yuan and an essay on Confucianism.

Po Chü-i (772–846). Poet, statesman. Like Li Po, Po Chü-i was amazingly precocious; he is reputed to have been able at the age of seven months to recognize a large number of the characters of the Chinese alphabet. He received a minor political position in 806, was banished in 815, and was reprieved in 820. Thereafter he rose rapidly, serving, in turn, as governor of Hangchow, governor of Soochow, governor of Honan, and president of the Board of War. He was stricken with paralysis in 839 and died several years later.

One of the most remarkable characteristics of the poetry of Po Chü-i is its simple and easy language. It is said that he would test his poems by reading them to an old peasant woman; he would change any words which she could not understand. He despised the preciosity and the display of erudition of which his contemporaries were guilty.

Po believed that all art should give instruction, but he did not always practice according to his own theory. Many of his poems are mere records of fleeting sensations, emotions, or events. His didactic poems are little more than "moral tales in verse";[4] these are often referred to as "satires," but the term is inaccurate because the poems lack wit — now usually considered an indispensable ingredient of satire. Some examples of his didactic verse are "The Dragon of the Black Pool," "The Man Who Dreamed of Fairies" (a censure of the Emperor Hsien Tsung's interest in magic), and "The Two Red Towers" (an attack on clericalism[5]).

Far more popular are his poems of sentiment and his miscellaneous descriptive and narrative pieces. The "Lute Girl" is an exquisite description of a maiden who moves her listeners to tears by the sadness and beauty of her song. "The Everlasting Wrong" is a sensuous account of the ascent to power of Yang Kuei-fei, the concubine of the Emperor Ming Huang (685–762), the insurrection of the Emperor's soldiers, Yang's death, and her sad message from the world of spirits. Other charming pieces by Po Chü-i are "Golden Bells" and "Remembering Golden Bells" (poems about his daughter who died at the age of three), "Planting Bamboos," "Watching the Reapers," "Rain," and "Lazy Man's Song."

HISTORY

Ssu-ma Kuang (1019–1086). Statesman, historian. After resigning as Minister of State, Ssu-ma devoted the remainder of his life to the writing of his *T'ung Chien*, or *Mirror of History*, an account of the period from *c*. 450 B.C. to A.D. 960.

Chu Hsi (1130–1200). Historian, philosopher. His revision of the history of Ssu-ma Kuang (above) "is still regarded as the standard history of China."[6] He is also one of the leading interpreters of Confucianism.

DRAMA

Songs and dances with gestures accompanied some religious rites in China as early as the sixth century B.C. These performances, however, appear to have little to do with the development of Chinese drama; at least, no steps in such development can be traced. There are accounts of Tartar dramatic presentations in the eleventh century A.D.; perhaps, then, the Chinese drama is derived from Tartar sources. All that is really known is that in the thirteenth century under the Mongols there was a Chinese drama.

Apparently the trade guilds in China — like those in medieval England — were instrumental in dramatic production. They built stages and presented performances free to all who wished to stand in the courtyard and watch. Powerful and wealthy individuals also sponsored private performances.

The plays were generally presented on a stage with no curtain, no wings, and almost no properties. Costumes, however, were elaborate and expensive. In order to compensate for the lack of properties and of realism, the actors had to be extraordinarily skillful in the representation of each scene.

Early Chinese drama is "simple in construction and weak in plot."[7] There is no such thing as genuine tragedy — no passion or emotional purgation. Instead of falling into the traditional Western categories of comedy, tragedy, and history, medieval Chinese plays may be classified as either "military" or "civil." The former deal with historical events and historical characters, and often include scenes of battle and of physical violence. The "civil" drama is concerned with ordinary people and especially with domestic life. It is usually farcical and, when actually presented on the stage, often interlarded with ad libs (many of them indecent) by the actors.

Most medieval Chinese drama is anonymous. Perhaps the most memorable dramatist whose name is known is the thirteenth-century WANG SHIH-FU. Thirteen of his plays survive. One of these, *Story of the Western Pavilion*, tells how a young scholar saves a lady and her daughter from brigands and as a reward is promised the hand of the daughter in marriage. When the mother reneges on her promise, the lady's maid of the daughter cleverly maneuvers a happy ending.

THE NOVEL

Like the drama, the Chinese novel is obscure in its origin. Although tales had been familiar to the Chinese long before the Mongol invasion, the novel proper seems to have been introduced from central Asia early in the thirteenth century. It was to reach its highest development about three centuries later.

The medieval Chinese novels may be classified as to subject-matter as follows: (1) novels of usurpation and plotting, (2) novels of love and intrigue, (3) novels of superstition, and (4) novels of brigandage and lawlessness.[8]

The most popular novels of the period are two:

THE STORY OF THE THREE KINGDOMS (*c.* 1250?). Attributed to Lo Kuan-Chung, this is a historical novel dealing with the wars of the third century A.D. There are many bloody scenes and many accounts of brave deeds. The style is facile and entertaining.

RECORD OF TRAVELS IN THE WEST (*c.* 1325?). Anonymous. Though ostensibly an account of a journey by Hsuan Tsang to India for the purpose of collecting Buddhist books, images, and relics, most of the *Record* has absolutely nothing to do with Hsuan's journey. Instead it is filled with delightful, irrelevant, and unrelated tales, many of which recount wondrous or miraculous events.

13

Arabian and Persian Literature

A. Arabian Literature

Historical Background. Before the seventh century A.D. the history of Arabia is almost negligible. For hundreds of years Semitic nomads had inhabited the peninsula and had occasionally wandered as far as Egypt and Mesopotamia. The various bands of nomads waged almost continuous warfare against each other; consequently Arabia had neither unity nor significance as a nation.

Between 622 and 632 Mohammed (Mahomet, Muhammad), by virtue of his doctrines and his military conquests, made himself master of the whole country. Fired by religious zeal, the Mohammedan Arabs under the caliphs ("successors" to Mohammed) attempted to subjugate the world. They swept through Persia, Asia Minor, northern Africa, Spain, and parts of India. Though later weakened by decadence and religious schisms, the Arabs were able to withstand the six Crusades against them, and they were not driven from Spain till late in the fifteenth century.

Despite the cruelty and ruthlessness of the medieval Arabs, the world is indebted to them for the development, preservation, and dissemination of many types of culture. They established universities at Bagdad, Cairo, and Cordova. It is hardly too broad a statement to say that between 650 and 1300 the Arabians made greater contributions in the fields of mathematics, chemistry, medicine, astronomy, and philosophy than any other people made.

General View of the Literature. Prior to the Mohammedan era, there was little Arabian literature. There were a few tales and legends and a number of short, passionate love poems — poems which Wilfrid S. Blunt has called "the most delightful wild flower of literature the Eastern world can show."[1]

From the seventh to the thirteenth century literature flourished. Although there were no epics and no dramas, and although there were no literary giants, a great number of writers of varying stature

156

produced hundreds of lyrics, panegyrics, satires, epigrams, elegies, biographies, histories, sermons, lectures, commentaries, and fables. Two works have achieved universal fame and influence. These are the Koran and *The Arabian Nights.*

THE KORAN or **ALCORAN** ("The Reading"). The sacred book of the Mohammedans. It consists of a hundred and fourteen chapters or *suras,* which, according to Mohammed, were given to him piecemeal in moments of inspiration. The inspired bits were taken down by scribes but were not collected till after the Prophet's death. Then they were arranged according to length (the longest first, the shortest last) with a total disregard for both logic and date of composition.

The book is written in rhymed (and sometimes rhythmical) prose; there is some alliteration. The style is uneven. In the shorter chapters (written principally at Mecca before 622), the expression is forceful and curt; in the longer ones (written at Medina between 622 and 632), Mohammed becomes less a prophet and more a legislator and statesman; consequently, his sentences are milder and more gently persuasive.

The subject matter of the Koran is derived almost entirely from Hebrew and Christian sources. Mohammed's central message is monotheism — the belief in Allah, of whom Mohammed, Moses, and Jesus are the chief prophets. Great emphasis is laid on the afterlife. Every believer is to be rewarded with eternal bliss; he is to receive seventy-two wives and eighty thousand servants. Every nonbeliever is to suffer eternal punishment.

Though distinctly lower than Christian ethics, the ethics of the Koran are not lacking in nobility. They teach honesty, kindness, and the brotherhood of the faithful. Four main duties are prayer, alms-giving, fasting, and making a pilgrimage to Mecca.

THE ARABIAN NIGHTS' ENTERTAINMENTS or *The Thousand and One Nights.* The most widely popular of all Arabian literature. It is a series of a thousand and one tales bound together by a framework device. The parts vary in origin and date. The framework appears to have been brought from India by the Persians and then translated into Arabic in the tenth century. One group of the stories, too, is probably of Indian origin and probably very ancient. A second group revolves around Bagdad and deals with the era of Haroun-al-Raschid (763–809). A third and later group deals with adventures around Cairo. A fourth group, of uncertain date but probably fairly late, is of Jewish origin.   As we now know it, the whole book was drawn up about 1450, probably in Cairo. A few stories were added during the sixteenth century.   The oldest extant manuscript is dated 1548.

"The style of the *Arabian Nights* is absolutely popular and local."[2] The language is colloquial, and the dialect varies according to the source.   The spirit is romantic.

The framework which binds the stories together is well known. King Shahriyar of India, in order to be sure that he will never be married to a faithless wife, executes each of his brides the morning after the consummation of their marriage.   When Scheherazade, daughter of Shahriyar's vizier, marries the king, she forestalls execution for a thousand and one nights by telling part of a story to the king each night but withholding the end till the following evening. At last Shahriyar relents and gives up the plan for execution.

The most popular of the tales told by Scheherazade are "Sinbad the Sailor," "Ali Baba and the Forty Thieves," and "Aladdin and His Lamp."

B. Persian Literature

Historical Background.   In 651 the Sasanian Empire of the Persians was overrun by the Arabs; Persia became a tributary province of the caliphs; Mohammedanism replaced Zoroastrianism as the dominant religion; and Arabic superseded Pahlavi as the official language.   The resilient and adaptable nature of the Persians, however, enabled them to preserve much of their culture and to absorb and color Arabian life much as the Anglo-Saxons did the civilization of the conquering Normans.

From 651 till the early part of the ninth century little of importance happened inside Persia.   By 820 the Arabian caliphate at Bagdad had been so weakened that independent dynasties began to spring up within Persia, some of them of Sasanian origin.   Ancient Persian culture revived somewhat between 820 and the date of the Mongolian conquest of Arabia and Persia in 1258.   The Mongolian period, which came to an end with the death of Tamerlane in 1405, was one of much warfare and internal conflict, but Persian was re-established as the official language early in the era.

General View of the Literature.   Although there were some history and philosophy written in medieval Persia, the only literature of world significance was poetry.   Most of the poets of any consequence were sponsored by the local rulers, and literally dozens of poets turned out epics, romances, lyrics, epigrams, and especially panegyrics to please their noble patrons. Most of the poetry was rich in imagery and romantic in sentiment. "Philosophical and worldly feelings, contempt for the world and enjoyment of its pleasures, mystic faith and sophisticated skepticism, existed side by side in the golden age of Persian literature."[3]

Rudagi (Abu Abdillah Jafar bin Mohammed) (*c.* 880–954). "The first great classical poet of Persia."[4] Rudagi was also the first Persian to write court poetry — poetry which was, in the main, extravagant flattery of some patron. In addition to such panegyrics, Rudagi wrote many odes (e.g., "Bring Me Yon Wine" and "April's Moon"), three (lost) historical romances, and some epigrams. In his poetry one may see the beginning of the conflict — so prominent in later Persian verse — between physical, worldly pleasures and the strict Mohammedan theology. Though Rudagi's style was usually simple and direct, sometimes it was marred by artificiality and elaborateness.

Firdausi (Firdawsi) (*c.* 935–1020). At the beginning of the eleventh century the powerful Sultan Mahmud of Ghazna gathered about himself an illustrious group of scientists, historians, and poets. Unsuri, Farrukhi, and Asjadi all became famous for their odes, elegies, and panegyrics. Far greater than these was a fourth poet of Mahmud's circle, Firdausi, who brought to court his *Shah Namah*, the product of thirty-five years of labor. This exceedingly long epic (60,000 couplets) attempts to chronicle the history of Persia from 3600 B.C. through the end of Sasanian rule in A.D. 651. It includes a large number of heroic legends about ancient Persia, the biographies of fifty kings, and numerous miscellaneous narratives of adventure (from one of which Matthew Arnold drew his story of *Sohrab and Rustum*).

As a work of art the *Shah Namah* has many defects. It is repetitious, its meter is monotonous, its descriptions of both scenes and characters are stereotyped, and it lacks historical perspective. But its subject matter is what counts. The poem is intensely patriotic, and it is generally considered the Persian national epic.

In addition to the *Shah Namah* Firdausi wrote *Yusuf and Zuleikha* (in rhyming couplets), a poem about the Biblical Joseph and Potiphar's wife, in which the hero is depicted as the paragon of virtue, loyalty, and male perfection.

Omar Khayyám (Omar ibn Ibrahim al Khayyám) (died *c.* 1123). Best known of all Persian poets. As a reaction against the "ecstatic spiritualism"[5] of the Sufis (a group of pantheistic mystics noted for the strange symbolism of their religious poetry), Omar the Tentmaker of Nishapur — scientist, mathematician, astronomer, and philosopher — wrote his *Rubaiyat.** These "Quatrains" were apparently written at many different times and consequently reflect many different moods and points of view — often conflicting with each other. If any trend can be traced at all, it is the transformation of a pious Moslem into an avowed skeptic. What are believed to be the later quatrains show Omar as a freethinker, satirizing all religious dogma. Sometimes he depicts God as malign and cruel, sometimes as merely blind. Everything — even pleasure — is vain and futile, but wine is a wonderful aid toward momentary exaltation and oblivion. Omar ponders about the meaning of life and concludes that the best doctrine is to "eat, drink, and be merry, for tomorrow we die."

The quatrains do not form an organic whole; instead ,almost every stanza repeats the melancholy burden of futility. But there is perhaps no other poem in world literature which expresses so epigrammatically and appealingly the pessimistic philosophy of *carpe diem.*

Nizami (*c.* 1141–1203). "The second great classical poet of Persia."[6] Nizami has become famous for his romances of love. His works are characterized by sweetness, pathos, elegance of diction, colorful imagery, psychological truth, and the frequent use of anecdotes. His five major works are grouped under the title *Khamsa* (*Quintet*) or *Panj Ganj* (*Five Treasures*).

THE TREASURE HOUSE OF SECRETS or *Makhzanu 'l Asrar.* The earliest of Nizami's five works. This is a collection of religious and ethical maxims, freely interspersed with anecdotes.

KHOSRU AND SHIRIN. An idyllic tale of the love of Prince Khosru for the Armenian Princess Shirin, who, however, loves Farhad, a master builder. The plot is resolved by the tragic death of Farhad.

LAYLA AND MEJNOUN. A sad story of two lovers whose

---

* The form of the *rubai* (rhyming *aaba*, with the third line a suspension of thought from the first two lines to the fourth) was originated by Abu Shuku of Balkh (fl. *c.* 950). The form was admirably followed by Fitzgerald in his version of Omar's *Rubaiyat.*

families, like the Montagues and the Capulets, are enemies; the two lovers persevere in their love but are joined only in death.

THE SEVEN EFFIGIES or *Haft Paykar*. A collection of seven tales, "each told to the king by one of his seven wives, somewhat after the style of the *Arabian Nights*."[7]

BOOK OF ALEXANDER or *Iskandar Namah*. An epic based on the life of Alexander the Great.

Sa'di (*c.* 1184–1291). Philosopher, poet. After a life of much traveling, Sa'di settled down in the south of Persia, where he was relatively undisturbed by the Mongols. His style is fresh, simple, epigrammatic, and tender. His main theme is practical expediency, which sometimes becomes ethically questionable. Although he is remembered chiefly for his *Gulistan* and *Bustan*, he was a prolific writer and turned out poems of many genres and verse forms, especially odes and jests (*mulaybat*).

THE BUSTAN or *The Fruit Garden*. Made up of ten sections of facile poetic essays on justice, contentment, humility, and other virtues, which are illustrated by innumerable anecdotes about warriors, kings, saints, and other famous people.

THE GULISTAN or *The Rose Garden*. Made up of prose as well as poetry. This work is similar to *The Fruit Garden*, but is lighter and more humorous; it contains a large number of stories drawn from history or from Sa'di's personal experience.

Hafiz (Mohammed Shamsu 'l Din Hafiz) (d. 1389). "The prince of Persian lyricists."[8] The genius of Hafiz lies not in the originality of his theme but in his exquisite treatment of age-old themes. Some of his poems are religious and reflective; he is better known, however, for his odes celebrating wine, love, and beauty, and hence he is known as "the Anacreon of the East."[9] In much of his poetry there is a distinct touch of Sufi mysticism, but this is usually combined with a sensuous and physical charm. "In depth of vision, felicity of language, and beauty of imagery he stands easily and incomparably first amongst the poets of Persia."[10] Some of his best known lyrics are "A Persian Song," Ode 11 ("I Have Borne the Anguish of Love"), Ode 12 ("I Said to Heaven That Glowed Above"), and Ode 13 ("Oft Have I Said, I Say It Once More").

Bibliography for Medieval Oriental Literature

General

Thompson, Stith, and John Gassner. *Our Heritage of World Literature*. New York: Dryden Press, 1942.

Chinese

Giles, Herbert A. *A History of Chinese Literature*. New York: D. Appleton and Co., 1928.

Waley, Arthur (trans. and ed.). *Translations from the Chinese*. New York: A. A. Knopf, 1945.

Arabian

Huart, Clement. *A History of Arabic Literature*. New York: D. Appleton and Co., 1903.

Nicholson, Reynold A. *A Literary History of the Arabs*. New York: Charles Scribner's Sons, 1907.

Persian

Browne, Edward G. *A Literary History of Persia*. New York: Charles Scribner's Sons, 1902.

Jackson, A. V. W. *Early Persian Poetry*. New York: Macmillan Co., 1920.

Levy, Reuben. *Persian Literature*. London: H. Milford and Oxford University Press, 1923.

Part Five
Medieval Western Literature

14
Germanic Literature

Historical Background. The Germanic peoples are a branch of the Indo-European family of nations — a family which, it is believed, had its origin at some unknown time either near the Vistula or in central Asia. Various groups of Indo-Europeans migrated to India, others to Asia Minor, and still others to Europe. Among those who went to Europe were the Germanic branch, who settled in the northern and north-central part of the continent. At least as early as the third century B.C. these tribes had established themselves in the region bounded by the Vistula River on the east, the Main on the south, the Weser on the west, and the North and Baltic seas on the north; later they extended their boundaries and made new settlements in all directions except east.

By the first century A.D. the Germanic peoples could be divided linguistically into three groups: (1) East Germanic, or Gothic; (2) West Germanic; and (3) North Germanic, or Scandinavian. East Germanic virtually became a dead language about the sixth century. West Germanic split into (1) High German, the dialect of central and southern Germany and the ancestor of Modern German, and (2) Low German, the dialect of north Germany and the ancestor of English, Frisian, and Dutch. The North Germanic group is made up of Norwegian, Danish, Swedish, and Icelandic.

The early Germans were a crude and warlike race, characterized by "grim humor, violent passions, and . . . brute courage."[1] Their primitive religion was a worship of gods more noteworthy for strength and bravery than for ethics and wisdom.* Many pagan rites, traditions, and superstitions were retained even after the coming of Christianity (*c.* 400).

After the fall of the Western Roman Empire, Theodoric and his Ostrogoths established a powerful but shortlived empire. The Vandals, the Visigoths, and the Franks all rose to political and military importance. But it was not till the reign of Charlemagne (768–

* See Appendix.

814) that a successful attempt was made to unite the intensely individualistic tribes into a nation. A period of relative anarchy and decentralization after the death of Charlemagne was followed by the era of the Saxon emperors (919–1024) — rulers who did a great deal toward making Germany aware of itself as a nation. During this period Germany was brought into close contact with Roman civilization. The Franconian emperors (1024–1125) were too busily occupied with struggles against both the Church and the nobles to contribute much toward the political and cultural development of the nation. The Hohenstaufens (1138–1254) probably did more than any previous dynasty toward the development of a national consciousness, and under these monarchs intellectual activity was quickened both by royal encouragement and by a renewed and increased intercourse with Italy. In Germany, as in some other European countries, the Crusades of the twelfth and thirteenth centuries helped to weld the knights together as a social class, to lay additional emphasis on religious devotion, and to introduce much foreign culture.

In Scandinavian lands, there was much less emphasis on strong monarchy and political progress than in the regions around the Rhine and the Weser. Norway and especially Iceland (colonized by a band of select Norwegians determined to escape the tyranny of King Harold Fairhair) preserved longer than any other sections the ancient Germanic ideas — "the love of an independent life, the ideal of the old-fashioned Northern gentleman, who was accustomed to consideration and respect from the freemen . . . and . . . who would not make himself the tenant, vassal, or steward of any king."[2]

*General View of the Literature.** Only one piece of East Germanic (Gothic) literature survives — a translation of the Bible, attributed to Wulfila.

West Germanic literature is much richer. Numerous heroic lays were written in Old High German (750–1100). Many of these were collected by Charlemagne, but were destroyed by his successors as being pagan and therefore unworthy of preservation; only a fragment of one lay (*The Lay of Hildebrand*) is extant. During the three hundred years following the death of Charlemagne (814) most Germanic literature was written in Latin. In Middle High German (1100–1500) there were epics, lyrics, sermons, tales, didactic

* For a discussion of Germanic, or Norse, mythology, see Appendix.

poetry, histories, biographies, and dramas.   This literarily prolific period may be divided into three parts: the beginnings (1100–1180), the classical period (1180–1250), and the decline (1250–1500).³

North Germanic (Norse, Scandinavian) is noted for its vigor, crudeness, and intensity.   It is in this language that the ancient Germanic mythology and culture were preserved in their most intact form.   There are three principal types of Norse literature: (1) the *Eddas* (written *c.* 900–1100), which are poems about myths, heroes, and love; (2) *skaldic*, or court, poetry (written *c.* 1100–1200), which tells about kings and their deeds; and (3) *sagas* (written 1100–1400), which are prose narratives made up of history and biography. Most of the sagas are either partially or entirely fictitious.

EAST GERMANIC (GOTHIC)

Wulfila (Ulfilas, Ulphilas) (*c.* 311–383).   The only extant manuscript of Gothic literature is a translation of the Bible, attributed to Wulfila, a Christian bishop and teacher who lived in the region directly north of the Danube estuary.   Wulfila is credited with inventing the Gothic alphabet — a combination of Greek, Roman, and Runic characters.   His version of the Bible is a skillful translation of the Greek original — "not a mere slavish rendering, but a work of intellect, the dialect of the woods asserting itself vigorously according to its genius — not straitened to conform to the idioms of more polished tongues."⁴   Only a few fragments of the Old Testament and a major portion of the New Testament have been preserved.

WEST GERMANIC (GERMAN)

Old High German*
(750–1100)

Only two surviving works of Old High German merit discussion. In addition, there are two charms, small fragments of two epics, and a few heroic songs, of which *The Lay of Ludwig* is most noteworthy; this lay tells of the victory of the West Franks over the Normans in 881.   Also several pieces of Latin prose and poetry were written during this period.⁵

---

* The only early work of any consequence in Low German was the *Heliand*, an anonymous poem, written *c.* 830 in Old Saxon.   It is about 6000 lines of alliterative verse telling the life of Christ.

THE LAY OF HILDEBRAND (*Hildebrandslied*) (first composed *c.* 600; extant version, *c.* 820). Only sixty-eight lines of this pagan heroic epic exist today. This fragment is made up of alliterative, four-stress lines, marked by Germanic parallelism — that is, repetition of an idea without repetition of words. The subject matter is part of the East Gothic saga cycle, and it tells part of the story of Hildebrand, a rugged old chieftain, who, after a thirty-year sojourn with the Huns, returns to fight against his native land. He meets his son Hadubrand, who refuses to believe that Hildebrand is his father and insists on fighting. The fragment ends as the duel begins, but the tragic implication is that Hildebrand kills Hadubrand.

THE BOOK OF THE GOSPELS (*Evangelienbuch*) (*c.* 868). By OTFRID (OTFRIED) OF WEISSENBURG. This is a 15,000-line Christian epic telling the life of Christ. It is said to be the first Germanic poem employing end-rhyme instead of alliteration. The preface is an interesting eulogy of the Franks. The style of the poem is scholarly and didactic.

Middle High German: The Beginnings
(1100–1180)

Clerical Translations from French and Latin. The most memorable are *The Lay of Alexander* (*Alexanderlied*) (*c.* 1130), by LAMPRECHT, concerning the exploits of Alexander the Great; *The Lay of Roland* (*Rolandslied*) (*c.* 1130), an adaptation by KONRAD OF RATISBON of the French *Song of Roland;* and *The Chronicle of the Emperors*, also by Konrad of Ratisbon, an ambitious poem (of about 18,000 lines) which attempts to tell the history of the universe.

Minstrel Epics. Secular poems in a popular style. Noteworthy are *King Rother* (*König Rother*) (*c.* 1140), which tells about the romantic abduction of the Princess of Constantinople by a Lombard king; *Duke Ernest* (*Herzog Ernst*) (*c.* 1180), a fragmentary poem recounting the rebellion of Ludolf of Bavaria against his father, Otto I; and *Reynard the Fox* (*Reinhart Fuchs*) (*c.* 1190), the first beast epic in German; it is attributed to HEINRICH DER GLEISNER.

Minnesong. Love poetry which was an outgrowth of old Austrian folksong and Provençal lyrics. The minnesongs were "simple terse poems . . . artless [in their] mixture of narrative and subjective emotion."[6] The two earliest minnesingers whose names are known are the Austrian nobleman KÜRENBERG and DIETMAR VON AIST.

Middle High German: The Classical Period
(1180–1250)

Most of the authors of the Classical Period of Middle High German were either knights or clergymen, although some writing was done by commoners and wandering minstrels. There were six main kinds of literature: epic, lyric, and didactic poetry, sermons, and legal and historical prose.

EPIC POETRY. The greatest achievement of medieval German literature is the epic poetry of the Classical era. This poetry is of two distinct kinds: court and popular.

The Court Epic. Since this genre was written for the noblemen, it frequently shows signs of the author's pandering to the courtly taste for foreign customs. Its language is polite, cultivated, and generally lacking in dialectal forms; many French words are used. The court epics are tales of chivalry and consequently abound in long and detailed descriptions of horses, armor, tournaments, and the like. Their themes, which are usually borrowed from foreign sources, are the three "Matters" of medieval romance: Matter of France, stories of Charlemagne and his court; Matter of Britain, stories about King Arthur, his Round Table, and the quest for the Holy Grail; and Matter of Rome, stories about Greek, Roman, and Oriental antiquity.

The four major authors of court epics were as follows:

HEINRICH VON VELDEKE (fl. *c.* 1170–1200). The first author of a German court epic. His *Eneit*, written in rhymed couplets, was a medievalized version of Virgil's *Aeneid*. It is full of descriptions of courtly love and chivalric combats. It makes an attempt at logical construction of plot and at portrayal of "psychologically true and intelligible"[7] characters.

HERMANN VON AUE (d. *c.* 1215). His *Erec* was based on a romance by Chrétien de Troyes, and it introduced the Matter of Britain into Germany; though somewhat tedious, the poem has a noble theme: the fidelity of woman. *Iwein* is also borrowed from Chrétien. Though more artistically written than *Erec*, this second poem is on a lower ethical plane. Its theme is Iwein's chivalrous love for his lady and the miseries she inflicts on him because an exploit has made him late for an appointment with her. *Poor Henry (Der Arme Heinrich)*, on a German theme, is perhaps Hermann's best poem. It recounts how a knight stricken with leprosy at first refuses, then accepts, and finally refuses again to allow himself to be cured at the expense of the willing sacrifice of a young girl.   His humility causes God to cure him, and he and the girl marry.

WOLFRAM VON ESCHENBACH (c. 1170–1220).   "The profoundest and most original of all the epic poets of knighthood and the manliest man of them all."[8]   His *Parzifal* (based on Chrétien's *Percival* and on a lost Provençal poem) is a long (25,000 lines), deep, philosophical treatment of a man's redemption through the recovery (after a period of skepticism) of his belief in God.   Because of ignorance of chivalrous customs Parzifal is unable to free Anfortas, King of the Holy Grail.   After five years of doubt and melancholy he regains his faith, sets Anfortas free, and receives the crown.   In the middle of the poem Wolfram inserts some worldly adventures of Sir Gawain as a contrast to Parzifal's spiritual quest.

In addition to Parzifal, Wolfram wrote *Titurel*, a love story about Schionatulander and Sigune, now extant only in fragments, and *Willehalm von Oranse*, an (unfinished) account of Willehalm's struggles against the Mohammedans at the end of the eighth century.

GOTTFRIED VON STRASSBURG (fl. c. 1210).   His (unfinished) *Tristram* (*Tristan*), based on a poem by Thomas of Brittany, tells of the adulterous love of Tristram and Iseult.   Gottfried excels in character analysis and in the portrayal of emotions, and he is skillful in versification.

The Popular Epic.   At the same time that the court epics were being written, popular epics were being composed — primarily by knights — in Austria and Styria.   Unlike the court epics, the popular epics were not dependent on foreign topics or models. Their sources were ancient folk ballads or lays, dealing with such historical characters as Ermanarich, the East Goth; Theodoric, the Amal; and Attila (Etzel), the Hun.   Both the style and the diction of the popular epics are simpler than those of the court epics. Besides *The Lay of the Nibelungs* and the *Gudrun* (discussed below), the most noteworthy popular epics were *Albhart's Death*, *Laurin*, *The Lay of Ecke*, and *The Rose Garden* — all revolving around the figure of Dietrich of Bern (Theodoric).

THE LAY OF THE NIBELUNGS (*Das Nibelungenlied*) (c. 1200). The greatest German literary production of the Middle Ages.   The poem consists of nearly 10,000 lines arranged in the so-called Nibelung stanza — four rhyming lines, each line divided by a caesura;

the first half of each line contains three stresses, and the second half three stresses, except in the last line, where there are four stresses in the last half.

The Lay of the Nibelungs is an ingenious though not altogether harmonious blending of fairy tale (*Märchen*), myth, and history. Legends that grew up around some of the historical kings of the Burgundians, the Goths, and the Huns were fused with an ancient folktale about a dragon-slayer — a tale which probably antedates the Christian era in Germany. Christian ideals and the conventions of medieval chivalry are superimposed upon a culture which is essentially pagan and crude. It is believed that the author (probably an Austrian knight) gathered and welded together his diverse materials in somewhat the same way that Homer is believed to have created the *Iliad*.

The main plot is one of revenge. Before the action of the poem begins, Siegfried, a prince of the Netherlands, has killed a dragon and captured the gold-hoard of the Nibelungs. At the opening of the *Lay* he twice aids King Gunther of Burgundy — once in battle and again in Gunther's successful wooing of Princess Brunhild of Iceland. Siegfried marries Kriemhild, Gunther's sister. Several years later Kriemhild and Brunhild quarrel over the relative ranks of their husbands. As revenge for the slight to his mistress, Hagen, loyal vassal of Gunther, treacherously slays Siegfried. After many years of grieving and of yearning to avenge her husband's murder, Kriemhild marries Etzel (Attila), King of the Huns. Thirteen years later, Kriemhild invites Gunther, Hagen, and their followers to visit Etzel's court. When they unwisely accept, Kriemhild provokes a quarrel between the Burgundians and the Huns, which results in great slaughter on both sides. The Huns finally win, Gunther is killed, and Kriemhild herself beheads Hagen. She, in turn, is slain by Hildebrand, vassal of Dietrich of Bern.

The *Lay* has many shortcomings. It is full of contradictions, incongruities, and inconsistencies. The author "only half succeeds in clothing semi-pagan ideas and episodes with the knightly Christian garb which he and other medieval poets like to use."[9] The poem is prolix and repetitious; it abounds in tedious and irrelevant descriptions of clothes, armor, festivals, and the like. The author is a poor metrical technician, and he indulges in the lavish use of stereotyped phrases and stock rhymes.

The merits of the poem, nevertheless, more than counterbalance its defects.   Herein better than anywhere else, perhaps, can we see the ancient Teutonic people — their superstition, passion, courage, tenacity, and fierce pride.   We are made to sympathize with their ideals of *Treue*, or loyalty, the moral theme of the poem.   But the greatest merit of the *Lay* is the bold delineation of the four main characters: Kriemhild, a Fury whose thirst for vengeance leads her to exult in the slaughter of her native race, including her own brothers; Siegfried, the innocent victim of a jealous woman's wrath; Rüdiger, a blameless knight torn between his obligations as a host and his duty as a vassal; and — greatest portrait of all — Hagen, a Satanic villain-hero, whom loyalty to his overlord and his mistress leads knowingly into murder and to his own death.

Evaluations of the *Lay of the Nibelungs* range from that of Frederick the Great, who thought the poem "not worth a charge of powder,"[10] to those of Kurz and Carlyle, who considered it "by far the most important work which the Middle Ages have given us" and "the finest monument of old German art."[11]   Ludwig Baur calls it "the Iliad of the Germans."[12]   Saner opinion would place it somewhere between such extremes; certainly it is a poem not only of great historical and ethnological significance, but also of deep human interest and of tremendous power.

It has been especially influential on Hebbel and Wagner.

GUDRUN (*c.* 1225).   An anonymous poem, probably written by an Austrian knight, whose sources were Frisian and Frankish sagas and ancient German myths, and whose model was the *Lay of the Nibelungs*.   The poem is divided into three parts, of which each is the account of the abduction of a beautiful maiden.   The first part tells how the child Hagen (apparently unrelated to the villain of the *Lay of the Nibelungs*) is carried off by a griffin, grows up in a strange land, escapes with the princess Hilde, marries her, and becomes king of Ireland.   The second part is the story of the daughter of Hagen and Hilde.   This daughter — also named Hilde — goes willingly with the vassals of King Hettel of Friesland to become the wife of that monarch; Hagen gives chase, but is defeated in battle.   The third — and most important — part of the poem tells the story of Gudrun, daughter of Hettel and the younger Hilde.   She is betrothed to Herwig, prince of Zeeland, but is abducted by Hartmut, prince of Normandy.   She is held captive in Normandy for thirteen years, where she is treated cruelly by Gerlint, the Norman queen.   At last she is rescued by Herwig and her brother; Gerlint is killed; Hartmut is forgiven; and Herwig and Gudrun are happily married.

Though not so great as the *Lay of the Nibelungs,* the *Gudrun* is valuable for its preservation of the character of the northwestern part of the continent — its wild coasts and its daring people. The portrait of Gudrun herself as a princess of great dignity, fortitude, patience, and loyalty is "one of the noblest and most real in poetry."[13]

LYRIC POETRY.

Minnesong. Although the word *Minnesong* literally means "love song," it is broadly used to designate Middle High German lyric poetry, and its themes are not only love but also external nature, religion, patriotism, gratitude, and many others. Its most frequent theme is, however, romantic love. Woman is treated with the profoundest veneration; she is to be worshiped, served, and praised in accordance with the conventions of medieval courtly love.

The Minnesingers were influenced by the poets of France. The lyric poets of Bavaria and Austria showed less foreign influence and based their poems on native popular songs.

Lyrics by about a hundred and sixty Minnesingers have been preserved.

WALTHER VON DER VOGELWEIDE (*c.* 1170–1230). By far the greatest of the Minnesingers, "the most intense and most versatile German lyricist before Goethe, the most national German poet of the Middle Ages."[14] Walther "of the bird preserve" was probably born in southern Tyrol and was probably a knight. After serving several noble patrons and wandering all over central Europe (1194–1213), he became an adherent of the new Hohenstaufen Emperor Frederick II, who later rewarded him with a small fief.

Walther's poetry is noted for its earnestness and sensitivity and for a rare combination of artistry and simplicity. In addition to love poetry and nature poetry, he wrote patriotic pieces, dance songs, epigrams, gnomic passages, and poems admonishing political and religious leaders. He was especially critical of papal abuses.

Some of his best known lyrics are "Love Is Two Hearts' Happiness," "Springtime and Woman," "May Song," "An Ungrateful Mistress," "Unequal Justice," "Winter," "Equality before God," "The Times Are Out-of-Joint," "Kingless Germany," and "Farewell to the World."[15]

NEIDHART VON REUENTHAL (d. *c.* 1245). A Bavarian knight especially remembered for his deliberate avoidance of the artificiality of court poems. His best known poems are based on folk songs and deal with village life. They are fresh and popular in tone.

ULRICH VON LICHTENSTEIN (d. *c.* 1260). Famous not only for the melody of his songs but also for his autobiography, *Service of a Lady* (*Frauendienst*), which gives a valuable picture of life and manners in the German court of the thirteenth century.

Middle High German: The Decline
(1250–1500)

In the middle of the thirteenth century, chivalry and the power of the court began to decline. Robber knights were left unmolested by the emperors and the nobility, who seemed interested chiefly in their own safety or personal aggrandizement. The growth of business and commerce gave rise to a new sort of culture in the towns, but the refinement of the old civilization was gone, and national consciousness dropped to a minimum.

The results for literature were unfortunate. Instead of a polished and uniform language, many dialects were employed; metrical systems were barbarized; epics deteriorated into allegories; and lyrics degenerated into Mastersong (see below).

There were still, however, some writings worthy of the name of literature. Fables, beast epics, mock epics, rhymed chronicles, folk songs, sermons, prose tales, and histories were produced. But the most significant forms during the era were didactic poems, Mastersongs, and drama.

Sebastian Brant (d. 1521). Poet, jurist. His *Ship of Fools* (*Das Narrenschiff*), written in 1494, attacks the evils and follies of the age. The "fools" are really sinners — atheists, adulterers, corrupt Churchmen, and the like. The book was the first German work to achieve fame abroad.

Mastersong. Pedantic town poets, almost entirely lacking in inspiration, attempted to imitate Minnesong. Their poems were generally religious, didactic, historical, or allegorical. The Master-singers set up schools, run in much the same fashion as trade guilds; a very strict code governed both the form and the content of lyrics. An aspirant became a "Master" only after originating a new "tone" or Mastersong — both words and music. The Mastersingers insisted on mechanical correctness but seldom showed any real genius. The earliest school was said to have been founded at

Mainz about 1290 by Heinrich von Meissen. The most famous Mastersinger was Hans Sachs (1494–1576) of Nuremberg.*

Drama. As in Greece, France, and England, the drama in Germany arose out of religious rites. Some dramatic bits incorporated in early pagan celebrations were wiped out by Church persecution; but they were replaced in the eleventh century by *Spiele* ("plays" or "mysteries"), or representations of episodes from the Bible. First given in the Church as part of the rites at Christmas, Easter, and other holy periods, eventually the plays were moved into the market place. Comic and secular elements were added from time to time, and the language was changed from Latin to German. Passion plays (giving the life of Christ) were most popular, and the presentation of some of them (notably the one at Oberammergau) has survived till the present day.

The secular drama began in the fifteenth century. Young Shrovetide celebrators would wander from house to house presenting comic scenes from everyday life. Some were witty, many merely vulgar. The town most famous for these Shrovetide plays was Nuremberg, where Hans Sachs (above) gave them real significance.

NORTH GERMANIC (NORSE, SCANDINAVIAN)

Between 900 and 1300 a great deal of superior literature was produced in Scandinavia. Most of it falls under the headings of Eddas, skaldic poetry, and sagas.

The Eddas.[16]

THE ELDER EDDA (*Poetic Edda, Saemund's Edda, Codex Regius* [*R*]). A collection of mythological poems, legends, didactic poems, and gnomic bits. It was composed between 800 and 1150; the oldest manuscript is of the thirteenth century. SAEMUND SIGFUSSON THE WISE of Odde (d. 1133) is reputed to be the collector. The principal contents of the collection are: (a) *The Vision of the Prophetess* (*The Sibyl's Prophecy, Völuspá*), a description of the origin and doom of the world; (b) two tragic poems concerning the adventures of Helgi, a great hero; (c) a group of six miscellaneous mythological poems: "The Wooing of Frey," "The Flyting of Thor and Woden," "Thor's Fishing for the Midgard Serpent," "The Railing of Loki," "The Lay of Thrym" (see Appendix), and "The Lay of Weland"; (d) two groups of miscellaneous proverbial and didactic pieces;

---

* Sachs and the Mastersingers are celebrated in Richard Wagner's famous opera *Die Meistersinger von Nürnberg*.

and (e) a cycle of twenty heroic lays telling (with gaps) the story of the Volsungs (see below, *The Völsunga Saga*).

All these poems are written in alliterative verse. Most of them are extremely rapid in movement, terse, direct, objective, and dignified.

THE YOUNGER EDDA[17] (*Prose Edda*, *Snorri's Edda*). A work in prose and poetry, attributed to SNORRI STURLUSON (d. 1241). Intended as a guide for poets, it has five main parts: (a) the "Gylfaginning," a summary of Norse mythology; (b) "The Sayings of Bragi," a treatise on poetic diction and technique; (c) the "Skaldskaparmal," a glossary of synonyms and poetic expressions; (d) the "Hattatal," a list of meters and verse forms, with examples; and (e) an appendix containing a history of poetry and poets and a brief treatise on grammar and rhetoric.

Skaldic Verse. The *skalds* were minstrels or court poets. They flourished from the eighth to the fourteenth century. Whereas the poems of the *Elder Edda* deal principally with myths and legends of gods and heroes, most of the skaldic poems are about ancient or contemporary kings and leaders. The diction of these poems is highly polished and full of kennings and farfetched metaphors; and the versification and alliteration are unusually elaborate and intricate. Skaldic verse is less significant than Eddic verse, but the former has preserved for posterity a great deal of historical matter.

Sagas. Between 1100 and 1500 great numbers of prose narratives, or *sagas*, were written in Norway and Iceland. Entirely or partially fictional, extremely national and insular in character, they tell much of the history of the Northland and relate the lives of many of the countries' real and fictional heroes. The sagas are concise, objective, and nearly always tragic. Many of them show careful workmanship and narrative technique.

THE VÖLSUNGA SAGA (*c.* 1170). A prose paraphrase of the story of the Volsungs as found in the *Elder Edda;* it is likely that floating traditions and some popular songs, now lost, were also used as sources. The saga tells the story of Sigurd the Volsung — an earlier version of the Siegfried legend told in the *Lay of the Nibelungs*. Sigurd (Siegfried of the *Lay*) is a grandson of Volsung, King of Hunland. After slaying Fafnir the dragon and taking a magic ring and a hoard of gold which Fafnir has been guarding, Sigurd rides through a wall of flame to awaken Brynhild (Brunhild), a Valkyrie. These two fall in love with each other, but Grimhild, wife of King Giuki of the Nibelungs, administers to Sigurd a magic potion, which causes him to forget Brynhild. He then marries Gudrun (= Kriemhild), Grimhild's daughter; and Brynhild marries Gunnar (= Gunther), the brother of Gudrun. In jealous wrath Brynhild persuades Guttorm, another of Gudrun's brothers, to murder Sigurd in his sleep; as the fatal blow is struck, Sigurd hurls Gram, his sword, and cuts Guttorm in half. Brynhild wounds herself and dies on Sigurd's funeral pyre. Gudrun marries Atli (= Etzel) the Budlung, who, in order to obtain the gold-hoard of Sigurd, treacherously slays Gudrun's brothers; but the gold has been concealed in the Rhine. Gudrun kills Atli, burns his hall, and escapes to the land of King Jonakr, whom she marries.

The Völsunga Saga was the chief source of Wagner's *Ring* operas and of William Morris' *Sigurd the Volsung*.

THE CONFEDERATES (*The Bandamanna Saga*). The only intentionally comic saga, a piece of political satire. This tale is "an heroic work inspired with comic irony. . . . The main plot of the story is the reconciliation of a respectable son and the prodigal father."[18] The young man Odd leaves home because he and his father, Ufeig, are incompatible. After many years of prosperity, Odd is involved in a lawsuit and is about to lose his case because eight men, the "Confederates," resent his wealth and power. When the case is about to be decided against Odd, Ufeig, not recognized by his son, enters the debate and argues so cleverly that Uspak, the enemy of Odd, is outlawed. The Confederates plot to bring about Odd's downfall, but again Ufeig comes to the rescue and succeeds in causing the conspirators to betray each other. Father and son are reconciled, and Uspak meets an early death.

The Confederates is a superior saga, neat in details and organic in structure. Perhaps its chief virtue is its series of portraits: of the admirable but prosaic Odd; of the selfish and malicious Confederates; and — most delightful of all — of Ufeig, "the servant and deputy of the Comic Muse, . . . the ironical critic and censor of the heroic age."[19]

15

Celtic Literature*

Historical Background. Perhaps as early as the seventh century B.C. the branch of Indo-Europeans now known as Celts had settled western Europe, including France and possibly Spain.[1] The Galli, or Celts of Gaul, were absorbed by the Romans and the Germans. The Goidels, or Gaels, at one time apparently occupied a large portion of what is now England; about 400 B.C. they were probably driven west and north by a new wave of Celts, the Brythons, or Britons. The Goidels then settled principally in Ireland and western Scotland, and the Brythons took over the southern half of the larger island. When the Angles, Saxons, and Jutes invaded Britain in the middle of the fifth century A.D., some of the Brythons retreated to Wales and Cornwall, and others migrated to Brittany on the Continent.

The Gaels in Ireland were left relatively undisturbed from the beginning of the Christian era till the eighth century. Then for nearly three hundred years they were harassed first by the Norsemen and later by the Danes till 1014, when the Irish under King Brian Boru defeated the Scandinavians at Clontarf. Thereafter the former invaders were absorbed by the Celtic people. Subsequently Ireland was invaded and conquered by Henry II of England (1172).

The culture of the pre-Christian Celts — especially of the Irish — was decidedly barbaric. They killed male war-captives, made slaves of the females, and took great delight in displaying the severed heads of slain enemies. They even went so far as to make ball-shaped trophies out of the brains of their foes!

The chief occupations of the early Celts were cattle-raising, farming, and fighting.

Their pagan religion was a mixture of magic, superstition, and a worship of many local deities symbolizing the primitive forces of nature. The Celts believed in the transmigration of souls and in

* The term *Celtic* is here used to denote "Irish and Welsh"; the word is properly applied only to linguistics. See Kenneth Jackson, *Studies in Early Celtic Nature Poetry* (Cambridge, England: Cambridge University Press, 1935), p. vii, n.

human sacrifice. Their religious activities were directed and presided over by druids, highhanded priests who not only exercised religious power but also played an important role in political, military, and domestic affairs; the druids were, in addition, soothsayers and magicians. Christianity began to creep into the region in the third and fourth centuries, and St. Patrick succeeded in establishing it as the principal religion in the middle of the fifth century. Ireland soon afterwards became the center of Christian learning and culture, whence missionaries went out to England and France.

No summary of Celtic history can be complete without a few words concerning the essential nature of the Celts themselves. Despite their early barbarity, they were far less grim, somber, and melancholy than the medieval Germanic tribes. The Celts were romantic people — proud, passionate, volatile, imaginative, fanciful, superstitious, sensitive, and impractical. Like the Germanic peoples, they loved justice and bravery, but they also loved fun and love and mystery and the delicate beauties of nature.

It is not surprising that the Celts never achieved great political power in Europe; their accomplishments were in other realms. They contributed charm, humor, and playfulness to the culture of medieval Europe — contributions more lasting and ultimately more important, perhaps, than the founding of an empire.

General View of the Literature. Although some traditions hold that Irish poetry was written as early as the first century A.D., it was not till the time of St. Patrick (*c.* 432) "that Ireland may be said to have become, properly speaking, a literary country."² The Gaels remained literarily active till 1172, when Henry II's conquest put an end to "any true Celtic literature and art in Ireland."³ The Brythons in Wales apparently began their literature later and stopped later than did their Irish kinsmen. Neither the date of oral composition nor the date of original writing of any of the works may be determined exactly; it is almost certain, however, that many of them existed in either oral or written form for many years — perhaps centuries — before reaching the state in which they have been preserved. Hundreds of medieval Celtic manuscripts have been saved — most of them from the period 1100–1400. The most important Gaelic ones are: (1) *The Book of the Dun Cow* (*c.* 1100), (2) *The Book of Leinster* (*c.* 1150), and (3) *The Yellow Book of Lecan* (*c.* 1391) — all devoted chiefly to romances and all repetitious of each other. The principal Brythonic manuscripts are: (1) *The Black Book of Carmarthen* (twelfth century), a book of poetry; (2) *The Book of Aneurin* (thirteenth century), also poetry; (3) *The Book of Taliesin* (fourteenth century), poetry; and (4) *The Red Book of Hergest* (fourteenth century), prose and poetry.

Both the Irish and the Welsh produced great quantities of prose and poetry — hymns, love lyrics, nature lyrics, histories, laws, ballads, heroic lais, romances, and others. Although all of these are of historical interest, the lais and romances are the types holding the greatest appeal for students of comparative literature and for the average reader.

As in Greece and the Germanic lands, the romances and heroic lais were probably transmitted orally for many decades. The transmitters and composers were bards — poets who in authority and social importance were second only to the kings. In order to attain the rank of ordinary bard, an aspirant had to study for seven years; and to reach the highest rank — that of *ollamh* (*ollave*), he had to labor twelve years and memorize three hundred and fifty tales and many other short poems. Unfortunately, no great genius came along to consolidate these tales into great epics like the *Iliad* and the *Lay of the Nibelungs*. Although a number of the tales are related, they are preserved in many different manuscripts of various dates and various places; the task of creating a continuous and consistent narrative remained for modern editors to accomplish.

Despite the amorphous state of the lais and romances, there are many characteristics, merits, and defects which one finds common to nearly all of them. Most of them are lacking in courtliness and sophistication; instead, they are crude and unpolished, sometimes even brutal. The tales are almost completely pagan; Christian elements are usually incongruous late interpolations. Other characteristics are dramatic force, a robust sense of humor, pathos, tenderness, and brilliance of description. The tales are marred by exaggeration and by repetitiousness of epithets and descriptive details. Some of the poetic narratives employ rhyme.

GAELIC TALES

There are three main cycles of Gaelic (or Irish) tales plus many lesser cycles and independent narratives.

The Mythological Cycle. Narratives of the Mythological Cycle attempt to trace the history of Ireland from its earliest settlement down through the successful invasion by the Milesians (possibly the Celts of history). These accounts tell of the coming of Ceasair and later of Partholon — both descendants of Noah; of the advent of the Nemedians; of the battle of the Nemedians against the Fomorians; of the two battles of Moytura between the Tuatha De Danaan and the Fir Bolg — both races descended from the Nemedians; and finally of the conquest of the Tuatha De Danaan by the Milesians from Spain. The most popular individual tales are the accounts of the two battles of Moytura, "The Wooing of Etain," "The Fate of the Children of Tuirenn," and "The Fate of the Children of Lir." (The last two tales plus "The Exile of the Children of Usnach" [of the Red Branch Cycle] form the famous "Three Sorrows of Story Telling.")

The Red Branch Cycle. The tales of the Red Branch (or Cuchulain) Cycle revolve around King Conchubar of Ulster and his warriors, who, according to tradition, lived in the first century A.D. Most of the tales are about the birth, the mighty deeds, and the death of Cuchulain, the greatest hero of Irish legends.[4] A large percentage of this cycle is devoted to a series of events known as "The Cattle Raid of Cooley." The best known tale from the Red Branch Cycle is "The Exile of the Children of Usnach."

"THE CATTLE RAID OF COOLEY" ("Tain Bo Cuailnge"). "The great epic of ancient Ireland."[5] Queen Medb (Maeve) of Connacht requests from Dare of Ulster the loan of his bull. When he overhears an insult by one of Medb's men, Dare haughtily refuses the loan, whereupon Medb decides to take the animal by force. Her large army is opposed by that of Conchubar, and Cuchulain slays countless numbers of her men. The most ferocious battle is that between Cuchulain and Ferdiad; the latter is finally slain by means of the *gae bulga*, a barbed torpedo, which Cuchulain launches with his foot. Eventually the Ulstermen kill or put to flight all the army from Connacht. In the meantime, however, Medb has captured Dare's bull. When she brings him to her home, he kills her husband's bull, returns to his native Cooley in Ulster, and then bellows so loud that his heart bursts and he dies.

"THE EXILE OF THE CHILDREN OF USNACH." This is the touching story of Deirdre, the Helen of Irish legend. At Deirdre's birth, Cathbad the druid prophesies that she will bring woe to Ulster. Nevertheless, when she grows up, she is so beautiful that King Conchubar himself decides to marry her. She agrees to the marriage, but when she beholds Naisi (Naoise), she falls in love with him and persuades him to flee with her. Along with Naisi's two brothers, Ainle and Ardan, the two lovers find refuge in Scotland. Deceived by promises of amnesty, the four eventually return to Ulster, much against the better judgment of Deirdre. There the three men are treacherously attacked and killed, and Deirdre commits suicide. Cathbad and many of the warriors desert Conchubar and prophesy that misfortune will come to him because of his treachery.

The imaginative description of the heroine; the account of her childlike passion for Naisi; and the characterization of the three sons of Usnach as ingenuous, trusting, and courageous men — all these merits make the tale a superior one.

The Fenian (Ossianic) Cycle. Many Irish tales are concerned with Finn, the leader of a band of *fiana*, professional soldiers who attached themselves to various minor kings, protected the country from invasions, collected taxes, and partially supported themselves by hunting and fishing. According to the tales, Finn performed many miraculous feats as a boy, fought in many battles, had various domestic troubles, and finally was killed in the battle of Gabhra in A.D. 283. His son Ossian (Oisin) was at first renowned as both a warrior and a bard, but later tradition remembers him chiefly as a poet. He is reputed to have lived in Ireland till the days of St. Patrick. Another legend tells that he was carried away by Niamh, a fairy, to the Land of Youth, where he lived three hundred years. And some of the stories say that Finn himself is not dead at all — that he still lives with his *fiana* in the hills of Ireland and will come again, when he is needed, to help fight his country's enemies.

BRYTHONIC TALES

The Brythonic (Welsh) tales are neither so numerous nor so artistic as the Irish stories. They are historically significant, however, not only because they are records of ancient Brythonic customs and attitudes, but also because they contain the earliest references to Arthur, who, according to tradition, was the last King of the Brythons before the coming of the Anglo-Saxon invaders. There is no distinct "cycle" in Welsh literature as there is in Irish, but there are about nine references to King Arthur in medieval Welsh.[6]

"THE TALE OF PWYLL."[7] By assuming the shape of the

King of Hades (Pen Annwyn), Prince Pwyll of Dyved succeeds in marrying Rhiannon, despite her betrothal to Gwawl. Pwyll tricks Gwawl into a bag and refuses to release him till he relinquishes all claim to Rhiannon. Pryderi, the son of Pwyll and Rhiannon, disappears soon after his birth, and his mother is accused of having eaten him. Pryderi reappears several years later.

"KILHWCH AND OLWEN." At King Arthur's order, Kay, Bedivere, and Gawain aid Kilhwch in his attempt to secure as a wife Olwen, daughter of Hawthorn, chief of giants. The knights succeed in acquiring thirteen treasures as a "brideprice" for Hawthorn; each treasure involves a very difficult quest.

The story is memorable for its picture of Arthur — not as a king of the age of chivalry, but as a fairy king. His followers are superhuman warriors, and Arthur's magic powers aid them in their mighty exploits.

This work appears to have influenced Geoffrey of Monmouth and Chrétien de Troyes.

16

French Literature

Historical Background.   The earliest known inhabitants of the country now known as France were the Galli, a branch of the Celtic race, who had been in western Europe perhaps since the seventh century B.C.   Nothing is known about the Galli before the Roman conquest, which began in 154 B.C. and which was completed in 50 B.C. The Celtic people and their civilization were almost completely absorbed by the Romans.

The invasions by the Barbarians (Germanic tribes) had two important effects on France.   First, those Barbarians — despite their inferior culture and their willingness to adopt Latin culture — eventually became the rulers of France.   And second, the invasions of England by the Anglo-Saxons drove many Brythonic Celts into the northwestern peninsula of France, now known as Brittany.

The history of France from the sixth century to the eleventh is mostly a tale of battles for supremacy among the different bands of Germanic invaders.   A few dates, events, and eras are worthy of note.   In 507 Clovis became King of the Franks and established Christianity as the religion of his country.   In 732 at the battle of Tours, Charles Martel defeated the Moors, who had conquered Spain and invaded France.   By 800 Charlemagne had succeeded in consolidating a large portion of France and Germany and in having himself crowned emperor.   During the tenth century bands of Norsemen took over northeast France (whence the name Normandy) and in 1066 conquered England.

The eleventh century is especially memorable for the rise of feudalism and chivalry.   The nobility became more refined, and woman's role in society became more exalted.   It was not till the twelfth century, however, that feudalism and chivalry reached their peaks and began to decline.   By causing the death of many nobles and impoverishing many others, the Crusades helped to increase the power both of the monarchy and of the bourgeoisie.   The marriage of Eleanor of Aquitaine to Henry II of England in 1152 brought France and England closer together culturally as well as politically. Toward the end of the century the cathedral school at Paris developed into a university, and the city soon became the cultural center of Europe, to which scholars flocked from all over the Continent.

The thirteenth century saw a further decrease in the power of the nobles and a concomitant increase in the power of the king and the common people; the flourishing of industry and commerce added to the strength and importance of the towns. The rise of the scientific spirit led to a questioning of some of the doctrines of the Church; there was increasing opposition to the Church's dominance of moral and intellectual matters.

The Hundred Years' War (1338–1453) between France and England reversed for a while the trends of the preceding hundred and fifty years: cultural progress and commercial activity came almost to a standstill, and some of the importance of the aristocratic and military classes was restored. At the end of the war, however, trade and industry were resumed, medieval feudalism expired, and the bourgeoisie regained all it had lost except political power. The monarchy was strengthened immeasurably, and the victories of Joan of Arc brought France a national unity and a patriotism she had never had before. Thus the Middle Ages came to an end in France.

General View of the Literature. The French language is a direct outgrowth of Latin, which had been established by the Romans as the official language of the government, of the schools, and — later — of the Church; this language was classical Latin, as written by Cicero and Caesar. Among the soldiers and less educated classes there developed what is known as Low Latin or Vulgar Latin, a "more clipped, more careless, less grammatically correct"[1] language. By the fifth century Low Latin had undergone some changes and was called Gallo-Latin. The destruction of the schools and governmental system by the Barbarians helped establish this more popular speech as the national tongue; eventually the Church, which had clung to classical Latin, was forced to capitulate so that its priests and bishops could communicate more readily with the people.

In 842 Charles the Bald and Louis the German took the famous *Oaths of Strassburg* against their brother Lothair. Louis took his oath in French; this oath is considered the "birth certificate of the French language."[2]   There were two main tongues spoken from the tenth to the fourteenth centuries: the "langue d'oc" south of the Loire River and the "langue d'oïl" north of the Loire (*oc* and *oïl* were the two ways of pronouncing the French word for "yes"). After the fourteenth century the northern dialect prevailed and became the ancestor of modern French.

Four short works,* chiefly of linguistic interest, were written in the tenth century.   "It is however with the eleventh century that the history of French literature properly so-called begins."[3]   The literary works produced before 1480 fall into three principal categories: literature of the Church and cloister, literature of the castle and court, and literature of the towns.[4]

In the eleventh century the importance of the Church and of feudalism are indicated by the three types of literary productions: saints' lives, neo-Latin religious works, and *chansons de geste* (poems concerning the mighty deeds of heroes; see below).

Both the large number and the excellence of *chansons de geste*, poetic romances, and lyrics written during the twelfth century have led critics to call this era "the Golden Age of medieval French literature."[5]   This poetry shows an increase in polish, in sophistication, and in social consciousness over that of preceding centuries.

The thirteenth century is noteworthy for its prose romances, its drama, its satire, its lyrics, and its allegory.   Much of the literature of this century reflects the rise of the bourgeoisie.   It shows an increasing tendency toward rationalism, realism, and cynicism.

The literature of the fourteenth and fifteenth centuries shows the disastrous effects of the Hundred Years' War.   There was little opportunity or inspiration for imaginative works.   A few narrative poems, a few prose chronicles, and a few lyrics were written; but as a whole the centuries were for the most part literarily sterile.

"LITERATURE OF THE CHURCH AND CLOISTER"

As "the strongest unifying and civilizing force in the Middle Ages,"[6] the Church naturally exerted a tremendous influence on early French literature.   For several centuries all French philosophical and theological writing was in neo-Latin, inasmuch as only the Churchmen, as a rule, were interested in such writing, and

---

* A song of St. Eulalie (possibly of the late ninth century), a poem on Christ's Passion, a life of St. Leger, and a poem about Boëthius.

furthermore, the French language was for a long time inadequate for abstract thought. Saints' lives and poems about the miracles of the Virgin Mary were written in both neo-Latin and the vernacular. The Church employed satires and allegories (especially tales of beasts and stones) for purposes of instruction in ethics. Finally, the liturgical drama was begun in the Church, but soon moved outdoors and became a secular production.

"LITERATURE OF THE CASTLE AND COURT"

The works produced by and for the noblesse may be subdivided into the literature of feudalism (principally of the eleventh and the twelfth centuries) and the literature of chivalry (written chiefly between 1150 and 1300).

The Literature of Feudalism

THE CHANSONS DE GESTE. The customs, ideals, and psychology of the early days of French feudalism have been preserved in the ninety-five epic poems known as *chansons de geste* (literally, "exploit songs"). These are narratives concerning the adventures of heroes who lived during the eighth and ninth centuries, but the poems breathe the atmosphere of the days of feudalism and the Crusades. The *chansons* are only semihistorical, and often the deeds of two or more real personages are attributed to one hero. Great emphasis is laid on physical strength, bravery, fortitude, and loyalty to suzerain and to God.

The origins of the *chansons de geste* are uncertain. Perhaps some poet or scribe combined a number of cantilènes, or ballad-epics, which had been handed down orally for two or three hundred years. Or perhaps a medieval Churchman, eager to attract travelers to a certain shrine, would search written records and listen to jongleurs (wandering professional entertainers) in order to gather material about some hero whose exploits were in some way related to the shrine; then the Churchman would compose a *chanson* about the hero.

Most of the *chansons* were written in lines of ten syllables; some were composed in Alexandrines, lines of twelve syllables. In .the earlier *chansons* the lines were linked by assonance of the last syllable; later, rhyme succeeded assonance. The lines were grouped in *laisses*, strophes of varying numbers of lines; all the lines in each *laisse* employed the same assonance (or rhyme).

All of the *chansons de geste* deal with the "Matter of France" — stories about Charlemagne, his descendants, and other French noblemen. There are three main cycles: the Cycle of Charlemagne, the Cycle of Guillaume d'Orange, and the Cycle of Doon de Mayence.

The Cycle of Charlemagne (*Geste du Roi*). In this group are all the epics in which Charlemagne plays even a minor role.

THE SONG OF ROLAND (*La Chanson de Roland*) (*c.* 1100). The earliest and best French epic; in 4002 ten-syllable, assonating lines. The author is unknown; perhaps he is one TUROLDUS, whose name occurs at the end of the Oxford manuscript; but it is more likely that Turoldus was only the scribe who copied the manuscript. The historical basis of the poem is slight: a chronicle by the monk Einhard tells that in 778 the rearguard of Charlemagne's army was ambushed in the Pyrenees by a band of Basques and that the prefect Hruodlandus was slain. From this tiny seed sprang what is often considered the national epic of "sweet France." A minor expedition against the Basques is transformed into a holy war against the Saracens in Spain, and the obscure Hruodlandus becomes Roland, the beloved nephew of Charlemagne and the ideal of French knighthood.

The story of *The Song of Roland* is as follows: After seven years of war against the Saracens in Spain, Charlemagne has conquered every city but Saragossa, held by Marsile, the Moorish king. When Marsile sues for peace, Charlemagne sends Ganelon, the stepfather of Roland, to arrange the terms. Turning traitor because he is jealous of Roland, Ganelon conspires with Marsile to prepare at Roncevaux an ambush for Charlemagne's rearguard, which will be under the command of Roland. The trick works, and the rearguard is annihilated, but not before Roland and his men have slain 20,000 of the Saracens. Just before he dies, Roland blows his horn to recall Charlemagne, who then returns and wipes out the remaining Saracens. Another Moorish army has to be defeated before the French king takes Saragossa. Returning to Aix-la-Chapelle, Charlemagne punishes Ganelon by having him torn apart by horses. Roland's fiancée, Aude, falls dead from grief upon hearing of the death of her betrothed.

The epic is marred by exaggeration, dull cataloguing, and repeti-

tion.   Character portrayal is crude: each person is either almost
entirely good or entirely bad.   But the poem is an eloquent expression of French patriotism and "the spirit of militant Christendom."[7]

THE PILGRIMAGE OF CHARLEMAGNE TO JERUSALEM
(*Le Pèlerinage de Charlemagne*) (*c.* 1115).   In twelve-syllable lines,
possibly composed to account for and glorify the relics of St. Denis.
When Charlemagne's queen hints that Hugh, the Emperor of
Constantinople, is taller and handsomer than her husband, Charlemagne journeys to Jerusalem, acquires some sacred relics, and then
goes to Constantinople.   There, after some magic feats have been
performed by virtue of the relics, Charlemagne compares himself
with Hugh and discovers that he himself is a foot taller than Hugh;
thereupon he returns to France, forgives the queen, and presents
the relics to the Abbey of St. Denis.   The poem has many humorous
passages; it is amusing rather than inspirational.

HUON OF BORDEAUX (*c.* 1200).   Influenced by the romances
of adventure (see below).   In self-defense Huon, the son of the
Duke of Bordeaux, kills Charlot, the son of Charlemagne.   Sen-
tenced to perform some apparently impossible tasks, he is aided by
the dwarf Auberon (Shakespeare's Oberon).

The Cycle of Guillaume d'Orange.   This cycle is made up of
tales about Guillaume d'Orange, who is the protector of the weak
and cowardly Louis, son of Charlemagne.   Guillaume is also a
mighty champion of Christianity against the Saracens.   The finest
chansons in this cycle are *The Song of Guillaume* (*c.* 1120), *Aliscans*
(1150), *The Coronation of Louis* (1150), and *Aymeri de Narbonne*
(1150).   This cycle is more unified than the Cycle of Charlemagne.

The Cycle of Doon de Mayence.   This group is concerned with
unruly vassals who rebel against their overlords and especially
against Charlemagne.   The best single poems of the group are
Ogier the Dane and *Renaud de Montauban* (both *c.* 1175–1225).   Most
of the poems in the cycle are full of violence, cruelty, and savagery.

The Literature of Chivalry

ROMANCES.   Like the *chansons de geste*, the early French
romances are poetic narratives.   There are, however, some important differences between the two types: (1) the romances have no
historical basis such as the *chansons* have; (2) the romances are, in
general, more artistic and more refined; (3) the romances are far

more concerned with love; and (4) the romances deal more with the marvelous, the magical, and the fantastic than with mere feats of strength and courage.

There are three principal cycles of this genre: romances of antiquity, whose subject matter is virtually synonymous with the "Matter of Rome"; Breton romances, whose subject matter is virtually synonymous with the "Matter of Britain"; and romances of adventure.

Romances of Antiquity.

THE ROMANCE OF ALEXANDER (*Roman d'Alexandre*). Perhaps begun about 1147 by LAMBERT LE TORT and finished about 1176 by ALEXANDRE DE BERNAY.* This poem, written in twelve-syllable lines (hence the English term *alexandrine*), gives a fantastic biography of Alexander the Great.

THE ROMANCE OF THEBES (*Roman de Thèbes*) (*c.* 1150). Anonymous; tells the legend of ancient Thebes.

THE ROMANCE OF AENEAS (*Roman d'Enéas*) (*c.* 1155). Anonymous; retells much of the story of Virgil's *Aeneid*.

THE ROMANCE OF TROY (*Roman de Troyes*) (*c.* 1165). By BENOÎT DE SAINTE-MAURE. It is a poem of about 30,000 lines in octosyllabic rhyming couplets. Among Benoît's sources were Dares Phrygius, Guido della Colonna, Dictys Cretensis, and some epitome of Homer. Though repetitious and windy, this poem is of great importance because it began the Troilus and Cressida story, which Boccaccio, Chaucer, Shakespeare, Dryden, Morley, and many others have retold.

Breton Romances.

The Norman interest in Celtic legend combined with Provençal interest in courtly love and chivalry to inspire the romantic tales about King Arthur and his knights, about Tristram and Iseult, and about the Holy Grail; these three elements (at first unrelated) eventually were brought together as parts of one cycle. Geoffrey of Monmouth's Latin *History of the Kings of Britain* (1147) and Wace's *Brut* (1155) were the two most important written sources of French Arthurian romances.

It is impossible to do more here than merely to hint at the enormous influence and vogue of the "Matter of Britain." Eschenbach, Chaucer, Malory, Spenser, Dryden, Tennyson, Swinburne, Wagner, Bédier, J. R. Lowell, and E. A. Robinson are only a few of those

---

* Scholarly arguments concerning the dates and authorship are still in progress.

who have found inspiration in the legends about Tristram and the other knights of Arthur.

TRISTRAM AND ISEULT. Both BÉROUL (*c.* 1150) and THOMAS OF BRITTANY (*c.* 1170), Anglo-Norman poets, wrote poems telling the love story of Tristram and Iseult; of these poems only fragments have survived. This legend was extraordinarily popular and soon was retold all over Europe. There were many variants. One version[8] is as follows: Tristram is sent by his uncle, King Mark of Cornwall, to Ireland to bring back Iseult, who is to marry King Mark. On the trip back to Cornwall, Iseult and Tristram by mistake drink a magic philter and fall in love with each other. Mark discovers their affair and at first banishes them, but later forgives Iseult. Tristram goes to Armorica in Brittany, where he marries another Iseult. When he is seriously wounded, Tristram sends a messenger for Iseult of Cornwall and tells him to hoist white sails on his return if his mission is successful. Iseult of Cornwall renounces everything to come to Tristram, but Iseult of Brittany tells her husband that the ship has black sails. Tristram dies of a broken heart, and Iseult of Cornwall, too, dies of grief when she learns of her lover's death.

THE HOLY GRAIL. Another legend which had great vogue and which became attached to the Arthurian cycle was the story of the Holy Grail (the vessel in which Joseph of Arimathea caught the blood of Christ, or the vessel used for wine at the Last Supper). The Grail took on mystical significance, and the quest for it became — for the legendary knights — a sort of crusade. In the earlier accounts Percival was the hero of the quest; in later legends he was superseded by Galahad.

MARIE DE FRANCE (fl. *c.* 1147–1189). Norman poetess and fabulist, who lived for many years in England at the court of Henry II. Marie is most famous for her *lais*, short narrative poems "which are to the romances what the short story is to the novel of to-day."[9] About fifteen of her lais are extant; these are characterized by simplicity, directness, passion, sentimentality, and an excellent understanding of human love. Her most famous lais are (a) *Lanval*, the story of a knight who loses his beautiful fairy-lover because he cannot keep his promise of secrecy; (b) *Le Lai du Fresne*, a story about a patient woman; (c) *The Two Lovers*, a sentimental tale about a young man who dies in an attempt to win a princess by carrying the princess up a hill; (d) *Bisclavret*, a story about a werewolf; and (e) *The Honeysuckle,* an episode in the love affair of Tristram and Iseult — Tristram sends a code-message on a hazel twig to his beloved. She also wrote a hundred and three fables, collected under the title *Ysopet.*

CHRÉTIEN DE TROYES (*c.* 1130–1180). The greatest of the French romancers and the first to organize the Arthurian tales into a cycle. He was also the first to introduce into written literature Lancelot and his love for Queen Guinevere. Chrétien served for many years at the court of Marie de Champagne. Learned and resourceful, he was an excellent psychologist and narrator, and his style is facile and charming. His *Erec* is the story of a patient and long-suffering wife — the story which Tennyson retells in *Geraint and Enid. Lancelot, the Cavalier of the Cart,* tells of the amour of Lancelot and Guinevere. Other surviving works by Chrétien are *Cligès; Yvain, the Cavalier of the Lion; Percival the Gallois (Conte dou Graal);* and (doubtful) *William of England.*

ROBERT DE BORON (or Borron) (*c.* 1170–1212). Principal successor to Chrétien. He wrote an Arthurian trilogy (*c.* 1210) composed of: *Joseph of Arimathea,* or *The Great Holy Grail,* which tells the early history of the Grail; *Merlin,* in which the magician is the central character; and *Perceval,* which tells about the winning of the Grail and about the "end of the Arthurian world of legend."[10]

Romances of Adventure. Here are grouped poems of Eastern origin and short tales (hardly *romances* in the strict meaning of the term) dealing with western European subjects. These *romans d'aventure,* written chiefly from the twelfth to the fifteenth century, are romantic descendants of the old *chansons de geste.* They are full of highly improbable incidents, passionate love, and gallantry.

FLORE AND BLANCHEFLEUR (12th century). This poem tells how Flore rescues Blanchefleur, a Christian maiden, from captivity in Babylon; the lovers return to Spain, which becomes Christian for sake of Blanchefleur.

AUCASSIN AND NICOLETE (12th century). Unique in its combination of poetry and prose. The story is fantastic and poorly organized; one event often follows another with no attempt at transition being made. But as an account of romantic love, *Aucassin and Nicolete* has rarely been surpassed.* The hero renounces every-

---

* Many contemporary scholars now consider it a burlesque of the old romances. As evidence they point to the unusually ludicrous events and the extravagant exaggeration.

thing for sake of his amour; and Nicolete, in accordance with the conventions of courtly love, gives herself joyously to her lover. The story is as follows: Count Garin de Biaucaire refuses to allow his son Aucassin to marry Nicolete because she is believed to be a commoner. The lovers escape and wander through many incredible adventures. At length Count Garin dies, Nicolete is discovered to be a princess after all, and she and Aucassin marry and live happily ever after.

CHRONICLES. Till the latter part of the twelfth century, there was no genuine French history in the vernacular. For the learned, the Churchmen had written Latin accounts of local and national affairs, but the average Frenchman had depended on what little history was contained in the *chansons de geste*. From 1150 onwards, however, chronicles in both prose and verse appeared in great numbers.

In Verse.

WACE. The most famous chronicler in verse was the Anglo-Norman Wace (*c.* 1119–1175). His *Romance of Brutus* (*Roman de Brut*), or *Exploits of the Britons* (*Geste des Bretons*) (*c.* 1170), in octosyllabic couplets, attempts to trace the origin and history of the Britons from Felix Brutus, a descendant of Aeneas; the work is little more than a paraphrase of Geoffrey of Monmouth's Latin *History*. Wace's other work, *The Romance of Rou* (*Le Roman de Rou*), or *Exploits of the Normans* (*Geste des Normands*) (left incomplete, finished by Benoît de Sainte-Maure), gives the early history of the Normans and Anglo-Normans.

In Prose.

GEOFFROI DE VILLEHARDOUIN (*c.* 1150–1218). The first important French prose historian. His *Conquest of Constantinople* (*c.* 1205) recounts how the Fourth Crusade abandoned its aim of recapturing the Holy Sepulchre and became instead an expedition against Constantinople. The chronicle is notable for its clear, sparse, logical, and eloquent prose style, which (according to Gaston Paris) led the way to modern French prose. Villehardouin is trustworthy in dates and chronology, but he is too diplomatic to be a good interpreter of motives.

JEAN DE JOINVILLE (*c.* 1224–1317). The seneschal of Louis IX. In 1304 Joinville wrote *The Life of St. Louis* (*La Vie de Saint Louis*), a formless, gossipy narrative which is important for its pictures of thirteenth-century life in France. The work gives, incidentally, a delightful character sketch of its author, who is often shown in contrast with the good king.

JEAN FROISSART (1333–*c.* 1410). The greatest French chronicler of the Middle Ages. About 1405 Froissart wrote a work in four volumes entitled *Chronicles of France, England, Scotland, Spain, Brittany, Gascony, Flanders, and Other Places*. The purpose of the chronicles was ostensibly to narrate the feats of arms of France and England during the last three quarters of the fourteenth century; actually, the work gives the history of western Europe from 1325 to 1400. Froissart is often inaccurate and partial. His attitude is aristocratic; he despises the common people and glorifies court life and its pomp. He revels in descriptions of tournaments, battles, pageants, armor-clad knights, and beautiful ladies. His chronicles have been called "the swan-song of chivalry."[11]

Though best known for his chronicles, Froissart wrote also many ballades, *virelais*, and rondeaus.

PHILIPPE DE COMMINES (1447–1511). "The first modern historian."[12] Commines is a critical thinker with a real philosophy of history; he delves into motives, causes, and results. He is far less personal than Froissart and Joinville. His *Memoirs* (*c.* 1500) "are a general history"[13] — a history of France from 1464 to 1483 and from 1494 to 1495 (the intervening years are not covered).

LYRIC POETRY.

Early Northern Lyrics. In the sixth century a sermon was preached protesting against the wickedness of northern French lyrics — either on the ground of the frivolity which they indicated or on the ground of their pagan origin. At any rate, in northern France during the sixth century and later there were lyrics, often probably accompanied by dancing. Most of these have been lost; a few, however, have been preserved. The oldest date from the early part of the twelfth century. There are the four following types: (1) Work Songs (*chansons de toile, chansons d'histoire*), semi-narrative poems sung by women while they engaged in spinning or weaving; (2) Songs of the Unhappily Married (*chansons de mal-mariée*), complaints of a young wife about her husband; (3) Pastorals (*pastourelles*), songs in which a shepherdess either accepts or spurns a knight; and (4) Crusade Songs (*chansons de croisade*), lyrics occasioned by the Crusades — perhaps the knight is urged to fight for Christ; perhaps the knight who is about to depart for the Holy Land expresses sadness in departing from his beloved; or perhaps the maiden pours out her grief or her anxiety for the departing Crusader.

Troubadours and Trouvères (11th–13th century). The southern (Provençal) region of France was more deeply influenced by Roman and Saracen culture than the northern section was. Feudal society, therefore, was more highly refined in the south, and chivalry found early expression in lyrical poetry. Noblemen either became *troubadours* themselves or patronized troubadours — lyrical poets whose main theme was courtly love (*amour courtois*).* The names of more than four hundred troubadours who lived between 1090 and 1292 are known. Among the most famous are GUILLAUME DE POITIERS, JAUFRE RUDEL, BERNARD DE VENTADOUR, GUIRAUT DE BORNEIL, and BERTRAN DE BORN.

The unifying effect of the Crusades and the marriage of Eleanor of Aquitaine to Louis VII (1137) helped to spread Provençal culture to northern France. There the *trouvères*, or professional minstrels, adopted the themes and techniques of the troubadours. In the hands of the trouvères the code of courtly love became even more rigid, and their poetry was, on the whole, less natural and less spontaneous than that of their southern prototypes. The most famous trouvères were CHRÉTIEN DE TROYES; BLONDEL DE NESLE (who, according to the legend, freed Richard the Lion-hearted from prison): GUI, CHATELAIN DE COUCY; and THIBAULT DE CHAMPAGNE.

Later Lyricists (14th and 15th centuries). Many of the French lyrics in the latter part of the Middle Ages were as artificial as they formerly had been, and the poetic forms employed were often more intricate and complicated, especially the rondeaus, the *chants royals*, and the ballades.

---

* The conventions of courtly love are too numerous and too complicated to be discussed fully here. Briefly, the system reflects an illicit relationship between lover and lady (usually a lady married to somebody else). "Love is a cult, a religion, and the lady an idol, a goddess, sometimes almost an abstraction" (Kathleen T. Butler. *A History of French Literature* [New York: E. P. Dutton and Co., 1923], I, 50). And sometimes love is almost a disease, of which the lover can be cured only by the complete surrender of his beloved. In order to prove himself worthy of such surrender, the lover must submit to every whim of the lady and often must perform whatever feats of strength or bravery she assigns him. According to the code the greatest sins in the sight of the god of love are faithlessness and violation of secrecy; a lady's giving herself to a proven lover is considered not a vice but a virtue. This artificial code was to a large extent the result of the medieval practice of arranging marriages for political, social, or financial expediency rather than for mutual affection of the principals.

GUILLAUME DE MACHAUT (*c.* 1305–1377). Machaut was famous more for his technique than for his emotion or his subject matter. He took especial pride in the intricacy of his ballades and lais. His "Speech of the Amorous Fountain" ("Dit de la Fontaine Amoureuse") influenced Chaucer's *Book of the Duchess.*

EUSTACHE DESCHAMPS (*c.* 1340–1407). Composed more than 80,000 lines of verse. In addition to love lyrics, he wrote many satirical and historical pieces. Most of his poems are ballades, rondeaus, and other short types. He, like Machaut, influenced Chaucer.

CHRISTINE DE PISAN (*c.* 1363–1431). A widowed noblewoman with three children, Christine decided to earn her living by writing. Her *Book of Three Virtues* attacked the antifeminist attitude of Jean de Meun's part of the *Romance of the Rose.* She also wrote many graceful and sincere ballades expressive of her own personal emotions.

ALAIN CHARTIER (*c.* 1385–1433). "The father of French eloquence,"[14] Chartier wrote a large number of courtly and allegorical poems. He was familiar with the classical Latin poets and helped to make them popular in France. He was also intensely patriotic and wrote many poems urging France to reform itself internally and to drive the English back across the Channel.

CHARLES D'ORLÉANS (1391–1465). Father of Louis XII. He entertained himself during twenty-five years of captivity in England by writing *The Book of the Prison*, a volume of rondeaus and ballades. Though artificial and almost entirely void of either thought or emotion, these lyrics are so technically perfect that their "very artificiality seem[s] natural."[15]

"LITERATURE OF THE TOWNS"

With the decline of feudalism and the increase in commerce and industry, the towns became wealthy and powerful; and the bourgeoisie (Third Estate, *tiers état*) began to feel its own importance and to make itself felt culturally and intellectually. By the middle of the thirteenth century there was a considerable body of bourgeois literature. Lacking from this literature were the heroism and the romanticism of the courtly writings. Instead, it was permeated by the *esprit gaulois* — an attitude of mocking and satirical, yet jovial criticism; it was often realistic and rationalistic. People, institutions, and ideas that had formerly been idealized and venerated were now held up to ridicule or scathingly attacked; woman, the Church, and chivalry were favorite objects of criticism.

The principal types of bourgeois literature were satire, drama, and allegorical, didactic, and lyrical poetry.

Satire

Rutebeuf (*c.* 1230–1285). Jongleur, gambler, "perhaps the most vigorous poet of his time,"[16] "the greatest [French] writer of the thirteenth century."[17] Little is known of his life except that he lived in poverty; he was probably born in Burgundy or in Paris. His works fall into three clearly defined divisions.

PERSONAL AND COMIC POEMS. In this group we find poems complaining of his personal lot (e.g., "Rutebeuf's Poverty"), in which there is some satire. Others are more sarcastic, especially those attacking hypocrisy and some of the religious orders (e.g., "Song of the Orders"). In all of the first group "there are many lively strokes of satire, and not a little of the reckless gaiety, chequered here and there with deeper feeling. . . ."[18] Some poems in this group may be considered fabliaux (see below).

OCCASIONAL POEMS. These are somewhat more elevated than the poems of the first group. Some are defenses or elegies of distinguished persons (e.g., "The Speech and Complaint of Master Guillaume de Saint Amour"); others are satirical commentaries on current events (e.g., "Speech of the University of Paris").

DEVOTIONAL POEMS. In this group one finds saints' lives (e.g., "Life of St. Mary of Egypt"), personal confessions (e.g., "The Death of Rutebeuf"), various poems to the Virgin, and the miracle play *Théophile*.

Fabliaux. It is in the fabliau that the *esprit gaulois* is most readily recognizable. A fabliau is a tale in verse (usually octosyllabic couplets), "for the most part comic, of a real or possible event occurring in the ordinary conditions of human life."[19] The fabliaux banteringly ridicule every section of society — especially women, nobles, and the clergy. Many of the tales are indecent and even bawdy, and they abound in trickery and practical jokes.

There are about two hundred extant French fabliaux, varying in length from thirty to several hundred lines; nearly all are anonymous or are attributed to authors of whom nothing is known but the name. Their period of composition was from about 1150 to about 1340. Opinions of the merit of the fabliaux vary widely.

Professor Wright thinks them worthless except for the one merit of
"realistic observation."[20]   Other critics have considered them
delightfully humorous pictures of the manners and customs of the
people of the twelfth and thirteenth centuries.   Whatever their
intrinsic merit, they have been profoundly influential on Boccaccio,
Chaucer, Molière, La Fontaine, and many other writers.

"THE PEASANT DOCTOR" ("Le Vilain Mire").   Source of
Molière's *Doctor in Spite of Himself* (*Le Médecin malgré lui*).   In order
to repay her husband for many beatings he has given her, a peasant
woman tells two royal messengers that her husband is a famous
physician.   Brought to the court to remove a fishbone from the
throat of the prince, the peasant makes such funny faces that the
prince laughs the bone out.   Then when the peasant is beset by
multitudes who wish treatment, he tells them that the only way
he can cure them is to burn the greatest sufferer among them.   All
thereupon declare themselves well.

"THE PARTRIDGES" ("Les Perdrix").   A greedy woman
eats some partridges which her husband had destined for himself.
She calms his wrath by one of the "endless stratagems which these
tales delight in assigning to womankind."[21]

Beast Fables and Satires.   During the Middle Ages there were
numerous fables because they were convenient vehicles for moral
instruction.   The fables of Phaedrus, Avianus, and Aesop were
widely popular.   In France there were written many beast tales
derived from folklore and Aesop.   Some were employed for
satirical rather than strictly didactic purposes.

THE BOOK OF REYNARD (*Le Roman de Renart*).   By far the
most popular of all medieval beast epics.   This work is more than a
fable: it is a group of four cycles, consisting of twenty-five poems
("branches") written at different times by different authors.   The
oldest "branches" (*c.* 1174) were written chiefly to amuse; as additional "branches" were added from time to time, more and more
satire and allegory crept in, so that by the time the last of the
"branches" were written, the beasts were only thinly veiled representations either of types (e.g., friars) or of specific individuals.
The earliest cycle (*The Old Reynard, L'Ancien Renart*) tells about
various beasts — Reynard the Fox, Noble the Lion, Chanticleer
the Cock, and so on.   These are entirely normal animals — types,
yet at the same time individuals — except that they are endowed
with speech and reason.   The second cycle (*The Coronation of*

Reynard, Le Coronement Renart, c. 1260) is a satire against the Franciscans and the Dominicans; this cycle is of little merit. The third cycle (*The New Reynard, Renart le Nouvel,* written in 1288 by Jacquemart Giélée) is better than the second but not quite so fresh as the first. The animals virtually become medieval knights: they dress in armor, ride horses, fight with weapons, and so on. The cycle is marred also by too much allegory. The fourth cycle (*The Counterfeit Reynard, Renart le Contrefait, c.* 1335) is an enormous collection (one manuscript is 32,000 lines). It is openly satirical and allegorical, and it contains a vast amount of moralizing. Included in some of the manuscripts are many amusing fabliaux and romances, and in some versions there are pointed allusions to the grievances of the common people.

FAUVEL (*c.* 1310–1314). By the Norman GERVAIS DE BUS, *Fauvel* is an allegorical poem in two parts which owes a great deal to *The New Reynard.* Fauvel is a horse, whose name is made up of the initial letters of the words *flatterie, avarice, vilenie, vanité, envie,* and *lâcheté* (cowardice): the horse symbolizes all evil and especially falseness. In the first part of the poem many people — kings, nobles, clergymen, even the Pope — try to gain his favor ("curry Fauvel," whence our expression "curry favor"). In the second part of the poem Fauvel is rejected as a suitor by Fortune; then he marries Vainglory, and their offspring soon infest the world. The poem ends with a prophecy of the end of Fauvel and all his evil.

Allegorical and Didactic Poetry

The people of the Middle Ages were inordinately fond of allegory. There were, in addition to the beast fables, many poems in which abstract ideas were symbolized by people or things, usually with a view toward teaching some moral lesson. The Church smiled on such literature and even went so far as to condone pagan mythology by interpreting it as an allegorical representation of Biblical tradition. In the early fourteenth century Ovid's *Metamorphoses* were translated and commented upon in the popular *Book of the Fables of Ovid the Great* (*Le Roman des Fables d'Ovide le Grand*). Even more popular, however, was *The Romance of the Rose.*

THE ROMANCE OF THE ROSE (*Le Roman de la Rose*). This was one of the most influential works of the Middle Ages: Chaucer borrowed from it and translated part of it into Middle English.

It is in two parts, each by a different author: these parts are very different in spirit and style.

Part I (4058 lines) was composed *c.* 1230 by GUILLAUME DE LORRIS near Orleans.   It is a highly romantic, symbolical tale of a knight's courtship of a beautiful maiden (represented by the Rose).   The Rose dwells in the Garden of Love and is shut in by a wall from the annoyances and dangers of the outside world — for example, Old Age, Envy, Poverty, Hatred, and the like.   A knight enters the garden, is shot with one of Cupid's golden arrows, falls in love with the Rose, and attempts to reach her.   He is aided by Welcome (*Bel-Accueil*), but is hindered by Danger, Shame, Fear, Anger, and Slander (*Malebouche*).   He succeeds in kissing the Rose, but Slander sees him and awakens Jealousy, who imprisons Welcome and builds a wall around the Rose, leaving the lover outside to lament his fate.

At this point in the story de Lorris died.   If he had lived, the ending would almost certainly have included the knight's freeing of Welcome and subsequent success in his affair with the Rose.

Part II (about 18,000 lines) was written *c.* 1277 by JEAN DE MEUN, or MEUNG.   This part is an unwieldy and formless attack on all that Guillaume de Lorris had held sacred.   Whereas Guillaume, on the one hand, was a "courtly idealist,"[22] who worshipped at the shrine of Woman and Love, who glorified chivalry, who revered the Church and the clergy, and who admired and respected the nobility — Jean de Meun, on the other hand, was a "cynical realist,"[23] who treated woman, chivalry, the Church, the clergy, and the nobility with mordant sarcasm.   He turned the cold light of reason onto all these and searched out their fallacies.   Woman he found to be foolish and fickle; the Church was too ascetic; and the nobility and the monarchy were motivated entirely by selfishness.

The second part of *The Romance of the Rose* is filled with de Meun's erudition — long excursions into philosophy, mythology, and medieval science.   Almost incidentally, it seems, he tells of the lover's struggles and the final plucking of the Rose.   Though literarily inferior to de Lorris' composition, de Meun's sequel is perhaps more interesting and is certainly more informed by the inquisitive, satirical, rationalistic spirit of the rising bourgeoisie.

Drama

Serious Drama.

LITURGICAL.   As in Greece, Germany, and England, the serious drama in France was an outgrowth of religious rites.   Since

Church services were held in Latin, the spectacular element was very important. The reading of the Gospels was rendered in dialogue, interrupted by hymns. Gradually more and more spoken bits were added with accompanying gestures. Eventually at Christmas and Easter the whole stories of the Advent and the Resurrection were enacted by the priests on the altar steps; the language was still Latin. This was real drama — liturgical drama — and it was probably presented as early as the tenth century.

Somewhat later as the plays became longer and the settings more elaborate, the presentation was moved into the churchyard and then into such unconsecrated places as innyards. Secular bits were added, and actors other than priests played various roles. Finally, perhaps late in the eleventh century, the plays were given in French.

The Play of Adam (*c.* 1215) is the oldest extant French drama. It is an example of the transition from the liturgical play to the next stage of development — the *mystery* play. *The Play of Adam* is in Anglo-Norman French, but its stage directions are in Latin. It tells the stories of the fall of Adam and Eve and of Cain's slaying of Abel. It ends with a prophecy of the coming of Christ.

THE MYSTERY PLAY. This type of drama may be defined as a representation of some historical or Biblical event; most of the mystery plays are on religious subjects, but a few are on secular ones. About sixty mysteries have survived, most of them from the fifteenth century; nearly all the earlier ones have been lost. Those on religious subjects may be grouped into three cycles: (1) Cycle of the Old Testament, which begins with the Garden of Eden and goes down to the reign of Augustus Caesar; (2) Cycle of the New Testament, which begins with the birth of Christ and continues through the activities of the apostles after Christ's death; and (3) Cycle of the Saints, of which each play deals with the life and death of some saint. Many of the mysteries were almost interminable, requiring several days for a performance. Furthermore, they were rather chaotic; comic and profane elements were admixed almost at will by the dramatists. There was rarely any observance of the unities. The stage settings and costumes were elaborate.

Originally the mysteries were put on by volunteer actors. Later special guilds were formed. Sometimes hundreds of actors — once five hundred — took part in one play. In 1402 Charles VI granted permission to the Confrères de la Passion to perform mysteries.

Performance of this genre came to an end in 1548, when mysteries were banned for having degenerated into indecency.

The most famous single mysteries were: (1) *The Passion* (*c.* 1450), by ARNOUL GRÉBAN, which gave the whole life of Christ in 34,574 lines; (2) *The Acts of the Apostles* (*c.* 1450), by ARNOUL and SIMON GRÉBAN; (3) *The Siege of Orléans* (1439), a secular play about Joan of Arc; and (4) *The History of the Destruction of Troy* (1452), by JACQUES MILLET.

THE MIRACLE PLAY.   Nearly every miracle play portrays the intervention of some saint — most often the Virgin Mary — in human affairs.   Though a somewhat later development, the miracles flourished concurrently with the mysteries; the extant manuscripts of the miracles, however, antedate those of the other genre.   Most of the miracles are melodramatic, and often the dénouement is affected by the sudden appearance of Mary "*dea ex machina.*"[24]   The "human and realistic interest is much stronger than the religious intention."[25]   Unlike the mysteries, the miracles were generally presented by a cast of only five or six players.

The oldest extant miracle is Jean Bodel's *Play of St. Nicholas* (*c.* 1250).   Another interesting one is Rutebeuf's *Miracle of Théophile* (*c.* 1260), perhaps the earliest story in which a human being makes a pact with the devil.   The largest collection of miracles is the group of forty-one plays[26] known as *The Miracles of Our Lady*, preserved in a fourteenth-century manuscript.   *The History of Griselda* (1393), a secular miracle, is the earliest known serious secular play in the French language; it is a dramatization of the well-known Patient Griselda story.

THE MORALITY PLAY.   A morality play is a dramatization of the conflict between good and evil which takes place in the human soul.   This type of drama reflects the medieval fondness for allegory: all the characters in the morality are mere personifications of abstractions.   The morality was a distinct step forward in the development of French drama, inasmuch as the representation of a conflict introduced a real plot and suspense.

The morality flourished chiefly in the late fifteenth and early sixteenth centuries.

Some of the most famous French moralities are: (1) *The Well-Informed* (*Le Bien-Avisé*), in which the hero succeeds in the world and proceeds to heaven by virtue of Reason, Faith, Contrition, Confession, and Penitence; (2) *The Poorly Informed* (*Le Mal-Avisé*), in which the hero is a failure and proceeds to hell; and (3) *The Children of the Present* (*Les Enfants de Maintenant*), in which two children tread the primrose path till one dies on the scaffold of Perdition; the other repents, embraces Discipline, and is saved.

Comic Drama.

ORIGIN.   The origin of French comedy is obscure.   Apparently the jongleurs carried about in their repertoires — along with *chansons de geste*, romances, and fabliaux — dramatic bits of three types, known as "disputes" (*débats*), "speeches" (*dits*), and "happy sermons" (*sermons joyeux*).   A *débat* is a dialogue in which the speakers defend the merits of two persons or things which are opposed to each other; for example, there are *The Dispute between Winter and Summer* and *The Dispute between Water and Wine*.   The *dit* is a dramatic monologue, the most famous being *The Speech of the Franc-Archer of Bagnolet*, in which a *miles gloriosus* boasts of his bravery till he thinks he sees a knight; then he cowers till he discovers that the "knight" is only a scarecrow, whereupon his courage and boastfulness return. A *sermon joyeux* is a parody of a part of a church service.

ADAM DE LA HALLE (fl. *c*. 1260).   The first writer of French comedy whose name is known.   He wrote two comedies: *The Play of the Bower* (*Le Jeu de la Feuillée*) and *Robin and Marion*.   The former is made up of three loosely connected scenes.   In the first scene the hero Adam decides to desert his wife and go to school; there is much satire directed at Adam's father and wife and at the bourgeoisie of Arras.   In the second scene two fairies present gifts to Adam, but a third fairy, who has been slighted, condemns him to remain with his wife.   The third scene shows how a monk is swindled of his valuable relics.   *Robin and Marion* is little more than a dramatized *pastourelle*.   The plot is slight, but the play abounds in rustic songs, dances, and games.   It is a forerunner of the *opéra comique*.

FIFTEENTH–CENTURY COMEDY.   By the fifteenth century two distinct types of French comedy had been established: the *sotie* and the *farce*.   The *sotie*, at first a burlesque in which inferior Churchmen satirized their superiors, was later a satirical piece "attacking the King, the government, the nobility, or the Church."[27] The most famous example is *The Play of the Prince of Fools* (1512), which attacks Pope Julius II and the Church.   The *farce* is comparable to the interlude in English literature.   This genre is a short, dramatized fabliau, originally intended as a comic skit in the mystery plays.   It is characterized by coarse, boisterous humor.

About a hundred and fifty farces have been preserved. The genre is the only type of French drama not swept away by the Renaissance. Two of the most entertaining farces are: (1) *The Wash-tub* (*Le Cuvier*), in which a henpecked husband turns the tables on his wife; and (2) *Lawyer Pathelin* (*L'Avocat Pathelin*), in which a shrewd lawyer teaches his client a way to avoid paying debts and the client uses the trick to avoid paying the lawyer his fee.

Lyrical Poetry

François Villon (1431–c.1480). "The greatest French poet of the middle ages."[28] Born François de Montcorbier (or des Loges or Corbueil or Corbier), he assumed the surname of his foster father, Guillaume Villon. François received a Master's degree at the University of Paris (1452) and seemed destined to be a clergyman; but he became associated with a band of vagabonds and thieves and got himself "in prisons oft." Three times he was in serious trouble: once for murder (1455), once for theft (1462), and once for brawling (1462). His last sentence was commuted to banishment. Nothing is known of his life after 1463.

Villon's poetic output was small. His two longest works are *The Little Testament* (*Le Petit Testament*) (c. 1456) and *The Great Testament* (*Le Grand Testament*) (1461), in which he bequeathes many imaginary objects and qualities to his friends and enemies — who range from dignitaries to ruffians. Inserted within the *Testaments* are many short lyrics, chiefly ballades and rondeaus. Two famous lyrics are the "Ballad of Lost Ladies" ("Ballade des Dames du Temps Jadis") and "Ballad of the Hanged" ("Ballade des Pendus").

Villon is justly praised for the depth and sincerity of his emotions and for the vigor and precision of his style. He combines "deep feeling [with] a lively sense of humor."[29] He can weep over the transiency of beautiful things and yet jest grimly about his approaching execution. He has an infinite zest for all physical pleasures — wine, food, warm shelter in winter, beautiful women. Nature for him is nearly always harsh or cruel, and he has great pity for poor, suffering rascals. Yet he never whines with self-pity, nor does he blame his own miseries on Fate; he confesses his guilt and prays only for God's mercy and forgiveness.

Villon's preoccupation with death, combined with his gusto for life, makes him a suitable figure to serve as a transition from the Middle Ages to the Renaissance in France.

Spanish Literature

Historical Background. At some unknown time several hundred years before Christ, the peninsula now made up of Spain and Portugal was populated by the Iberians (of unknown origin) and the Berbers from North Africa. The Celts invaded the peninsula in the fifth century B.C., and there followed a fusion of the races. The Iberic peoples (ancestors of the Basques) remained concentrated in the eastern portion and the Celts in the west — what is now Portugal and Galicia. Even before the Celtic invasion, the Phoenicians, the Greeks, and the Carthaginians had made some settlements along the coast; and Carthage was the dominant power on the peninsula. In 206 B.C. the Romans destroyed Carthage and proceeded to occupy and latinize Spain. Roman power remained unbroken till A.D. 409, when Spain was overrun by the barbarian Suevi, Alani, and Vandals. The Visigoths followed five years later; they adopted Roman civilization to a large extent, but effected some changes in law and social customs.

In 711 the Moslem invasion began, and by 758, when the caliphate of Cordova was established, the Moors had conquered all the peninsula except the northwest mountainous portion, which was, no doubt, considered both difficult to conquer and relatively worthless. The Spanish Christians did not abandon their country to the Moslems; instead, the two races lived side by side for centuries, and the Spaniards absorbed much of the superior culture of their conquerors. The Moors imparted to the Spaniards a great deal of knowledge in the fields of medicine, mathematics, and engineering. Moslem literary influence was slight.

The reconquest of Spain began in 1085, when Toledo was taken back from the Moors. Cordova and Seville were recaptured in 1236 and 1248 respectively. Almost nationwide unity was achieved in 1469, when Ferdinand of Aragón married Isabella of Castile. Granada, the last Mohammedan stronghold, fell in 1492.

The characteristics of the Spanish people — determined to a

large extent by the geography of the land and the history of the nation — which have most influenced Spanish literature are stoicism, dignity, individualism, democracy, and humor.

General View of the Literature.   In 206 B.C. Latin became the official language of Spain; nearly all traces of Celtic were soon obliterated. As in France, the populace spoke Vulgar Latin, which at some indeterminate date and after many gradual changes had taken place, became the national language.   The conquests by the Barbarians and the Moors had little permanent effect on the Spanish tongue.

Spanish literature "dates roughly from the twelfth century."[1] From about 1140 till the beginning of the Renaissance in Spain (*c.* 1469), a considerable amount of both prose and poetry was written; little, however, was literature of the first rank.   A large percentage was either an imitation or a translation of French works. There were tales of various sorts (especially apologues, *exempla*, and adaptations of French romances), law, satire, allegory, and religious and didactic poetry.   Drama developed from the Church ritual in much the same way as in France, but Spanish miracles and mysteries never attained either the originality or the excellence of the French ones.   The most significant literature of medieval Spain was in the realms of the epic, the chronicle, the lyric, and the ballad.

THE EPIC

There is much disagreement as to whether the Spanish epic is of French or of Germanic origin.[2]   However the case may be, both French and German influences are strong.   Some of the *cantares*, or folk-epics, may have been composed orally in the tenth century; the oldest extant version, however, is dated about 1140.   The *cantares* are rougher and less artistic than the French *chansons de geste*, and the line-length in the Spanish epics is highly irregular. Six principal cycles of *cantares* were developed around such historical or legendary Spanish heroes as Rodrigo the Goth, Barnardo del Carpio, and Rodrigo Díaz (the Cid).   Only fragments of three epics have been preserved: *The Song of My Cid* (*c.* 1140), *Roncesvalles* (extant manuscript, *c.* 1310), and *The Rhymed Chronicle* (*c.* 1410). Many *cantares* have been paraphrased ("prosified") in *The General Chronicle* (see below).

THE SONG OF MY CID (*El Cantar de Mío Cid, Poema del Cid*). Probably written about 1140 by a Castilian.   This poem, greatly influenced by the *Song of Roland*, is the only Spanish epic which has survived almost in its entirety. There are 3735 lines; the first few lines — probably about fifty — are lost. The poem concerns the latter part of the life of the historical figure Rodrigo (or Ruy) Díaz de Bivar (*c.* 1040–1099), who served Sancho II of Castile and Alfonso VI of Leon. The story (as told in the epic) is as follows: King Alfonso falsely accuses Rodrigo the Cid (from the Arabian *sidi*, meaning "lord" or "leader") of withholding tribute money; the king decrees exile. Sorrowfully Rodrigo obeys the decree, withdraws to the mountains, and gathers about himself many faithful followers, with whose help he wages war against the Moors. After every victory he sends presents to Alfonso in hope that the king will revoke the decree of exile. After Rodrigo has captured Valencia and become virtually an independent monarch himself, Alfonso relents and welcomes back his loyal vassal. At Alfonso's insistence, the Cid reluctantly agrees to marry his daughters to the Infantes de Carrión, who, after the marriage, turn out to be cowards and wifebeaters. When the Cid demands their punishment, they are tried by judicial combat and ignominiously defeated. Rodrigo's daughters then marry the princes of Navarra and Arragon.

Since *The Song of My Cid* was written only forty years after the death of its hero, it is "the most realistic of epics."[3] It is unusually accurate historically; no magic appears, and there are few Christian miracles; exaggeration is almost entirely lacking. The tone is dignified and austere. There is no element of romantic love. The poem is especially valuable as a reflection of Castilian laws, customs, and modes of life in the eleventh century.

The epic has been influential on de Castro, Corneille, Herder, and Southey.

THE CHRONICLE

From the fifth century on, many religious establishments kept chronicles in Latin. Most of these, however, were sketchy and dull. RODRIGO JIMÉNEZ DE RADA (1170–1247) and LUCAS DE TUY (d. 1249) made attempts to trace chronologically national and world events, and they succeeded in writing real history; but these men, too, wrote in Latin. The first vernacular chronicle of importance was written by Alfonso the Wise.

Alfonso the Wise (1226–1284). King of Castile, scholar, poet, historian. Inspired by the examples of Rodrigo and Lucas, Alfonso wrote (or compiled) in Castilian a *General Chronicle* — "by far the most important work of history anywhere undertaken during the Middle Ages."[4] The *Chronicle* begins with the Flood and then relates the entire history of Spain from the days of the Greek and Carthaginian settlements down through the reign of Ferdinand III (1252). It is entirely untrustworthy as history, inasmuch as its author made little effort to distinguish between fact and fable; but it is unfailingly interesting. As far as literature is concerned, its most valuable portion is a large number of prose paraphrases of the old epics, which it accepts as genuine historical accounts.

THE LYRIC

Almost no primitive Spanish lyrics have survived. There is reason, however, to believe that large numbers were written during the Middle Ages. There were watchmen's songs, Christmas songs, love songs, and *serranillas* (songs in which a mountain maid accepts or rejects a lover; cf. the French *pastourelle*). The influence of the Provençal troubadours was strong during the twelfth and thirteenth centuries, especially in Cataluña and Galicia.

Juan Ruiz (fl. *c.* 1283–1351). Archpriest of Hita, the first Spanish humorist, perhaps the greatest medieval Spanish lyricist. It is difficult, however, to classify Juan Ruiz. His fame rests on only one work, *The Book of Good Love* (by which he means the book of the love for God and goodness); but this work contains bawdy tales, a prayer, hymns, *exempla*, *serranillas*, love songs, and apologues. Ruiz's ostensible purpose is to point out morals by showing the contrast between love for righteousness and sensual love; but it is clear that his main interest is the latter. The principal charms of the book are its revelation of the author's personality and its wealth of intimate details about fourteenth-century life.

THE BALLAD[5]

The form of medieval Spanish literature which is probably most widely read today is the *ballad*, which here denotes a short epico-lyric poem. Some scholars think that many of the ballads were early and were the raw material out of which the *cantares de gesta* were made; others believe that most of the ballads were late and were mere remnants or débris of the epics. The matter is still in dispute.[6] At any rate, it is likely that many of these short narrative poems were orally preserved for a long time — perhaps for hundreds of years. Most of the traditional ballads were probably written (at least in their present form) after 1400. There are several important collections, but all of them were compiled during the sixteenth century or later and so belong to the period of the Renaissance.

Many of the traditional ballads are joyfully romantic and evoke the splendor, the bitterness, the bravery, and the rivalry of the days when Christians were struggling against Saracens. Some tell of the gallant deeds of the heroes of the epic cycles; some are love stories; some give accounts of historical events; some recount humorous incidents.

Some of the best known ballads are "Abenamar, Abenamar," "The Lamentation of Don Roderick," "The Cid's Courtship," "The Lamentation for Celin," "Lady Alda's Dream," and "Count Arnaldos."

18

Italian Literature

Historical Background. "The essential characteristic of Italian History is diversity — diversity of race and dialect, diversity of political interests, of internal development, of traditional customs."[1] From A.D. 476, when the last Western Roman emperor was dethroned by the Barbarians, till the latter part of the nineteenth century, Italy knew little unity of any sort. Mr. Symonds' comment is particularly applicable to the medieval period. Ostrogoths, Visigoths, Vandals, and Byzantines kept the country in a turmoil during most of the fifth and sixth centuries. In 568 the Langobards (Lombards) invaded Italy and for two centuries dominated the land, despite the fact that they never succeeded in conquering the eastern portion of the peninsula, a part of the south, Rome, Sicily, Sardinia, and Corsica. The Langobards were overthrown in 774 by Charlemagne, who was crowned Emperor of the Holy Roman Empire in 800; his dynasty ruled till 888. Thereafter followed a period of anarchy till the Saxon Otto (the Great) became emperor in 962. The Normans infiltrated southern Italy early in the eleventh century and by 1137 had made themselves rulers of Sicily, Naples, Capua, and Apulia. The southern kingdom was united to the Holy Roman Empire in 1197 under the House of Suabia.

The two historical trends during the twelfth and thirteenth centuries which were the most significant for a student of Italian literature were the rise of the city-states of the north and the Pope's struggle for political power.

By virtue of the rise of the burgher class and by virtue of the increase in commerce resultant from the Crusades, many cities in central and northern Italy amassed great wealth and developed so much political power that they were able — though nominally subject to the Holy Roman Emperor or the Byzantine Emperor — to demand considerable autonomy. Florence, Venice, Genoa, Pisa, Milan, Bologna, Pavia, and Cremona became commercially, politically, and culturally important.

The Emperor Henry VI's appointment of Pope Innocent III as guardian of Prince Frederick began a bloody controversy which lasted well into the fourteenth century.   When Henry died in 1197, Innocent assumed more and more political power, and he was aided by Otto of Brunswick of the Welf (Guelf) family, who claimed the imperial throne.   The young Emperor Frederick II, of the Waibling (Ghibelline) house, led the opposition.   Rivalry between one city-state and another led many of them to side with one faction or the other, and often there were factions within a city.   Numerous bitter battles were fought, but none were sufficiently decisive. Eventually foreign monarchs were called on to help in the struggle, which was still being carried on at the time of the death of Dante (1321).

General View of the Literature.   The Italian language is a natural outgrowth of Latin — principally of so-called classical Latin.   Its development was, of course, gradual; it was not recognized as a new language till about 915.

The veneration for the great authors of the old Roman Empire plus the reluctance to admit that Italian was a new language — not merely a vulgar dialect — led most Italian writers of the Middle Ages to employ Latin for their compositions.   Consequently there is no medieval Italian literature in the same sense that there is medieval French, German, and Spanish literature.   It is true that in the thirteenth century GUIDO GUINICELLI, GUIDO DELLA COLONNA, ST. FRANCIS OF ASSISI, GUIDO CAVALCANTI, and CINO DA PISTOIA wrote some commendable lyrics; and BRUNETTO LATINI compiled an encyclopedia and wrote *The Tesoretto*, a long didactic poem in the form of a vision.   It remained for Dante, however, to produce the first Italian literature of universal significance.

DANTE (DURANTE) ALIGHIERI
(1265–1321)

Dante Alighieri, poet and statesman, was born in Florence of a prominent Guelf family.   Little is known of his early life, but it is believed that he studied under the learned Brunetto Latini.   Dante tells us that in May, 1274 — when he was about nine years old — he met Beatrice Portinari, the daughter of a rich Florentine citizen. He immediately fell in love with her.   Nine years later she spoke to him for the first time — and "it made Dante a poet."[2]   From a

distance he continued to worship her, even after she married somebody else. Her death in 1290 plunged the poet into the deepest
despair. In 1289 he fought with the Guelfs against the Ghibellines
and helped the former win a great victory. He apparently played
a leading part in Florentine politics during the following ten years.
In 1300 he rose to the highest local political position: he became one
of the six Priors who governed the city. Soon afterwards the Guelfs
split into two parties, the Whites (*Bianchi*), or moderates, and the
Blacks (*Neri*), or radical propapists. Dante was a White. When
violence flared in 1301, the Blacks were victorious, and the Whites
—including Dante—were exiled from Florence. Dante never
returned, but spent the last twenty years of his life wandering from
city to city as one patron after another seemed eager for his services.
He died in Ravenna, an ardent Ghibelline.

Works.

THE NEW LIFE (*Vita Nuova*) (*c.* 1291–1300). *The New Life**
is a commemoration of Dante's love for Beatrice. It is a series of
thirty-one poems — principally sonnets and *canzoni* — set into a
prose background. The first division (containing ten poems) tells
of the effects of Beatrice's beauty on the poet; the second section
(containing ten more poems) gives an account of "the miracles
wrought by the splendour of her soul";[3] and the third section deals
with Beatrice's death and Dante's memories of her. Toward the
latter part of the third section the poet begins the process of trans-
forming Beatrice into a symbol of heavenly or spiritual love — a
process which was to be completed in the *Paradise*.

The New Life closes with an epilogue in which Dante hints of the
writing of the *Divine Comedy*. He says that in a vision he has seen
things which cause him to cease writing about Beatrice till he can
"discourse more worthily concerning her . . . [and till he can]
utter concerning her what hath never been said of any woman."[4]

THE BANQUET (*Convito, Convivio*) (*c.* 1301–1309). An attempt
by Dante to bring philosophy to the layman — to provide a feast
from the crumbs from the table of the great philosophers. The
work is little more than a popular rendering (in Italian) of the Aris-
totelian works of Albertus Magnus and Thomas Aquinas; it was
also influenced by Boëthius. .

* The term *Vita Nuova* seems to have the double meaning of "young life" and
"regenerated life," the latter referring to the effect on Dante of his love for
Beatrice.

Dante intended to write first a general introduction and then a commentary on each of fourteen *canzoni*, which, apparently, he had already composed. He completed only the introduction and three of the commentaries.

Here Beatrice appears as an allegory of divine philosophy — "a phase in the apotheosis of Beatrice herself."[5]

ON THE VULGAR TONGUE (*De Vulgari Eloquentia, De Volgari Eloquio*) (*c.* 1304). A document in Latin prose in which Dante defends the use of Italian (versus Latin) for literary works. The document is significant not only for its spirited defense of the vernacular but also for its account of current Italian dialects and its precepts on Italian metrics. Dante completed only one and a fraction of the proposed four books.

ON MONARCHY (*De Monarchia*) (*c.* 1313). A pro-Ghibelline treatise in Latin prose in which Dante expounds his beliefs concerning the separation of the temporal and spiritual spheres of government. The treatise is in three books. The first attempts to show that temporal monarchy is necessary for the good of the world; the second argues that the Roman people should rule by Divine will; and the third tries to prove that emperors receive their authority directly from God and not from the Pope.

THE DIVINE COMEDY (*Divina Commedia*[6]) (begun *c.* 1307, finished 1321).

Environmental and Literary Influences. To attempt an account of all the environmental matters which influenced the *Divine Comedy* would be to write both a detailed history of thirteenth-century Florence and an intimate biography of Dante. The corruption of the Church, the struggle between Guelfs and Ghibellines, the split of the Guelfs into Blacks and Whites, Dante's exile, his bitterness toward Florence, his gratitude to his various patrons, and finally (and, of course, most important of all) Dante's love for Beatrice — all are reflected in the vast panorama of the *Comedy*.

A few of the authors who most directly affected Dante's masterpiece were Homer, Aristotle, the Biblical writers, Cicero, Virgil, Statius, Lucan, Boëthius, Albertus Magnus, Thomas Aquinas, Guido Guinicelli, Guido Cavalcanti, Cino da Pistoia, and Brunetto Latini.

Nature and Meaning of the Poem. The *Divine Comedy* is an allegory[7] of a human soul's journey through hell and purgatory and on to heaven. Lost and in danger, the soul is led by Reason (represented by Virgil) through the realms of torment; then, edified and chastened by witnessing such terrifying punishments, the soul — now led by Theology (represented by Beatrice) — makes a tour of the nine heavenly spheres.   Many of the symbols may have a double or even triple meaning — ethical, religious, and historical; and some of the symbology is now obscure.   Many historical and fictional characters are used to personify specific virtues or vices; Dante wreaks vengeance on his enemies and heaps praises on some of his friends by depicting them, respectively, suffering torments in hell or purgatory or rejoicing in the delights of one of the heavens.

Much use is made of mystical numbers, especially three, seven, nine, ten and one hundred.

The *Divine Comedy* is a literary epic; unlike the *Iliad* and the *Song of Roland*, which were formed largely from orally transmitted legends and songs, it is the almost entirely fictional creation of the genius of one man.   Nor is it a national epic like the *Aeneid*, for its protagonist (Dante himself) is not an embodiment of the traditional virtues of the country; it might, however, be considered a national epic because it reflects so well the Italian turmoil of the thirteenth century.   Perhaps the most accurate label for the *Divine Comedy* is Epic of the Middle Ages, inasmuch as its theme is preparation for the life after death — which was the principal concern of medieval man.

Structure and Meter.   Dante makes great use of the mystical number *three* in both the structure and the rhyme-scheme of his *Comedy*. The poem consists of three books (*Hell*, or *Inferno; Purgatory*, or *Purgatorio;* and *Heaven*, or *Paradiso*).   *Purgatory* and *Heaven* each contain thirty-three cantos, and *Hell* has thirty-three regular cantos plus one of introduction.   Thus there are one hundred (the "perfect" number) cantos in the entire work.   There are 14,230 lines in the poem.

Each line has eleven syllables, with an accent normally on the penultimate syllable, but sometimes either on the antepenultimate or the final syllable.   The rhyme-scheme is *terza rima* (invented by Dante himself): *aba, bcb, cdc,* and so on; thus each group of three lines forms a unit.

Dialect.   The dialect of the *Divine Comedy* is Tuscan, which Dante was most instrumental in establishing as the predominant dialect of the country.   It is the basis of modern Italian.

The Story.

For Dante the earth is the center of the universe. When Lucifer and his angels were cast down from heaven to earth, the impact created a conical cavity, with its apex at the center of the planet. This cavity is hell, which is divided into nine circles of decreasing size. Jerusalem is directly over the center of the cone. On the other side of the globe, diametrically across from Jerusalem is a mountain. This is purgatory, which consists of seven cornices, or levels, of punishment. On the top of the mountain is Eden, the Earthly Paradise. Around the earth there are nine concentric spheres or heavens, and surrounding the outmost sphere is a spaceless region known as the empyrean, the dwelling place of God.

(a) *Hell (Inferno).* Dante has a vision, in which he seems to be in a Dark Wood, threatened by wild beasts. Virgil (Human Reason) appears and offers to lead Dante on a journey (which has been proposed by Beatrice as a means of instructing and purifying her lover). They proceed to the Gate of Hell and to Ante-Hell, where timid and neutral souls reside. Next the travelers visit *Circle One*, or *Limbo*, where the unbaptized children and virtuous heathen are placed; Virgil himself is a permanent inhabitant of this circle. From here on various classes of impenitent sinners are punished; the severity of the sin and of the punishment increases with the descent, and the punishment is suited to the crime. In the next four circles the travelers see the punishment of incontinence: *Circle Two*, the lustful; *Circle Three*, the gluttonous; *Circle Four*, the avaricious and the prodigal; *Circle Five*, the slothful and the angry. In *Circle Six* are the heretics, and in *Circle Seven* are the violent and the bestial: tyrants, murderers, suicides, squanderers, and those violent against God, nature, or art. *Circle Eight (Malebolge)* is subdivided into ten gulfs wherein, respectively, are punished (a) panders and seducers, (b) flatterers, (c) simoniacs, (d) soothsayers and sorcerers, (e) barterers and peculators, (f) hypocrites, (g) thieves, (h) evil counselors, (i) scandal-mongers and schismatics, and (j) impostors, alchemists, forgerers, and miscellaneous falsifiers. *Circle Nine* is reserved for the direst of all offenders — those guilty of treachery and malice. There are four gulfs, in which are punished, respectively, (a) traitors to their kindred, (b) traitors to their country or party, (c) traitors to their guests, and (d) traitors to their lords or benefactors. Nearly immersed in ice at the bottom of the fourth gulf — at the center of the earth — is Lucifer, who continuously grinds Judas, Brutus, and Cassius in his teeth.

At Lucifer's back is a secret passage through the earth, by which Virgil and Dante reach the base of the purgatorial mount.

(b) *Purgatory (Purgatorio)*.   The second section of the *Divine Comedy* is far less dire in tone than that of *Hell*.   Though filled with suffering, purgatory is pervaded by an atmosphere of hope, for here are only penitent sinners — sinners who will eventually reach heaven. Near the foot of the mount there is an Ante-Purgatory, in which those guilty of negligence through lack of love are being purged. As the poets ascend the mountain, they perceive that the punishments become decreasingly severe.   The crimes are the Seven Deadly Sins: pride, envy, anger, sloth, avarice or prodigality, gluttony, and lust.   Each (in order) is purged on a separate cornice or terrace.

As Dante and Virgil near the top of the mountain, Beatrice replaces Virgil as the guide.   She rebukes Dante for insufficient devotion but takes him on into Eden and then into the heavens.

(c) *Heaven (Paradiso)*.   As Beatrice bears Dante aloft, he sees the glories of the various heavens.   In the first three spheres he beholds those souls whose virtue has been sufficiently great to assure them of a place in paradise but still not great enough to win for them the highest bliss: on the *moon* are those who have been inconstant in their vows; on *Mercury*, those imperfect in justice; on *Venus*, those defective in temperance.   On the following four spheres are those exemplifying the four Cardinal Virtues: on the *Sun*, the prudent and wise; on *Mars*, the brave — especially warriors; on *Jupiter*, the just — especially rulers; and on *Saturn*, the temperate — especially the ascetic and contemplative spirits.   The eighth heaven is the *Sphere of Fixed Stars*, the heavenly counterpart of the Garden of Eden; here Dante is shown a vision of man's redemption, Christ's triumph, and the new Adam.   This sphere represents the three Heavenly Virtues — faith, hope, and charity.   The ninth heaven is the *Crystalline Sphere*, or *Primum Mobile*, wherein all nature, time, and motion begin.   Outside the *Primum Mobile* is the *Empyrean*, "the true Paradise of vision, comprehension, and fruition, where man's will is set to rest in union with universal Good, and his intellect in the possession of universal Truth."[8]   Here God has beatified all "the saints and Angels in the vision of His Essence."[9]   This is the real intellectual paradise of which all the other heavens are mere intimations. Now Dante is shown the mystery of the Trinity and of man's union with God. This being the whole purpose of his journey, the poem is brought to an end.

Summary of Criticism. At least one critic considers Dante one of the "three poets who have most profoundly stirred man's imagination."[10] Despite some adverse criticism, most scholars and literary historians agree that he is one of the five or six greatest poets who have ever lived. His greatness may be seen in both technique and content.

One of Dante's most wonderful endowments is his pictorial imagination. His descriptive method may profitably be contrasted with that of Milton. In depicting hell, the English poet uses broad, exaggerated strokes — and achieves "imaginative sublimity."[11] Dante, on the contrary, gives an exact and minute delineation — and achieves "unflinching realism."[12] Where Milton is abstract and indefinite, Dante is concrete and detailed. Symonds says that Dante is "unique among the poets of the world"[13] for his faculty of vision.

Other features of technique for which Dante has been praised are his "symmetry, balance, antithesis, climax."[14]

He has been censured for tediousness, prosiness (especially in philosophical passages), obscurity, and grotesqueness.

Though Dante is a master of technique, his greatest virtue as a poet lies in his thought, his attitudes, his points of view, and his religious and moral scope. He has been blamed, to be sure, for occasionally displaying hatred and bitterness toward his enemies, whom he subjects to the tortures of hellfire; and he is sometimes guilty of egotism and pride. Nevertheless, the *Divine Comedy* is a profoundly moral poem. It is "the epic of Man, considered as a moral being, exercising free will under the eye of an inexorable judge, who punishes and rewards according to fixed laws. . . . The real sublimity of Dante is not pictorial. It is moral. . . . The whole *Purgatorio* is a monument to the beauty and tranquility of Dante's soul. The whole *Paradiso* is a proof of its purity and radiance and celestial love."[15]

Furthermore, the poem is of universal application. "What more could a poet do? Dante poetized all life and nature as he found them. His imagination dominated and focused the whole world. . . . His poetry covers the whole field from which poetry may be fetched, and to which poetry may be applied."[16]

X In summary, "Force, depth, definiteness, brevity, sincerity, intensity, subordination to fixed purposes — these are the great qualities of Dante's genius."[17]

Influence.   Dante's influence has been very strong on Petrarch, Boccaccio, Chaucer, Milton, Byron, Shelley, Longfellow, Chateaubriand, and Goethe.

Bibliography for Medieval Western Literature

General

Chadwick, H. Munro, and N. K. Chadwick. *The Growth of Literature.* Vol. I. Cambridge, England: Cambridge University Press, 1932.

Ker, William P. *Epic and Romance.* London: Macmillan and Co., 1926.

Thompson, Stith, and John Gassner. *Our Heritage of World Literature.* New York: Dryden Press, 1942.

Weatherly, Edward H., and Others. *The Heritage of European Literature.* Vol. I. Boston: Ginn and Co., 1948.

German

Francke, Kuno. *A History of German Literature as Determined by Social Forces.* 4th ed. New York: H. Holt and Co., 1901.

Friederich, Werner P. *History of German Literature*, College Outline Series. New York: Barnes & Noble, 1951.

Hosmer, James K. *A Short History of German Literature.* Revised ed. New York: Charles Scribner's Sons, 1910.

Liptzin, Sol. *Historical Survey of German Literature.* New York: Prentice-Hall, 1936.

Priest, George Madison. *A Brief History of German Literature.* New York: Charles Scribner's Sons, 1909.

Robertson, John G. *A History of German Literature.* Rev. ed. London: Blackwood, 1949.

Thomas, Calvin. *A History of German Literature.* New York: D. Appleton and Co., 1909.

Celtic

Cross, Tom Peete. *Harper and Bard.* Chicago: Thomas S. Rockwell Co., 1931.

De Blácam, Aodh. *Gaelic Literature Surveyed.* Dublin and Cork: Talbot Press, 1929.

Hull, Eleanor. *A Text Book of Irish Literature.* Dublin: M. H. Gill and Son, n.d.

Hyde, Douglas. *The Story of Early Gaelic Literature.* London: T. F. Unwin Co., 1922.

Jackson, Kenneth. *Studies in Early Celtic Nature Poetry.* Cambridge, England: Cambridge University Press, 1935.

Rhys, John. *The Welsh People.* 2nd ed. New York: Macmillan Co., 1900.

French

Butler, Kathleen T. *A History of French Literature.* Vol. I. New York: E. P. Dutton and Co., 1923.

Dowden, Edward. *A History of French Literature.* New York: D. Appleton and Co., 1898.

Holmes, Urban Tigner. *History of Old French Literature from the Origins to 1300.* New York: F. S. Crofts & Co., 1937.

Nitze, William A., and E. Preston Dargan. *A History of French Literature.* Revised ed. New York: H. Holt and Co., 1927.

Saintsbury, George. *A Short History of French Literature.* 5th ed. Oxford: Clarendon Press, 1897.

Schwarz, H. Stanley. *An Outline History of French Literature.* New York: A. A. Knopf, 1924.

Wright, Charles H. C. *A History of French Literature.* New York: Oxford University Press, 1925.

Spanish

Fitzmaurice-Kelly, James. *Chapters on Spanish Literature.* London: A. Constable and Co., 1908.

————. *A History of Spanish Literature.* New York: D. Appleton Co., 1898.

Ford, Jeremiah D. M. *Main Currents of Spanish Literature.* New York: H. Holt and Co., 1919.

Northup, George Tyler. *An Introduction to Spanish Literature.* Chicago: University of Chicago Press, 1925.

Peers, E. Allison (ed.). *Spain: A Companion to Spanish Studies.* 3rd ed. London: Methuen and Co., 1938.

Italian

Brooks, Alfred M. *Dante: How to Know Him.* Indianapolis: Bobbs-Merrill Co., 1916.

Butler, Arthur John. *Dante: His Times and His Work.* London: Macmillan and Co., 1902.

Cosmo, Umberto. *A Handbook to Dante Studies.* Tr. by David Moore. New York: Barnes & Noble, 1950.

Croce, Benedetto. *The Poetry of Dante.* Translated by Douglas Ainslie. New York: H. Holt and Co., 1922.

Dinsmore, Charles Allen. *Aids to the Study of Dante.* Boston: Houghton Mifflin Co., 1903.

Foligno, Cesare. *Epochs of Italian Literature.* Oxford: Clarendon Press, 1920.

Friederich, Werner P. *Dante's Fame Abroad,* 1350–1850. Rome: Edizioni di Storia e Letteratura, 1950.

Gardner, Edmund G. *Dante.* New York: E. P. Dutton Co., 1923.

_____ (ed.). *Italy: A Companion to Italian Studies.* London: Methuen and Co., 1934.

Garnett, Richard. *A History of Italian Literature.* New York: D. Appleton and Co., 1898.

Grandgent, Charles H. *Dante.* New York: Duffield and Co., 1921.

_____. *Discourses on Dante.* Cambridge, Mass.: Harvard University Press, 1924.

_____. *The Power of Dante.* Boston: Marshall Jones Co., 1918.

Santayana, George. *Three Philosophical Poets.* Cambridge, Mass.: Harvard University Press, 1910.

Scartazzini, Giovanni A. *A Companion to Dante.* Translated by Arthur John Butler. London: Macmillan and Co., 1893.

Symonds, John Addington. *An Introduction to the Study of Dante.* 4th ed. London: Adam and Charles Black, 1899.

Appendix

Appendix

Mythology

Two bodies of mythology have greatly influenced world literature, art, and music: classical and Norse (Germanic). Several theories have been advanced to explain the origin of these myths, whose types are common to all mythology.

Nature Theory. Myths arose as attempts by primitive man to explain natural phenomena — storms, sunrise, the change of season, etc.

Psychoanalytic Theory. Myths were expressions by concrete symbols of sexual or emotional conflicts.

Anthropological Theory. Myths were created to narrate, to establish, to codify, to justify, and to enhance primitive customs, rituals, and moral and religious precedents. According to this theory (advanced by Malinowski in 1926 and most widely held today), a myth is a "narrative resurrection of a primeval reality, told in satisfaction of deep religious wants, moral cravings, social submissions, assertions, even practical requirements. . . . It vouches for the efficiency of ritual and contains practical rules for the guidance of man."*

Classical Mythology

Myths of Creation.†
ORIGIN OF HEAVEN AND EARTH. Accounts are confused and conflicting as to the prime elements: (a) the River Ocean encircling all sea and land (Homer); (b) Night and Darkness, from which sprang Light; (c) Time, from whom sprang Chaos, whence came Night, Mist, and Ether (fiery air); Time caused Mist to swirl around Ether till the mass became an egg, which broke into halves — Heaven and Earth; Love came from the center of the egg; (d) Chaos, composed of Void, Mass, and Darkness, whence emerged

* Bronislaw Malinowski, *Myth in Primitive Psychology* (New York: W. W. Norton and Co., 1926), p. 19. Malinowski cogently discredits the other theories; see pp. 11–35.

† Charles M. Gayley, *The Classic Myths in English Literature and Art*, rev. ed., (Boston: Ginn and Co., 1911), pp. 3–9. Most of the mythological material in this appendix has been derived from Gayley.

Ge (Mother Earth), Love, and Night; from Ge came Uranus (Heaven) and then Earth.

ORIGIN OF THE GODS.

First Dynasty: Ge and Uranus.   Their offsprings were thirteen* Titans, all giants personifying some mighty natural or physical force or phenomenon, the most famous of whom are Hyperion, Oceanus, Cronus, Atlas, and Prometheus; three Cyclopes, one-eyed, cannibalistic giants, representing lightning and thunder; and three Hecatonchires, hundred-handed monsters, possibly personifying earthquakes.   The end of the reign of Ge and Uranus was brought about thus: fearing the power of the Cyclopes and the Hecatonchires, Uranus imprisoned them in Tartarus (within Ge). At the plea of Ge, Cronus mutilated Uranus with a scythe and freed the imprisoned ones.†   From the blood of Uranus sprang giants with legs of serpents, the Furies (goddesses of vengeance, with hair made of snakes; also called the Erinys and the Eumenides), and the Melic nymphs (warlike maidens, from whose bodies spears were made).   Uranus was deposed.

Second Dynasty: Cronus and his Sister-Titan Rhea.   Their offsprings were the beings who later became the Olympic deities: Zeus, Poseidon, Hades, Hera, Demeter, and Hestia.   The end of the reign of the second dynasty came about thus: from fear Cronus swallowed his first five children.   A battle between the Titans and the progeny of Cronus and Rhea followed.   The Titans were defeated and Cronus was deposed.   All Titans except Atlas (who bore the world on his shoulders), Prometheus, and Oceanus were confined in Tartarus.

Third Dynasty: Zeus and Hera.   The principal deities under this dynasty were as follows:

Greek Name	Roman Name‡	Function
Zeus, son of Cronus and Rhea	Jupiter, Jove	King of the gods and the sky
Hera, sister and wife of Zeus	Juno	Queen of the gods, patroness of marriage

* Alexander S. Murray, *Manual of Mythology* (Philadelphia: D. McKay, 1895), p. 42, lists only twelve.

† Gaylev, pp. 4–6.   Other accounts say that the Titans also were imprisoned within Ge.   See Murray, p. 43.

‡ The Greek and Roman Olympic deities are not entirely identical, but for all practical purposes, Zeus = Jupiter, etc.

Greek Name	Roman Name	Function
Poseidon, brother of Zeus	Neptune	God of the sea
Aphrodite, daughter of Zeus and Dione	Venus	Goddess of love
Ares, son of Zeus and Hera	Mars	God of war
Hades, brother of Zeus	Pluto	God of the underworld (which is, incidentally, also called Hades)
Hestia, sister of Zeus	Vesta	Goddess of the hearth, the fireside, and domestic life
Demeter, sister of Zeus	Ceres	Goddess of grain and agriculture
Hephaestus, son of Zeus and Hera	Vulcan	God of fire and forging, blacksmith of the gods
Apollo, son of Zeus and Leto	Apollo	God of the sun, lyric poetry, music, medicine, and archery
Hermes, son of Zeus and Maia	Mercury	Messenger of the gods, god of thievery, cunning, and commerce
Dionysus, son of Zeus and Semele	Bacchus	God of wine and vegetation
Persephone, daughter of Zeus and Demeter	Proserpina	Goddess of the underworld, wife of Hades
Artemis, daughter of Zeus and Leto	Diana	Goddess of the moon and of hunting, patroness of chastity
Athene, daughter of Zeus, sprung from his head	Minerva, Pallas	Goddess of wisdom, battle, spinning, weaving, and domestic arts

The Olympian gods were anthropomorphic, almost amoral, and powerful; they were subject to human emotions, such as jealousy, sexual passion, and hatred. Their food and drink, respectively, were ambrosia and nectar. Their home was Mount Olympus, really only an ideal, but symbolized by Mount Olympus in Thessaly.

ORIGIN OF MAN. There are variant stories: (a) man sprang from Ge (Mother Earth) and therefore is possibly as old as the Olympic gods; (b) he was created out of earth and water by Prometheus, and endowed by him and Epimetheus (Prometheus' brother) with various faculties.

Principal Characters of Some Famous Classical Myths.

ACTAEON. Actaeon saw Artemis bathing naked, was punished by being changed to a stag, and was killed by his own dogs.

ADONIS. He was a handsome youth who rejected the love of

Aphrodite. Though warned, he hunted a boar, which killed him. Aphrodite made the anemone spring from his blood.

ARACHNE. Arachne was turned into a spider for competing with Athene as a spinner.

ATALANTA. Meleager killed the boar of Calydon and then argued with his uncles over the spoils, which he gave to Atalanta. He killed his uncles, but died himself when his mother, Althea, burned a brand controlling Meleager's life span. Atalanta later raced Hippomenes, lost, and married him.

DAPHNE. She was beloved by Apollo, but fled his advances. She was subsequently changed into a laurel tree, which Apollo adopted as his own (hence "poet laureate").

ECHO. For loquacity, Echo was condemned to answer only — never could she initiate a conversation. She fell in love with Narcissus who shunned her. Echo languished away till only her voice was left. Narcissus fell in love with himself and pined for his own image till he died. A flower sprang up in his place.

HERCULES (HERACLES). Son of Zeus and Alcmene, Hercules aroused the jealousy and anger of Hera, who subjected him to Eurystheus. Eurystheus made him perform Twelve Labors: killing of the Nemean lion, slaying of the Hydra, capture of an Arcadian boar, capture of the stag of Cerynea, destruction of the Stymphalian birds, cleaning of the Augean stables, capture of the Cretan bull, capture of the horses of Diomedes, obtaining of the girdle of Hippolyta, capture of the oxen of Geryon, stealing of the golden apples of the Hesperides, and bringing of Cerberus] from the underworld.

HYACINTHUS. A young man beloved by Apollo, he was killed accidentally by Apollo's discus and was changed into a flower.

IO. Io, a mistress of Zeus, was changed into a heifer to escape the wrath of Hera, but was then chased by a gadfly. Finally she was restored to human form when Zeus promised to pay her no more attention.

JASON. Aided by Medea, a sorceress, Jason seized the Golden Fleece; he later deserted Medea.

MIDAS. Midas entertained Silenus and was rewarded by Dionysus with the gift of turning into gold everything he touched. He was freed of the gift at his own request when his food and drink became gold. Later his ears were made to resemble those of a jackass because he voted Pan's music superior to Apollo's.

NIOBE. Niobe, the daughter of Tantalus, dared to exalt herself, as the mother of fourteen children, above Leto, the mother of only two children — Artemis and Apollo. In punishment all Niobe's children were killed. Niobe wept so inconsolably that she was changed into a stone, from which flowed a never-ceasing fountain, symbolic of her tears.

ORPHEUS. The son of Apollo and Calliope, Orpheus was a superb musician. He married Eurydice, who, while fleeing the advances of Aristaeus, was bitten by a snake and died. Orpheus persuaded Pluto to allow him to bring Eurydice back to earth — but on the condition that Orpheus not look back at her till they reached the upper air. On the journey Orpheus' eagerness overcame him, he looked back, and Eurydice returned to Hades. Orpheus joined her there soon afterward to remain forever.

PANDORA. Curiosity led her to open a box left by Epimetheus; by so doing she released troubles on the world.

PERSEUS. He rescued Andromeda from a rock, where a sea-monster was about to devour her.

PHILOMELA. She was ravished by Tereus, the husband of Procne, her sister. She and Procne killed Itylus, son of Tereus and Procne, and fed him to his father. Philomela and Procne were pursued by Tereus. Philomela was changed into a nightingale, Procne to a swallow, and Tereus to a hawk.

PROMETHEUS. Prometheus stole fire from the sun and gave it to man. He was punished by Zeus by being chained on Mount Caucasus, where a vulture (or eagle) preyed on his vitals. Prometheus refused to tell Zeus a secret: that Hercules was the offspring who would dethrone Zeus. Hercules freed Prometheus and killed the vulture.

SYRINX. She was turned into a reed to escape Pan. Reeds were afterwards used to make the Pipe of Pan.

TANTALUS. Tantalus, King of Phrygia, betrayed the secrets of the gods, ridiculed their omnipotence, and fed them human flesh — his own son. He was punished in Tartarus by being made very hungry and thirsty and then being immersed to his neck in water which ebbed so that he could never drink and being offered trees of fruit which were jerked out of his reach before he could eat — hence our verb *tantalize*.

THESEUS. With the help of Ariadne, he killed the Minotaur in a labyrinth in Crete. Theseus later deserted Ariadne. When he failed to signal his success in the Minotaur venture, his father committed suicide. Theseus became king of Athens.

Norse (Germanic) Mythology

Myths of Creation.

ORIGIN OF HEAVEN AND EARTH. According to the Eddas, before there was a heaven or an earth, there existed "only a bottomless deep, Ginungagap, ... a world of mist, Niflheim,"* and Muspelheim, a world of light. From the midst of Niflheim sprang a fountain, Vergelmir, from which flowed twelve rivers; these rivers poured into Ginungagap, froze over, and filled up the deep. Warm winds from Muspelheim melted the ice and caused great clouds of vapor to form, from which clouds sprang Ymir, a frost-giant, and his cow Audhumbla, who was nourished by licking the salty ice. One day her licking revealed the presence of Bori, a god, who thereafter married a woman of the giant race and begat a son, Bor. Bor became the father of Odin, Vili, and Ve. These young gods killed Ymir. From his body they made the earth, from his blood the oceans, from his bones the mountains, from his hair the trees, from his skull the heavens, from his brain the clouds, and from his eyebrows a fence around the region between Muspelheim and Niflheim. This fenced-in area was Midgard, or Mid-Earth, the future abode of man.

Ygdrasil, a tremendous ash tree which sprang from the body of Ymir, was supposed to support the entire universe. One root of the tree extended into Midgard, another into Jötunheim (the place of giants), and a third through Niflheim on into Hel, the region of Death.

Directly above the top of Ygdrasil was Asgard, the dwelling place of the deities. This region was divided into two areas, Gladsheim for the gods and Vingolf for the goddesses. It could be reached only by crossing Bifrost, the rainbow. It was filled with gold and silver palaces, of which Valhalla, the hall of Odin, was the most beautiful.

ORIGIN OF THE GODS. Concerning the origin and the genealogies of the gods, Norse mythology is far less detailed and specific than classical mythology. The principal deities were as follows:

* Gayley, p. 373.

Odin (Woden, Alfadur*), son of Bor and a giantess; king of the gods.
Frigga (Fricka), wife of Odin.
Thor, son of Odin; strongest of the gods. He is equipped with a mighty hammer (thunderbolt), which returns to his hand after being thrown at an enemy; a belt which doubles his strength; and some iron gloves which increase the efficiency of his hammer.
Vidar, son of Odin; next in strength to Thor.
Bragi, son of Odin; god of poetry.
Iduna, wife of Bragi; keeper of the gods' apples of youth.
Balder, son of Odin; god of sunlight, springtime, and happiness.
Hödur, son of Odin; blind god of winter.
Freyr (Frey, Froh), god of rain and vegetation.
Freya (Freia), sister of Freyr; goddess of love. She is especially fond of music, flowers, springtime, and elves.
Tyr (Ziu, Tiw), a wrestler, god of battles.
Heimdall, watchman of the gods; he guards the borders of Asgard to prevent surprise attacks by giants.
The Valkyries, daughters of Odin; armed, warlike virgins, mounted on horses. They visit every battlefield and carry the bravest of the slain to Valhalla. These fallen heroes feast each night off the flesh of Serimnir, a boar which is cooked every morning but which becomes whole again every night. During the day the heroes fight and wound each other, but each evening their wounds are healed.

ORIGIN OF MAN. Soon after Odin, Vili, and Ve had created the world, they made a man out of an ashen spar and called him *Ask (Aske)*. They fashioned a woman out of a piece of elm; her they called *Embla*. Odin gave the new creatures life and soul; Vili endowed them with reason and motion; and Ve bestowed on them "the senses, expressive features and speech. Midgard was given them as their residence, and they became the progenitors of the human race."†

Other Famous Myths.

LOKI AND HIS CHILDREN. Loki, of the demon race, was the villain and trickster of Norse mythology. He had three offspring. The first was Fenris, a wolf, which the gods finally bound with Gleipner, a chain made of "the noise made by the footfall of a cat, the beards of women, the roots of stones, the breath of fishes,

---

* The term *Alfadur* (All-Father) sometimes is applied to Odin; but sometimes it seems to denominate a deity superior to Odin — an eternal and uncreated god.
† Gayley, p. 374.

the nerves (sensibilities) of bears, and the spittle of birds."* The second was the Midgard Serpent, which Odin threw into the ocean surrounding the earth; the monster was so huge that he encircled the world. The third offspring was Hela (Death), whom Odin cast into Hel, or the region below Niflheim; there she rules over all those who die of illness or old age (heroes are borne to Valhalla).

THE ASGARD WALL. The gods agreed to give a certain workman the sun and the moon as well as Freya's hand in marriage if he would construct a wall around Asgard and finish before the first day of summer. When it became obvious that the workman was going to fulfill his contract on time, Loki, at the request of the gods, contrived a trick. Svadilfari, the horse of the workman, was lured from helping his master by a mare which Loki released. The workman thereupon revealed his identity: he was a giant. He resumed his normal stature, but was killed by Thor, whose hammer shattered the giant's skull.

THE THEFT OF THOR'S HAMMER (*The Lay of Thrym*). Thrym, king of the Frost-Giants, stole Thor's hammer, buried it eight fathoms deep in Jötunheim, and refused to return it till he received Freya as his bride. At Loki's instigation Thor disguised himself as Freya, went to Jötunheim, was given the hammer, dropped his disguise, and then killed Thrym and his followers.

THOR'S VISIT TO JÖTUNHEIM. Thor, Loki, and Thialfi, Thor's servant, set out on foot to visit the abode of the giants. En route they encountered the giant Skrymir, whose snoring so disturbed Thor that the god thrice tried to kill the giant with his hammer, but the blows fell harmlessly on Skrymir's skull. After reaching Utgard, the capital of the giants, Thor and his two companions were challenged by the king, Utgard-Loki, to engage in several contests. Loki was defeated by Logi in an eating bout, and Thialfi lost a footrace to Hugi. Thor himself tried to drink in three drafts a horn full of mead, but he failed. Then he tried to raise a cat from the floor, but succeeded only in lifting one foot of the animal. Finally he was overcome in a wrestling match by Elli, an old woman. Later Utgard-Loki revealed that he himself, in disguise, was Skrymir and that Thor's hammer blows really fell on mountain sides and blasted great glens therein. The contests, too, were fraudulent. Logi was fire, Hugi was thought, the horn of mead was the sea, the cat was the Midgard Serpent, and Elli

* Gayley, p. 378.

was old age. Furious at having been tricked, Thor then tried to throw his hammer at Utgard-Loki, but the king, his followers, and the city had disappeared.

FREYR'S SWORD. Freyr had a wonderful sword which would by itself wreak havoc on a battlefield. One day while sitting on Odin's throne, Freyr saw Gerda, a beautiful maid, far away in Jötunheim. He fell in love with her, pined for her, and agreed to give his magic sword to Skirnir, his messenger, if Skirnir would procure Gerda for him. The messenger was successful and got the sword.

THE DEATH OF BALDUR. Tormented by dreams, Baldur told the assembled gods that he feared some imminent personal disaster. Frigga persuaded everything in the world to promise not to harm him — everything, that is, except mistletoe. The gods then amused themselves by throwing various objects at Baldur; all missiles were harmless. Hödur, being blind, was not participating in the pastime till Loki suggested his throwing mistletoe. Hödur agreed, Loki directed his aim, and the mistletoe struck and killed Baldur. Hermod, swiftest of the gods, rode Sleipnir, Odin's horse, to Hel in order to request Hela to let Baldur return to Asgard. The goddess of death granted the request on one condition — that all things in the world weep for Baldur. After Hermod's report to the gods, everything and everybody — except the hag Thok (believed to be Loki in disguise) — agreed to weep, but Thok's refusal kept Baldur in Hel. The god's body was burned on board his ship Hringham. Loki was punished by being chained and having a serpent eternally drop venom on his face. Siguna, Loki's wife, would catch the poison in a cup, but whenever she had to empty the cup, the poison would fall on Loki; his resultant writhing caused the earth to shake.

RAGNAROK (*The Twilight of the Gods*). The Norse believed that a time would come when all creation would be destroyed. After six harsh winters, the earth would quake, the sea would quit its basin, the heavens would burst asunder, and many men would die. Loki and Fenris would break their bonds and along with the Midgard Serpent, the Frost-Giants, and the inhabitants of Hel and Muspelheim would cross Bifrost to the battlefield Vigrid, where they would oppose the gods in a final conflict. Fenris would kill Odin, but would be slain by Vidar. Thor and the Midgard Serpent would kill each other, and so would Loki and Heimdall.

Surtur, leader of those from Muspelheim, would kill Freyr and then subject the whole universe to flames. The sun would dim, the earth sink into the sea, the stars fall, and time cease. Then the Alfadur (a deity here superior to Odin) would cause a new heaven and earth to rise from the sea, and a new age of happiness and plenty, free from sin and misery, would succeed, and men and gods would live happily thereafter.

Bibliography for Mythology

Fiske, John. *Myths and Myth-Makers.* Boston: J. R. Osgood and Co., 1874.

Gayley, Charles M. *The Classic Myths in English Literature and Art.* Revised ed. Boston: Ginn and Co., 1911.

Malinowski, Bronislaw. *Myth in Primitive Psychology.* New York: W. W. Norton and Co., 1926.

Murray, Alexander S. *Manual of Mythology.* Philadelphia: D. McKay, 1895.

Notes

Notes.

Notes to Chapter 1

1 Carl Holliday, *The Dawn of Literature* (New York: T. Y. Crowell Co., 1931), p. 50.
2 Alexander Heidel, *The Gilgamesh Epic and Old Testament Parallels*, 2nd ed. (Chicago: University of Chicago Press, 1949), p. 13.
3 Heidel, p. 3. Heidel disputes this, but agrees with other scholars that its date of composition is about 2000 B.C.

Notes to Chapter 3

1 Herbert A. Giles, *A History of Chinese Literature* (New York: D. Appleton & Co., 1928), p. 7.
2 Giles' figure quoted by Carl Holliday, *The Dawn of Literature* (New York: T. Y. Crowell Co., 1931), p. 311.
3 Giles, p. 128.

Notes to Chapter 4

1 Ernest S. Bates, *The Bible Designed to Be Read as Living Literature* (New York: Simon & Schuster, 1943), p. 513.
2 P. 559.
3 For other interpretations, see Bates, p. 771.
4 Carl Holliday, *The Dawn of Literature* (New York: T. Y. Crowell Co., 1931), p. 330.
5 For a list of the interpolations and an analysis of the original work, see Morris Jastrow, *A Gentle Cynic* (Philadelphia: J. B. Lippincott Co., 1919).
6 For a discussion of this problem see Bates, p. 900.
7 Quoted by Bates, p. 1113.
8 William Lyon Phelps quoted by Lawrence E. Nelson, *Our Roving Bible* (New York: Abingdon-Cokesbury Press, 1945), p. 1.
9 Cleland B. McAfee, *The Greatest English Classic* (New York: Harper & Bros., 1912), p. 130.
10 Albert S. Cook, *The Authorized Version of the Bible and Its Influence* (New York: G. P. Putnam, 1910), pp. 79–80.
11 John H. Gardiner, *The Bible as English Literature* (New York: Charles Scribner's Sons, 1906), p. 395.

Notes to Chapter 5

1 Edward Capps, *From Homer to Theocritus* (New York: Chautauqua Press, 1901), pp. 7–9, whence quotations in the paragraph.
2 Capps, p. 130.
3 Frank B. Jevons, *A History of Greek Literature* (New York: Charles Scribner's Sons, 1894), p. 83.
4 Wilmer C. Wright, *A Short History of Greek Literature* (New York: American Book Co., 1907), p. 58.
5 Wright, p. 58.
6 Jevons, p. 83.
7 Capps, p. 137.

Notes to Chapter 6

1 Wilmer C. Wright, *A Short History of Greek Literature* (New York: American Book Co., 1907), p. 76.
2 Quoted by Edward Capps, *From Homer to Theocritus* (New York: Chautauqua Press, 1901), p. 162.
3 T. A. Sinclair, *A History of Classical Greek Literature* (New York: Macmillan Co., 1935), p. 139.

Notes to Chapter 7

1 Edward Capps, *From Homer to Theocritus* (New York: Chautauqua Press, 1901), p. 320.
2 Capps, p. 320.
3 Thucydides' words (Book I) translated by Capps in *From Homer to Theocritus*, p. 319.
4 Wilmer C. Wright, *A Short History of Greek Literature* (New York: American Book Co., 1907), p. 182.
5 Wright, p. 321.
6 T. A. Sinclair, *A History of Classical Greek Literature* (New York: Macmillan Co., 1935), p. 330.
7 Capps, p. 334.
8 Capps, p. 334.
9 Philip W. Harsh, *A Handbook of Classical Drama* (Stanford, California: Stanford University Press, 1944), p. 47.
10 Wright, p. 211.
11 Harsh, p. 39.
12 Harsh, p. 118.
13 Wright, p. 234.
14 Richard C. Jebb, *Classical Greek Poetry* (Boston: Houghton Mifflin Co., 1897), p. 186.
15 Jebb, p. 189.
16 Harsh, p. 157.
17 Frank L. Lucas, *Euripides and His Influence* (New York: Longmans, Green & Co., 1928), p. 9.
18 Wright, p. 254.
19 Harsh, p. 236.
20 Wright, p. 262.
21 Jebb, p. 192.
22 Jebb, p. 192.
23 Quoted by Aristotle (*Poetics.* XXV).
24 *Poetics.* V.
25 Harsh, p. 276.
26 Louis E. Lord, *Aristophanes, His Plays and His Influence* (New York: Longmans, Green & Co., 1927), p. 71.
27 Capps, p. 341.
28 Wright, p. 168.
29 Capps, p. 339.
30 Capps, p. 364.
31 Paul Shorey, *What Plato Said* (Chicago: University of Chicago Press, 1934), p. 81.
32 Wright, p. 392.
33 Wright, p. 406.

Notes to Chapter 8

1 Quoted by Wilmer C. Wright, *A Short History of Greek Literature* (New York: American Book Co., 1907), p. 415.
2 Sainte-Beuve, quoted by Wright, p. 430.
3 Wright, p. 493.

Notes to Chapter 9

1 *Epistles* II. i ("To Augustus"). 62.
2 Philip W. Harsh, *A Handbook of Classical Drama* (Stanford, Calif.: Stanford University Press, 1944), p. 352.
3 Horace *Epistles* II. i. 74, tr. by Marcus S. Dimsdale.
4 Marcus S. Dimsdale, *A History of Latin Literature* (New York: D. Appleton & Co., 1915), p. 65.
5 J. W. Mackail, *Latin Literature* (New York: Charles Scribner's Sons, 1895), p. 92.
6 George D. Hadzsits, *Lucretius and His Influence* (New York: Longmans, Green & Co., 1935), p. 82.
7 Hadzsits, p. 112.
8 G. C. Trevelyan, *The Life and Letters of Lord Macaulay* (New York: Harper & Bros., 1876), I, 410.
9 "Frater, Ave atque Vale."
10 Herbert J. Rose, *A Handbook of Latin Literature* (London: Methuen & Co., 1936), p. 168.
11 Rose, p. 185.
12 Mackail, p. 62.
13 P. 159.
14 Mackail, p. 75.
15 Mackail, p. 80.

Notes to Chapter 10

1 George E. Woodberry, "Virgil," *Literary Essays* (New York: Harcourt, Brace, & Howe, 1920), p. 225.
2 Woodberry, p. 209.
3 Stith Thompson and John Gassner, *Our Heritage of World Literature* (New York: Dryden Press, 1942), p. 278.
4 Woodberry, p. 226.
5 Woodberry, p. 235.
6 Alfred Tennyson, "To Virgil."
7 Casper J. Kraemer, Jr., ed., *The Complete Works of Horace* (New York: Modern Library, 1936), intro., p. 1.
8 William Y. Sellar, *The Roman Poets of the Augustan Age: Horace and the Elegiac Poets* (Oxford: Clarendon Press, 1892), p. 192.
9 Marcus S. Dimsdale, *A History of Latin Literature* (New York: D. Appleton & Co., 1915), p. 306.
10 Dimsdale, p. 304.
11 Persius, quoted by Dimsdale, p. 305.
12 L. P. Wilkinson, *Horace and His Lyric Poetry* (Cambridge, England: Cambridge University Press, 1945), p. 86.
13 Herbert J. Rose, *A Handbook of Latin Literature* (London: Methuen & Co., 1936), p. 286.
14 Dimsdale, p. 315.
15 Rose, p. 287.
16 For her identity, see Dimsdale, p. 319; Rose, p. 290.

17 Dimsdale, p. 327.

18 I. viii. 43 — a quotation which Dimsdale (p. 335) amusingly calls "rather cynical."

19 Edward K. Rand, *Ovid and His Influence* (New York: Longmans, Green & Co., 1928), p. 20.

20 "*Nil nisi lascivi per me dicantur amores*" (III. 27).

21 Rand, p. 46.

22 Herman Frankel, *Ovid: A Poet between Two Worlds* (Berkeley, Calif.: University of California Press, 1945), p. 54.

23 Frankel, p. 89.

24 Alfred Church, *Ovid* (Philadelphia: J. B. Lippincott Co., 1880), p. 81.

25 Rand, p. 74. Frankel calls him an agnostic concerning the Roman gods (p. 90).

26 Frankel, p. 3.

27 Quoted by Church, p. 151.

28 Frankel, p. 73.

29 Church, p. 151.

30 W. Lucas Collins, *Livy* (Philadelphia: J. B. Lippincott Co., 1876), p. 183.

31 Dimsdale, p. 361; the second phrase is a translation of a passage from Quintilian.

32 Dimsdale, p. 361.

Notes to Chapter 11

1 Philip W. Harsh, *A Handbook of Classical Drama* (Stanford, Calif.: Stanford University Press, 1944), p. 417.

2 "The moral spirit of this play looks to the Christian future rather than to the Greek past" (Harsh, p. 432).

3 There is still much disagreement. See Harsh, p. 404.

4 T. S. Eliot, *Seneca, His Tenne Tragedies*, trans. and ed. by Thomas Newton (London: Tudor Translations, 1927), I, intro., p. xxv.

5 A. D. Goodley, quoted by Marcus S. Dimsdale, *A History of Latin Literature* (New York: D. Appleton & Co., 1915), p. 406.

6 "Nowhere else does Seneca descend quite so low. . . ." (Herbert J. Rose, *A Handbook of Latin Literature* [London: Methuen & Co., 1936], p. 365).

7 J. W. Mackail (*Latin Literature* [New York: Charles Scribner's Sons, 1895], p. 174) thinks it "silly and stupid."

8 *Annals*. XVI. 17–20.

9 J. Wight Duff (*Roman Satire: Its Outlook on Social Life* [Berkeley, Calif.: University of California Press, 1936], p. 97) calls it "the first picaresque novel."

10 J. M. Mitchell, ed., *The Satyricon* (London: G. Routledge & Sons, 1923), intro., p. 25.

11 Marcus S. Dimsdale, *A History of Latin Literature* (New York: D. Appleton & Co., 1915), p. 473.

12 Dimsdale, p. 472.

13 Rose, p. 408.

14 Dimsdale, p. 499.

15 Dimsdale, p. 504.

16 The manuscript gives the latter title. In IX. 985–986, however, Lucan says, "My *Pharsalia* will live" — a reference to the battle of Pharsalos, the climax of the story.

17 Quoted and partially denied by Dimsdale, pp. 463–464.

18 Rose, p. 396.

19 I. 17.

20 Dimsdale, p. 436.

21 His first name was either Publius or Gaius. See Rose, pp. 398–399, 401.
22 Dimsdale, p. 484.
23 Mackail, p. 211.
24 The second English title has been added by posterity; the adjective is descriptive not of the beast but of the splendor of the story.
25 Rose (p. 522) suggests that this ending — original to Apuleius — is perhaps symbolic and autobiographical.
26 Dimsdale, p. 526.
27 *The Reader's Encyclopedia* (New York: T. Y. Crowell Co., 1948), III, 967.

Notes to Chapter 12

1 An unnamed critic quoted by Herbert A. Giles, *A History of Chinese Literature* (New York: D. Appleton & Co., 1928), p. 143.
2 Titles by Arthur Waley, ed. and trans., *Translations from the Chinese* (New York: Alfred A. Knopf, 1945), pp. 118–122, 124.
3 Titles by Giles, pp. 162–163.
4 Waley, p. 134.
5 All titles of Po Chu-i's poems are derived from Waley, pp. 135–272, *passim*.
6 Giles, pp. 228–229.
7 Giles, p. 261.
8 Giles, p. 276.

Notes to Chapter 13

1 Stith Thompson and John Gassner, *Our Heritage of World Literature* (New York: Dryden Press, 1942), p. 481.
2 Clement Huart, *A History of Arabic Literature* (New York: D. Appleton & Co., 1903), p. 403.
3 Thompson and Gassner, p. 482.
4 Reuben Levy, *Persian Literature* (London: Oxford University Press and H. Milford, 1923), p. 18.
5 Levy, p. 37.
6 Levy, p. 46.
7 Levy, p. 47.
8 Thompson and Gassner, p. 483.
9 Thompson and Gassner, p. 483.
10 Levy, p. 76.

Notes to Chapter 14

1 Stith Thompson and John Gassner, *Our Heritage of World Literature* (New York: Dryden Press, 1942), p. 502.
2 William P. Ker, *Epic and Romance* (London: Macmillan & Co., 1926), p. 58.
3 George M. Priest, *A Brief History of German Literature* (New York: Charles Scribner's Sons, 1909), pp. ix–x.
4 James K. Hosmer, *A Short History of German Literature*, rev. ed. (New York: Charles Scribner's Sons, 1910), p. 5.
5 See Priest, pp. 16–19.
6 Priest, p. 25.
7 Priest, p. 31.
8 Priest, p. 33.
9 Priest, p. 43.
10 Calvin Thomas, *A History of German Literature* (New York: D. Appleton & Co., 1909), p. 51.
11 Quoted by Hosmer, p. 50.
12 Hosmer, p. 51.

13 Priest, p. 46.
14 Priest, p. 51.
15 Titles are by W. A. Phillips, quoted by Edward H. Weatherly and Others, *The Heritage of European Literature* (Boston: Ginn & Co., 1948), I, 514–519.
16 The origin and meaning of the word *edda* are obscure. Perhaps it means "great-grandmother"; perhaps it is related to the place name *Odde*, the home of Saemund; or perhaps it is derived from Icelandic *odhr*, which means "mind" or "poetry." See Charles M. Gayley, *Classic Myths in English Literature and Art* (Boston: Ginn & Co., 1911), pp. 458–459.
17 The term *edda* is properly applied only to this work.
18 Ker, pp. 229–230.
19 Ker, p. 232.

Notes to Chapter 15

1 There is a persistent Irish tradition that the earliest inhabitants of Ireland as well as a later group of invaders came from Spain.
2 Douglas Hyde, *The Story of Early Gaelic Literature* (London: T. F. Unwin Co., 1922), pp. 4–5.
3 Tom Peete Cross, *Harper and Bard* (Chicago: Thomas S. Rockwell Co., 1931), p. 18.
4 Lady Augusta Gregory has collected and unified the best of the cycle under the title *Cuchulain of Muirthemne* (London: J. Murray, 1902).
5 Cross, p. 72.
6 One in *The Book of Aneurin*, five in *The Black Book of Carmarthen*, two in *The Book of Taliesin*, and one in *The Red Book of Hergest*. From 1839–1849 Lady Charlotte Guest published *The Mabinogion*, a collection of eleven Welsh tales, of which five are about King Arthur.
7 One of the *Mabinogi* from Lady Charlotte Guest's collection.

Notes to Chapter 16

1 Kathleen T. Butler, *A History of French Literature* (New York: E. P. Dutton & Co., 1923), I, 4. A modification of Miss Butler's Table of Contents has been used as the outline of this section.
2 Butler, I, 5.
3 George Saintsbury, *A Short History of French Literature*, 5th ed. (Oxford: Clarendon Press, 1897), pp. 5–6.
4 Miss Butler's division.
5 Butler, I, 80.
6 Butler, I, 8.
7 Butler, I, 22.
8 As reconstructed by Joseph Bédier (b. 1864).
9 Butler, I, 38.
10 Charles H. C. Wright, *A History of French Literature* (New York: Oxford University Press, 1925), p. 35.
11 Butler, I, 46.
12 Butler, I, 47.
13 Wright, p. 47.
14 Translated from H. Stanley Schwarz, *An Outline History of French Literature* (New York: Alfred A. Knopf, 1924), p. 20.
15 Butler, I, 86.
16 Saintsbury, p. 59.
17 Butler, I, 57.
18 Saintsbury, p. 58.

19 Monsieur de Montaiglon, quoted and translated by Saintsbury, p. 41.
20 P. 60.
21 Saintsbury, p. 43.
22 Butler, I, 67.
23 Saintsbury, p. 43.
24 Wright, p. 76.
25 Butler, I, 73.
26 Schwarz (p. 22) gives the number as forty-two.
27 Butler, I, 77.
28 Schwarz, p. 21.
29 Butler, I, 88.

Notes to Chapter 17

1 James Fitzmaurice-Kelly, *A History of Spanish Literature* (New York: D. Appleton & Co., 1898), p. 24.
2 Familiarity with Germanic laws and customs seems to indicate a Gothic origin; but the Spanish name, *cantare de gesta*, is similar to the French *chanson de geste*, and the Spanish epics appear to imitate the French in the use of assonance rather than rhyme and in the division of the poems into *laisses*. See George T. Northup, *An Introduction to Spanish Literature* (Chicago: University of Chicago Press, 1925), pp. 26–30.
3 Northup, p. 46.
4 Northup, p. 74.
5 Sometimes called a "romance," but it is an entirely different genre from the French *romance* (above, pp. 189–193).
6 See Jeremiah D. M. Ford, *Main Currents of Spanish Literature* (New York: H. Holt & Co., 1925), pp. 35–46.

Notes to Chapter 18

1 John Addington Symonds, *An Introduction to the Study of Dante*, 4th ed. (London: Adam & Charles Black, 1899), p. 1.
2 Quoted by Symonds, p. 41.
3 Edmund G. Gardner, *Dante* (New York: E. P. Dutton Co., 1923), p. 72.
4 Translation by Gardner, p. 79.
5 Gardner, p. 98.
6 Dante's title for the epic was only *Commedia*, implying a narrative which ends happily. The adjective *Divina* was added by sixteenth-century editors.
7 Symonds (pp. 111–113) prefers to consider it an apocalypse. For the four types of symbolism employed by Dante, see Symonds, pp. 116–123.
8 Gardner, p. 216.
9 Gardner, p. 193.
10 C. H. Grandgent, *Dante* (New York: Duffield & Co., 1921), p. 3. The other two poets are Homer and Shakespeare.
11 Richard Garnett, *A History of Italian Literature* (New York: D. Appleton & Co., 1898), p. 50.
12 Garnett, p. 50.
13 P. 197.
14 C. H. Grandgent, *The Power of Dante* (Boston: Marshall Jones Co., 1918), p. 214.
15 Symonds, pp. 105, 238, and 161–162.
16 George Santayana, "Dante," *Three Philosophical Poets* (Cambridge, Massachusetts: Harvard University Press, 1910), p. 133.
17 Symonds, p. 199.

Quiz and Examination Questions

Quiz and Examination Questions

[The following questions may perhaps be found useful as a study-guide to students and as a list from which teachers may select questions for quizzes and examinations. Discussion Questions 1–55 and Definitions and Identifications 1–55 cover the literary works discussed on pages 3–97 and 225–230 of the text. Discussion Questions 56–115 and Definitions and Identifications 56–125 cover the works discussed on pages 101–221 and 230–234. This division may prove convenient in preparing separately for a mid-term test and for the final examination.]

Part A. Discussions

Write an essay on each of the following topics. *Think* before you *write*. Organize your material. Use only complete sentences. Illustrate your discussions whenever possible with direct references to (or quotations from) the pieces of literature under consideration.

1. The religious literature of the ancient Egyptians.
2. The story and the allegorical significance of the *Gilgamesh Epic*.
3. The structure and the contents of the *Mahabharata*.
4. The origin and characteristics of ancient Indian drama.
5. The contents of *The Five Classics*.
6. The early Hebrew conceptions of Yahveh (God) before the advent of Amos.
7. The book of Job as a treatment of the problem of evil.
8. The social and ethical messages of Amos.
9. The Unknown Prophet's doctrine of vicarious suffering.
10. Poetic techniques used in the Psalms.
11. Various interpretations of The Song of Songs.
12. The ethical lessons found in the book of Jonah.
13. A comparison of the aims, interests, and techniques of the Gospels of Mark, Matthew, and Luke.
14. Paul's teachings about marriage, personal pride, sympathetic understanding, and immortality as set forth in I Corinthians.
15. The purpose, tone, ethics, symbolism, and imagery of The Revelation of St. John the Divine.
16. The social, economic, religious, and political conditions in Greece between 900 and 700 B.C.
17. The origin and authorship of the *Iliad* and the *Odyssey*.

18. Achilles and Odysseus as personifications of the Greek ideals of bravery and wisdom.

19. *Hybris* (pride) as a motivating force in Greek tragedy.

20. Epic conventions established by Homer.

21. *The Battle of the Frogs and the Mice* as a burlesque of serious epics.

22. Topics and characteristics of the poetry of Sappho.

23. Anacreon as an author of *vers de société*.

24. The topics, structure, tone, merits, and defects of the poetry of Pindar.

25. A comparison of Herodotus and Thucydides as to accuracy, interest, style, technique, and philosophy of history.

26. The shortcomings and merits of Xenophon as a historian.

27. The origin of Greek tragedy and its development prior to the advent of Aeschylus.

28. The staging and production of a Greek tragedy in the last half of the fifth century B.C.

29. The structure, subject matter, and technique in Greek tragedy.

30. The *Oresteia* as a study of *hybris* (pride), the inheritance of guilt, and personal responsibility.

31. The merits and defects of the dramas of Aeschylus.

32. Sophocles' humanitarianism as shown in *Antigone*.

33. *Oedipus the King* as a study of the irony of fate.

34. Euripides' contributions to the development of tragedy.

35. *Alcestis* as a tragicomedy.

36. Euripides' *Medea* as a study of the passions of anger and jealousy.

37. A comparison of Aeschylus, Sophocles, and Euripides as to dramatic technique (plot, motivation, characterization, use of chorus), ethical and religious thought, diction, humor, and popularity.

38. The origin of Old Comedy.

39. The structure of an Aristophanic comedy.

40. Aristophanes' opinions about war as shown in *The Acharnians, The Knights,* and *Lysistrata.*

41. Aristophanes' satirization of Socrates and the Sophists in *The Clouds.*

42. Aristophanes' literary criticism in *The Thesmophoriazusae* and *The Frogs.*

43. The characteristics of New Comedy.

44. Demosthenes' rhetorical techniques as shown in *On the Crown*.

45. Plato's ideas and theories about immortality as set forth in the *Phaedo*.

46. Plato's conception of the ideal commonwealth.

47. Aristotle's ideas about plot construction, characterization, probability, and catharsis as given in the *Poetics*.

48. Aristotle's ideas about the soul and immortality as given in *On the Soul*.

49. Theophrastus' character sketches and their influence on later literature.

50. The conventions of pastoral poetry.

51. Epicurus' hedonism.

52. Plutarch's plan and purpose in *Parallel Lives*.

53. The characteristics of the satire of Lucian.

54. Some theories about the origin of mythology.

55. The three dynasties of the gods as given in classical mythology.

---

56. Plautus' use of intrigue and mistaken identity in *The Captives*.

57. Plautus' *Braggart Warrior* as a "character" play.

58. The characteristics, merits, and defects of Plautus' dramas.

59. A comparison of the plays of Plautus and Terence as to style, tone, plot construction, morality, characterization, diction, humor, and versatility.

60. Lucilius' debt to Old Comedy.

61. Lucretius' atomic theory.

62. Lucretius' theories about the soul, religion, and ethics.

63. A comparison of the lyrics of Catullus and Horace as to subject matter, restraint, and topics.

64. A criticism of Cicero as an orator and letter writer.

65. A comparison of Caesar and Sallust as historians.

66. Virgil's debt to Homer.

67. The significance for later literature of Virgil's *Eclogues* and *Georgics*.

68. The purpose, tone, style, technique, and criticism of the *Aeneid*.

69. A synopsis of the story of the *Aeneid*.

70. The contents and significance of Horace's *Art of Poetry*.

71. Horace as a satirist.

72. Ovid as a love poet.

73. The plan, contents, and importance of Ovid's *Transformations*.

74. The characteristics, merits, and defects of Livy's *Annals*.

75. The historical background of Latin literature during the period A.D. 14–476.

76. The characteristics of Senecan tragedy.

77. The tone and morality of *The Satyricon*.

78. A contrast of Martial and Juvenal as satirists.

79. Pliny the Elder as an author of natural history.

80. The philosophy of history and the ethical, religious, and political views of Tacitus.

81. Suetonius as a biographer.

82. The contents and influence of Boëthius' *Consolation of Philosophy*.

83. The significance of St. Augustine for later theological thought.

84. The poetry of Po Chü-i.

85. The origin, staging and technique of medieval Chinese drama.

86. The framework structure of *The Arabian Nights' Entertainments*, and the origins of the various groups of tales.

87. The religious and ethical ideas of Omar as set forth in *The Rubaiyat*.

88. The lyrics of Hafiz.

89. Some deities and stories in Norse mythology in comparison with similar ones in Greek and Roman mythology.

90. The origin, structure, merits, and defects of *The Lay of the Nibelungs*.

91. The origin of the miracle and mystery plays in France and Germany.

92. The contents of *The Elder Edda*.

93. Some similarities and differences in the stories of *The Lay of the Nibelungs* and *The Völsunga Saga*.

94. The origin of the Celts in Ireland and their culture and religion prior to A.D. 600.

95. The contents of the Red Branch Cycle of Celtic tales, with a detailed summary of *one* tale.

96. Some theories concerning the origin of the *chansons de geste*.

97. The Christian and patriotic elements in *The Song of Roland*.

98. The authorship, a synopsis, and a criticism of *The Song of Roland*.

99. The differences between a *chanson de geste* and a medieval French romance.

100. A summary of the contents of *The Romance of the Rose*, plus an explanation why it is a romance in name only.

101. Jean de Meun as a satirist.

102. The importance of the Breton romances, with special emphasis on Chrétien de Troyes and Marie de France.

103. *Aucassin and Nicolete* as a burlesque of medieval romances of adventure.

104. Some types of early lyrics (before 1200) in northern France.

105. The definition and characteristics of the fabliau.

106. The contents and vogue of *The Book of Reynard*.

107. The distinguishing characteristics of (1) mystery, (2) miracle, and (3) morality plays.

108. The origin and development of French comic drama prior to 1500.

109. Villon's attitudes towards sin, criminals, death, nature, and beauty.

110. The historical background of *The Song of My Cid*.

111. Some theories concerning the origin of the medieval Spanish ballad.

112. The historical and biographical influences on Dante's *Divine Comedy*.

113. The *Divine Comedy* as "an epic of the Middle Ages."

114. Dante as a transitional figure between the Middle Ages and the Renaissance.

115. A synopsis of the origins of heaven, earth, the gods, and man as given in Norse mythology.

Part B. Definitions and Identifications

Identify briefly but clearly and unmistakably each of the following:

1. Upanishads	7. Judas Maccabaeus	13. Polyphemus
2. Creon	8. Menander	14. Aegistheus
3. Leonidas	9. Stoicism	15. Mencius
4. Deus ex machina	10. Ashurbanipal	16. Longinus
5. Kalidasa	11. Cyrus	17. Jonathan
6. Pandora	12. Potiphar's wife	18. Josephus

19. Admetus
20. Tiamat
21. Sakuntala
22. Orpheus
23. Pericles
24. Philomela
25. Nehemiah
26. Zeno
27. Rosetta Stone
28. Hecuba
29. Jacob
30. Agon

31. Lao-tse
32. Saturn
33. Chryseis
34. Sennacherib
35. Xerxes
36. Iphigenia
37. Avesta
38. Bion
39. Polybius
40. Priam
41. Mordecai
42. Ares
43. Xanthias

44. Eabani
45. Demeter
46. Judith
47. Io
48. Esau
49. Parados
50. Noah
51. Thebes
52. Isaac
53. Krishna
54. Eve
55. Daphne

56. Maecenas
57. Ssu-ma Kuang
58. *Sha Namah*
59. Wulfila
60. Cuchulain
61. Minnesingers
62. Conchubar
63. Lesbia
64. *Oaths of Strassburg*
65. Psyche
66. Ganelon
67. Iseult
68. Agricola
69. Sebastian Brant
70. Wace
71. Trimalchio
72. Machaut
73. Juan Ruiz
74. Koran
75. Pathelin
76. Latini
77. Asgard
78. Ennius
79. Low German

80. Loki
81. Mecca
82. Gottfried von
    Strassburg
83. Ufeig
84. *On Monarchy*
85. Lucan
86. Guelphs
87. Catiline
88. Rudagi
89. Freya
90. Pwyll
91. Rutebeuf
92. Dido
93. Livius Andronicus
94. Thor
95. Walther von der
    Vogelweide
96. *Poems of Gloom*
97. Vulgate
98. Clovis
99. Niflheim
100. Statius
101. *Débat*
102. Balder

103. Li Po
104. Beatrice
105. Benoît de
     Sainte-Maure
106. Thrym
107. Amphitryon
108. *Ysopet*
109. Sigurd
110. Naevius
111. Hagen
112. Sa'di
113. Odin
114. Oedipus
115. Varro
116. Mastersong
117. Huon
118. *The City of God*
119. Fauvel
120. *The New Life*
121. Quintilian
122. *Terza rima*
123. Deirdre
124. Alexandrine
125. Skald

Index

Index

Index to Characters

Index to Characters

278